Long Swings in Urban Development

NATIONAL BUREAU OF ECONOMIC RESEARCH
URBAN AND REGIONAL STUDIES

Long Swings in Urban Development

by

Manuel Gottlieb
University of Wisconsin

National Bureau of Economic Research
New York 1976

Distributed by Columbia University Press
New York and London

Library of Congress Cataloging in Publication Data

Gottlieb, Manuel.

Long swings in urban development.

(Urban and regional studies; no. 4)

Bibliography: p. 345–356.

Includes Index.

1. Construction industry—United States—History. 2. Cities and towns—United States—History. 3. Business Cycles. I. Title. II. Series: Urban and regional studies (New York); no. 4.

HD9715.U52G66   338.4′7′6240973   74-15592

ISBN: 0-87014-226-7

Relation of the Directors to the Work and Publications of the National Bureau of Economic Research

1. The object of the National Bureau of Economic Research is to ascertain and to present to the public important economic facts and their interpretation in a scientific and impartial manner. The Board of Directors is charged with the responsibility of ensuring that the work of the National Bureau is carried on in strict conformity with this object.

2. The President of the National Bureau shall submit to the Board of Directors, or to its Executive Committee, for their formal adoption all specific proposals for research to be instituted.

3. No research report shall be published by the National Bureau until the President has sent each member of the Board a notice that a manuscript is recommended for publication and that in the President's opinion it is suitable for publication in accordance with the principles of the National Bureau. Such notification will include an abstract or summary of the manuscript's content and a response form for use by those Directors who desire a copy of the manuscript for review. Each manuscript shall contain a summary drawing attention to the nature and treatment of the problem studied, the character of the data and their utilization in the report, and the main conclusions reached.

4. For each manuscript so submitted, a special committee of the Directors (including Directors Emeriti) shall be appointed by majority agreement of the President and Vice Presidents (or by the Executive Committee in case of inability to decide on the part of the President and Vice Presidents), consisting of three Directors selected as nearly as may be one from each general division of the Board. The names of the special manuscript committee shall be stated to each Director when notice of the proposed publication is submitted to him. It shall be the duty of each member of the special manuscript committee to read the manuscript. If each member of the manuscript committee signifies his approval within thirty days of the transmittal of the manuscript, the report may be published. If at the end of that period any member of the manuscript committee withholds his approval, the President shall then notify each member of the Board, requesting approval or disapproval of publication, and thirty days additional shall be granted for this purpose. The manuscript shall then not be published unless at least a majority of the entire Board who shall have voted on the proposal within the time fixed for the receipt of votes shall have approved.

5. No manuscript may be published, though approved by each member of the special manuscript committee, until forty-five days have elapsed from the transmittal of the report in manuscript form. The interval is allowed for the receipt of any memorandum of dissent or reservation, together with a brief statement of his reasons, that any member may wish to express; and such memorandum of dissent or reservation shall be published with the manuscript if he so desires. Publication does not, however, imply that each member of the Board has read the manuscript, or that either members of the Board in general or the special committee have passed on its validity in every detail.

6. Publications of the National Bureau issued for informational purposes concerning the work of the Bureau and its staff, or issued to inform the public of activities of Bureau staff, and volumes issued as a result of various conferences involving the National Bureau shall contain a specific disclaimer noting that such publication has not passed through the normal review procedures required in this resolution. The Executive Committee of the Board is charged with review of all such publications from time to time to ensure that they do not take on the character of formal research reports of the National Bureau, requiring formal Board approval.

7. Unless otherwise determined by the Board or exempted by the terms of paragraph 6, a copy of this resolution shall be printed in each National Bureau publication.

(Resolution adopted October 25, 1926, as revised through September 30, 1974)

Contents

viii *Contents*

Appendixes:

Tables

Charts

Foreword

Work on this book was initiated some years ago as I tried to expand a chapter on long building cycles for use in a text on business fluctuations. While preparing to write that chapter, I had reviewed the available published literature, which I found meaty in some respects and thin in others. The descriptive portion of the literature had chiefly taken the form of local experience and was often insular in approach. Literature dealing with nationwide movements had chiefly concentrated upon the task of preparing usable national estimates of building activity from sample data. Systematic analysis of local swings had been commenced, but had not been carried to completion, by Arthur Burns, under the aegis of the National Bureau of Economic Research. Analysis on a somewhat larger scale, but with greater unevenness, had been undertaken in the older writings of Long and Pearson. A few daring econometricians had tried to distill patterns of behavior out of fragments of time series. Cairncross and Thomas in England, and Kuznets and Abramovitz in the United States, had traced many of the interconnections of building swings with over-all flows of output, capital, and labor.

While this literature pointed to the indubitable reality of long building swings and their systematic involvement with processes of economic growth and urban development, gaps in the treatment of the subject were conspicuous. First, apart from the decline in building associated with the catastrophe of World War I and the Great Depression, evidence of long swings in urban building in the United States was embarrassingly thin for the half-century preceding 1900. Available national measures for those early years were founded upon building-permit data for a handful of major cities; and there was some question of the reality of fluctuations apart from the disturbance in building and economic development generated by the Civil War. Thus, there was a need for a new source of information that would shed light on the pervasiveness and degree of independence of fluctuations in urban America during the later nineteenth century, and especially during the decades preceding and following the Civil War.

Secondly, there was a great need to canvass national experience among the industrially advanced peoples of the Western World so as to compare and relate forms of movement in America and elsewhere during the nineteenth and early twentieth century and, by doing so, to ascertain elementary properties of building fluctuations. Were durations and amplitude the same or different, did they become greater or lesser over time, and were the fluctuations interwoven to any perceptible extent? In many of the countries involved, national income accounts were in process of construction. During the period of gestation of this work, new sets of national accounts have become available, due in part to the prodding and encouragement of Simon Kuznets and to the efforts of research facilities which he has directed.

Thirdly, there was a great need to analyze some three hundred available time series, local and national, on a uniform basis and according to a definite statistical procedure capable of yielding comparable measurements which would shed light on long swings. Scattered through the literature was an enormous amount of statistical analysis by different investigators, but different methods were employed and the results were not easily compared.

Early in my research, I was fortunate in finding a nest of hitherto unused statistical information reaching back into the 1840's from a state in the heartland of North Central America, Ohio. It seemed to me that this information could illuminate processes of fluctuation and growth in the earlier period, when their exact nature and scope were somewhat obscure. With the encouragement of Moses Abramovitz of the National Bureau of Economic Research, whose own research interests at this time overlapped mine, and with the aid of research grants from the Rockefeller Foundation and from the Graduate School of my own university, the University of Wisconsin, it became possible to analyze and test the validity of the information, to collate it, and to put it in usable form. In an earlier publication, I have told the story of Ohio building statistics, which were projected back to 1837 and which were available by counties from 1858 onward [108]. In other works, I have coordinated Ohio records of building with other usable records of building, including Census records and building-permit estimates, to make up three basic sets of estimates needed to evaluate tendencies toward long swings in American economic history: the number of nonfarm housing units constructed annually, and the value in real dollars of new residential construction and of all buildings [108, 110]. In the present volume, I have utilized detailed Ohio records along with all other available statistics of real estate, demographic, and building experience in the process of urban growth. Ohio statistics loom prominently in the analysis, and for this reason many of our summaries distinguish between Ohio and non-Ohio coverage. In a special Appendix to this work (Appendix E), I have given a brief account of the procedures used and the legal basis and other essential characteristics of the Ohio statistical system. Attached to that Appendix are the basic time series with a full account of all adjustments performed on the raw data.

The second major task, that of systematic collection, standardization, and computer processing of all time series, was beyond the resources of a private investigator. To accomplish this end, I sought and obtained the assistance and facilities of the National Bureau of Economic Research, whose offices I visited for a four-month period in 1962. A vast collection of time series related to building and real estate market activity in various urban centers and for certain countries reposed in the archives of the Bureau. These had originally been compiled and evaluated by Arthur Burns, who had, in the thirties, launched an investigation and prepared a manuscript which he (unfortunately, in my opinion) did not think sufficiently complete to publish. To these data, I brought other series collected from various other urban communities, the corpus of my Ohio series, and national series for other countries, which were beginning to be available. All of these series were analyzed for long swings with the aid of a computer program for analysis of cyclical characteristics developed by the National Bureau for business-cycle analysis and adapted to meet our research needs. The officers of the Bureau, and especially Moses Abramovitz and Geoffrey Moore, gave much assistance over the years, helped to point up the problems of our research efforts, and reviewed the first drafts of many chapters of this book. They bear no responsibility for the initial design or methodology of the research nor can they be burdened with responsibility for any of its conclusions or findings.

Though the research effort has been under way for over a decade, few of its results have been published, apart from the new statistical series devised. In 1959, I released a paper which summarized the state of knowledge at that time and my tentative thinking on the problem [107]. Progress reports of the research were presented in various annual reports of the National Bureau of Economic Research [202, pp. 48–51; 203, pp. 46–47; 201, pp. 53–54]. With reference to demographic activities concerned with marriage and migration, a summary account of findings was presented to the 1965 United Nations World Population Conference at Belgrade [260, p. 464 (for summary only; the full text in mimeographed form was released to conference delegates)]. An extended statement of my views on certain critical statistical procedures was embodied in a review of a work on long swings by Moses Abramovitz [112, pp. 78–81].

The level of treatment embodied in the present volume involves what some may feel is a low degree of abstraction, since the analysis stays close to its materials, a general theory of long swings is not presented, "long chains of deductive reasoning" against which Marshall enjoined are not employed, and no effort is made to reduce our analyzed series to a generalized model whose structural relationships are extracted by econometric analysis. This must await, in my judgment, further study of influences emergent at the national level in the various countries of the Atlantic economy in which tendencies to long swings ran their course. Though we are concerned with the real long swings of urban development, and though we take note of the environment in which they occurred, still our method of treatment is not historical nor have we been preoccupied with analysis of temporal sequence as such. Rather, we have sought to bring out the general and essential characteristics of, and the interplay between, the different elements and processes at work in such swings: markets for new building, residential and realty markets for old building, markets for loan capital and capital flows, buildup of the labor force through migration and expansion of households through new marriages, and the interplay of financial and value margins of returns over cost. In pursuit of this interest, we have used an eclectic and opportunistic method. We have made broad historic comparisons, we have sought evidence in descriptive literature, and we have used partial-equilibrium analysis and multiple correlation.

The book was written for—and will be of interest to— professional economists and economic historians seeking to know more about long swings in urban development. These long swings embody a process of fluctuation which, in many respects, can be likened to the more frequently observed process of short cyclical fluctuation. Hence, I have freely referred to the literature of business cycles and have made frequent comparisons between characteristics of the two types of fluctuations. I have assumed in these references that readers come to this work with a general knowledge of macroeconomics and with an orientation to the theory and practice of business-cycle research. Readers who are somewhat backward in this respect may want to renew their acquaintance with some standard monograph on cyclical research.

Acknowledgments

I am grateful to many individuals who in numerous instances assisted in the research effort embodied in this work beyond the ordinary call of duty. I should like to cite specifically the following persons or groups: Mary D'Amico, who served as research assistant in the rough early years of the project, who translated endless rows of figures into meaningful chart patterns, and who mastered the statistical procedures of cycle analysis developed by the National Bureau of Economic Research; Asa Maeshiro, who helped especially in the regression analysis utilized in the research; Thomas Bochhaus, who was responsible for the preparation of the data sheets utilized in the redrawing of all the charts presented here; members of the business-cycle unit of the National Bureau of Economic Research, who helped in the preparation of the large number of charts utilized in the research; and Irving Forman of the Bureau staff, who with his usual high standards of performance produced the charts finally used in publication. My special thanks go to the members of the NBER Staff Reading Committee: Moses Abramovitz, Richard A. Easterlin, and Jack M. Guttentag; and to the NBER Directors' Reading Committee: Moses Abramovitz, Frank W. Fetter, and Gottfried Haberler. I am particularly grateful to Moses Abramovitz, who despite differences in philosophy and approach, gave unstintingly in counsel and comment as pages and pages of the manuscript came to him for review. Thanks go, too, to Joan Tron and Ruth Ridler, who exercised their editorial skills to good effect; to the Graduate School of the University of Wisconsin and to the Rockefeller Foundation, who provided some of the financing which made the work possible; and to officers of the National Bureau, and especially Geoffrey Moore, who retained faith that a usable work would ultimately emerge. Thanks, finally, go to my wife, Margaret R. Gottlieb, for her generous contribution of time and attention to this work in its various literary transformations.

CHAPTER 1

Introduction and Summary of Findings

A. HISTORICAL BACKGROUND

This work sets out the main results of an extended inquiry into the empirical characteristics of the urban growth process as manifested in long fluctuations in urban building and real estate market activity. Forms of urban growth were first examined by German scholars around the turn of the twentieth century in a series of case studies on urban growth affecting residential building, real estate activity, and land values.[1]

The tendency of residential building and associated real estate activity to grow in wavelike form was observed in many of the local studies. This wavelike tendency was traced back to the eighteenth century by Conrad [65], who studied the city of Freiburg for twenty selected years from 1755 to 1875. He found that waves in the rate of growth of population and of buildings tended to be about thirty years in length, whereas the rate of change in prices was about half that length, but of greater intensity (see Chart 1-1).

While Conrad's study of Freiburg stretched back farthest in time, the studies of Berlin between 1843 and 1910 by Emmy Reich, and of Rhine cities by Spiethoff, most clearly indicated the wavelike character of modern urban growth. It is perhaps characteristic that in Reich's and Spiethoff's work, long waves were not categorically marked off from the general business cycle to which they were accommodated and with which they were identified during major contractions.[2]

The tendency of urban growth to run in long waves was clearly formulated in the general work of Mangoldt. Land values and all associated real estate activity tended to rise by a process of wavelike terracing in which upward surges were followed by stepladdered plateaus, sometimes marked by absolute declines.

NOTE: Throughout the book, numbers in brackets refer to the bibliography at the end of the volume.

CHART 1-1
Per Cent Annual Change, Averaged over Periods 1775–1875,
Population, Residential Building, and House Prices, Freiburg, Germany

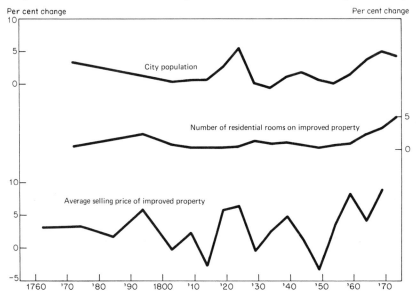

SOURCE: M. Conrad [65] as extracted in R. V. Mangoldt [179], p. 4.

He found that pattern so characteristic that he termed the tendency a law. Though his interest focused more on the rise than on its terracing, the phenomenon of local building cycles was distinctly observed.[3] The early German work was followed by intensive studies of urban building real estate patterns in major metropolitan communities of other countries.[4]

Aside from the summarization of these studies by Warren and Pearson,[5] the principal effort to collect the major findings on an international scale and in a comprehensive framework was undertaken in the 1930's by Arthur F. Burns at the National Bureau as a part of an over-all inquiry into cyclical characteristics of the building and construction industry. The first published expression of this research may be found in a paper by Burns calling attention to the "longer cycles" lasting from fifteen to twenty years in residential and urban building and in parallel long cycles in immigration, in subdivisions, and in real estate trading. In this study the mechanism of building cycles was explored theoretically [40]. The same mechanism was explored empirically in an extended manuscript written late in the thirties, utilizing some twenty-seven selected American long building series and seventeen foreign series. Summary results for American experience as distilled in this investigation were set forth later [41, pp. 418–428].[6] The central finding was that building construction is characterized by long cycles of "remarkably regular duration" running usually from fifteen to twenty years in length. These cycles were "clear-cut in outline, attain enormous amplitudes and are paralleled by long cycles in other real estate processes."

Although Burns took up other tasks, the study of long waves in construction was carried forward by other investigators at the National Bureau, under the general guidance of Simon Kuznets and Moses Abramovitz. Many of these studies, dealing with aggregate construction, demographic change, railroad and utility construction, and residential building, have already been completed, and still others are in process.[7] Other investigators in England and America have taken up the study of building cycles or long swings especially as they are propagated across national frontiers by migration of capital or labor.[8]

B. STATISTICAL COVERAGE OF THIS STUDY

This monograph is concerned predominantly with long waves in urban building and related real estate and demographic activities—in particular urban communities or regions. The statistical starting point was the fund of long time series collected and analyzed by the National Bureau of Economic Research. I dropped certain cities and areas included in the National Bureau tabulations, following an early decision to include only those communities for which two or more pre-1918 long cycles were available for study, and to exclude segments of time series depicting the behavior of building and real estate markets predominantly affected by wartime experience or by governmental activity and controls. This decision, which assigns greater weight to nineteenth-century experience, has theoretical implications which are developed at length in Chapter 2.

If the sample of the time series analyzed was narrowed by this decision, it was broadened by others. From nearly all of the surveyed regions I drew more abundantly from the statistical sources to bring under review additional measures of building, demographic, or real estate activities. From English investigators we added ten urban areas for which time series were available reaching far back into the nineteenth century.[9] More readily available were sets of building, demographic, or real estate time series for Amsterdam (three series), Stockholm (four series), Paris (five series), Sydney (three series), and Montreal (one series).

These additions were supplemented by records of building, real estate conveyance activities, and marriages in the eighty-eight counties of Ohio between 1857 and 1920 (see Appendix E). As adjusted and used in this investigation, these records were reduced to 125 time series covering the state as a whole, three large metropolitan counties, and five groups of counties selected to represent different degrees of urbanization, central-city size, and other economic characteristics.[10] These time series were analyzed in the same statistical format as my other series, thus putting all measures on a fully comparable basis. Because so much of my information regarding local building and real estate cycles stems from Ohio records, many of my summary tables and averages distinguish between Ohio and non-Ohio sources. This does not imply that Ohio experience is to be weighted equally with experience elsewhere; it rather warns against interpretation of averages resting upon Ohio and non-Ohio sources as having any semblance of the proper weighting. Unfortunately, outside of Ohio, available information was too fragmentary and scattered to make proper weighting feasible.

The analysis of *local* long cycles is supplemented in this work by a survey in Chapters 7 and 8 of long cycles as manifested on the nationwide level. For this purpose new and separately published estimates were prepared for (a) the number of nonfarm housekeeping residential units erected annually in the United States since 1840 and (b) the value (in 1870–1910 Ohio appraisal dollars) from 1850 to 1939 of total nonfarm building, residential and nonresidential. These estimates were in effect an average of the best available yearly index measures, aligned for trend and growth by use of benchmark estimates from the periodic Census returns, which were themselves adjusted for comparability to reflect building experience on the basis of the newly discovered Ohio sources.[11]

For England the process of estimation was considerably refined and extended by the work of Cairncross, Weber, and Parry Lewis for the nineteenth century and Mrs. Schumpeter and T. S. Ashton for the eighteenth century. For Germany it was found possible to construct a serviceable nationwide measure of urban residential building since 1867.[12] For France I was able to add nearly twelve years to an aggregative index based upon official French sources.[13] For other countries, such as Canada, Australia, Italy, and Japan, estimates prepared by recent investigators were used.

The analysis of national long cycles was not intended to be conducted on as exacting or on as comprehensive a scale as local long cycles. At the national level there are measurable influences affecting economic growth, the emergence of new technologies, and the role of finance which may not be directly felt at the local level. Quantitative evaluation of this complex of forces for any single country bristles with difficulties. The difficulties are compounded when processes within countries are affected by related processes abroad. My objectives at the national level were more limited. First, I wanted to collect and to appraise available measures of aggregated urban or nonfarm building and to compare tendencies to long cycles found at the national and at the local level. Second, it seemed desirable to shed light on the tendency to synchronization or inversion of different national movements. Third, I hoped to analyze demographic activities and shifts in price and value levels which played a role in long-swing movements. In these respects some contribution may have been made to the contemporary discussion of long swings, even though no formal effort at over-all synthesis has been attempted.

Both at the local and national level our inquiry was confined in principle to *urban building* as ordinarily measured by building permits and excludes many kinds of construction activity—including road building, canal and bridge construction, railway construction—which have played an important role in long-swing movements at the nationwide level.

C. FORM AND SCOPE OF ANALYSIS

An essential stage of the investigation of long-swing movements utilizing over two hundred long time series was the selection of appropriate statistical procedures to isolate the long-swing movement and to fix upon its measurable characteristics. This work of isolation involved three basic questions:

(a) Should underlying secular trends be presupposed separate from long swings and eliminated? (b) How could the irregular play of short cyclical fluctuations be taken out of our data without affecting the basic contour lines of the long-swing movement? (c) Could long swings be taken out of their historic context of antecedence and succession and shaped into some average pattern? The full statement and resolution of these issues makes up Chapter 2.

The advantage of trend elimination is that it facilitates the recognition and measurement of those essential characteristics of long-swing movements which take the form of acceleration and retardation of rates of growth. The disadvantage is that the force or tendency of secular growth is converted from a property of the long swing to a level plane around which long-swing fluctuations occur. I share the view of Schumpeter and Burns and Mitchell that the long swing tends to be a process of growth, and that we should envisage long swings as a *form of development* and not as separable from development. Hence I refrained from utilizing statistical procedures for trend adjustment.

I likewise disagree with methods of smoothing to eliminate from the time series the influence of short cyclical fluctuations. The two methods most commonly used, that of moving averages with a fixed period and that of overlapping reference-cycle periods fixed in a national chronology, are subject to two major biases. A fixed moving average is suitable for removing the effects of a periodic fluctuation with a relatively fixed period and amplitude. But with wide variability in both period and amplitude, use of a fixed short-term moving average will tend to give the appearance of long swings which do not exist. If a long-term moving average is employed, the effect is to smooth out unduly the form of the long swing itself, to convert short-period abnormalities into long-swing contours, and to shift turning points and bias measurements for amplitude. Use of a fixed reference-cycle period designed to approximate the succession of national states of cyclical "expansion" or "contraction" is a suitable smoothing device most of the time—but not all of the time, and especially not for periods of severe and sustained depression, such as 1873–79 and 1929–33, when a short cyclical reference "contraction" overlaps with a building decline or depression. The effect of the statistical procedure for these periods is to dampen unduly these downswings and thus to alter the appearance of essential characteristics of the long-swing movement.

For this reason I decided to use the mildest of smoothing procedures. As used by the National Bureau of Economic Research, this procedure allocates the entire expansion and contraction phases of long swings into "intervals" of approximately equal duration. These are "smoothed" over by "averaging" experience during the interval. In this procedure the annual values or "standings" at turning points are not themselves affected; averaging is confined only to values or standings within the three segments or "stages" of the long swing.

In removing these smoothed values from their time series array, I again diverged from prevalent practice, since other investigators are loath to cut the line of succession and antecedence which is inherent in the time series presentation. Without denying the influence of the preceding movement, it still seemed reasonable to me to believe that each long swing is substantially the outcome of its own processes; and that no violence is done to the essential nature of the long swing by separating each swing from its time series context to make it amenable to statistical manipulation. To this end, the "standings" were reduced to index relatives by division into the mean annual value for the entire cycle (or "cycle base"), thereby creating a "cycle pattern" for long cycles. Since the index relatives are expressed in homogeneous terms and all refer to the standardized stages or standings of a unit cycle, they can be consolidated by simple averaging into an "average cycle" pattern. This average pattern transforms the succession of long cycles and its stepladder growth into the intracyclical tilt of the average pattern itself. The amplitude of these patterns is then measured, as with short cycles, by the differences between cycle relatives at successive turning points. These cycle patterns are "specific" if resulting from use of the chronology of the analyzed series, or "reference," if resulting from the use of a reference chronology. For all activities within a given area, the reference chronology was derived from that used for residential building. A reference analysis for a local or regional residential-building series was provided by a national residential-building chronology. The composite of these measures of long swings was then easily manipulated to yield still other measures—of lead and lag, of secular trends, of rates of change—for which standard statistical procedures had been devised by the National Bureau of Economic Research.

This study was confined at the outset to three crucial questions:

1. How widespread in time and space are long urban-building fluctuations?
2. How similar are such fluctuations in various countries, over time, within different-sized communities, and with regard to different types of building?
3. How do urban-building fluctuations compare with business cycles with regard to duration, amplitude, timing, and form of movement?

An attempt to answer these questions led inevitably to real estate markets and to the underlying markets for building sites, building labor, building materials, and finance. These, in turn, revealed the influence of still more fundamental processes—migration from farms and villages, and marriages—by which labor supply is augmented and formed into households. Hence, the survey includes two additional questions:

4. How pervasive have been corresponding fluctuations in markets for undeveloped land, improved realty, rentals, mortgage credit, building labor and materials, as well as in migration and marriage?
5. What consistent relations exist between these different phases of urban growth and real estate market activity?

These questions can only be answered by an examination of the facts, particularly those derived from statistical time series. Needless to say, my interest is not in statistical measures as such but in the activities they represent. Since the statistical measures used here were incomplete and for many purposes fragmentary, our interpretations are often speculative. Many of the processes involved in *local* fluctuations are sustained and influenced by conditions in other urban communities, in the nation as a whole and, to a certain extent, in the entire world or at least its more advanced and integrated areas.[14] Our interpretations can be described, in Simon Kuznets' words, as "at best a sketch of possible but untested association between the findings and a set of known or reasonably acceptable general patterns of economic behavior, an indication of the directions in which specific tests of the suggested associations are to be sought, not a demonstration of the existence of such links. In short, explanations are conjectural rather than tested, partial rather than complete, suggestive rather than definitive'' [161, p. 6].

We have not sought to go beyond these conjectural, partial, and suggestive explanations, nor do we ask, as Easterlin [78, p. 47] did, ''Are the observations on long swings consistent with a model of relationships based on economic theory?'' The answers to this question depend upon presuppositions built into the theory or into the whole range of theories that may be relevant. These presuppositions in turn should be consistent with essential characteristics of the real world and it is one of the conclusions of this work that among these essential characteristics is a tendency toward long swings in urban growth in the unregulated markets of classical capitalism. Until we know more about these long swings, especially at the nationwide level, it is wiser to postpone or move cautiously in the work of modifying economic theory to be consistent with their reality.

D. SUMMARY OF FINDINGS

Natural and Local Swings

The findings of this work are presented separately for local long cycles in Chapters 2 through 6, and for national cycles in Chapters 7 and 8. This division corresponds to the distinction drawn early in the investigation between the local cycles in major urban communities, whose existence was more or less presupposed, and national cycles, whose existence was subject to question. Clarification of the relationship between local and national cycles was indeed one of the paramount objectives of the investigation.

As this objective was probed, it became increasingly evident that local and national cycles were not different species of behavior but the same field of behavior spelled out in different ways. Local cycles were simply a local phase of a national movement, while the national movement was in turn mainly a coalescence of local cycles. Our local building series included eighty-one long cycles averaging 19.7 years in duration per cycle, subject to a mean deviation of 5.0 years; our national series with 30.5 long cycles averaged 19.0 years per cycle with a mean deviation of 4.4 years, or virtually the same duration (Chapter 7, pp. 206 f.). We found that all of our regional areas exhibited regional and local cycles which matched the national movement, and that individual cities would only rarely "miss" a national set of turning points or possess an "extra" cycle (Chapter 7, pp. 208 ff.). Due to variation in timing and these occasional "misses" or "extras," the amplitude of the swings of cities and regions will run from a fourth to a third greater than the amplitude of the swings for the more inclusive aggregates (Chapter 7, pp. 207 f.). Substantial nonconformity in pattern and in dating was found characteristic only of the sample of rural Ohio counties with the lowest degree of urban influence and with a high responsiveness to shifts in agricultural conditions. Synchronization of local and national cycles was partly induced by major wars which caused all local building first to turn downward in major depressions in settled urban communities and then upward some time after the close of the war. Synchronization was to an even larger extent induced by the bond which ties together the little local economies whose outputs become each other's inputs. Because of this bond of integration, any prevailing national rate of growth will be translated into a schedule of counterpart local growth rates distributed around the mean as communities are favored or handicapped by innovation or by comparative advantage in resource layout (see Chapter 7, pp. 209 ff.).

Our surveyed long swings in building encompass the years between the early 1840's and the late 1930's. On the assumption that swings for a given area are to be dated by turns in their most common and fundamental component, residential building activity, twenty-four reference chronologies were constructed (see Chapter 2). These are detailed in Table 1-1, which groups reference chronologies under a set of master headings setting out the five long-swing movements which were found to be widely diffused through urban communities of North America, Western Europe, and related westernized communities. In only three cases were there extra or "skipped" cycles. Conformity to this Western World pattern was not, however, always positive. A tendency to counterwave with inverted timing was noticeable at times in Great Britain and, through the early years (1841–70), in Berlin, Amsterdam, and Paris. Dispersion in timing fell off discernibly for the two turns in the late seventies and late eighties but noticeably widened thereafter. A similar trend of dispersion of turning points, from American data only, has been found by other researchers [173, pp. 146, 152].

Other evidence not drawn from the patterns of building behavior attests to the presence of forces making for a tendency to counterwave or inversion in national and regional long-swing patterns. The evidence of marriage rates (Chapter 8, pp. 224 ff.) suggests that countries with primarily agricultural populations experienced a long-wave pattern between 1870 and 1913, with a duration of around twenty-five years and peaks in 1883–84 and 1907–8. Industrial countries exhibited nearly inverted but somewhat weaker marriage-wave patterns, with peaks in 1873 and 1897 and troughs in 1882–83 and 1910. During the seventy-five years before 1913, the three leading countries—England, Germany, and the United States—experienced long waves which at no time were completely in or out of phase with each other, partly because swing durations in the three countries differed. Between 1821 and 1861 England tended to be in phase with the U.S. 56 per cent of the time, but Germany was in phase only 32 per cent of the time. Between 1862 and 1913 the pattern shifted, with England inverting 37 per cent, and Germany 47 per cent of the years (Chapter 8, Table 8-3).

Duration

The findings with regard to local building activity are derived from the eighty-one long specific cycles of record for thirty urban areas located in eight countries. For national building activity, the records covered 28.5 long specific cycles in residential or total building in seven countries. Local cycles varied widely in duration, with a substantial clustering between fifteen and twenty-five years and with fewer than 5 per cent of the long cycles running over twenty-five years (Chapter 3, pp. 59 ff.). Longer rhythms may have run through our series but the time runs were too short to bring them to the surface. The lower limit of the local duration range is essentially indeterminate since the shorter *long* fluctuations (ten years and under) tend to fold into the longer *short* fluctuations of the business cycle proper. Nearly 14 per cent of the recorded building cycles had a total duration of under ten years, though only 3 per cent of the series had an average duration as brief as this (chiefly the industrial building

TABLE 1-1

Summary of Reference Chronologies (Based on Long Swings in Residential Building)

Area	Source (Series No.)	Trough, 1840's	Peak, 1850's	Trough, 1860's
United States				
1. Nationwide Total construction	*a*	1843	1854	1861
Residential building	0155[b]	1843	1857	1864
2. Ohio statewide	0147			1862
3. Cincinnati	0110			1863
4. Toledo	0115			1859
5. Cleveland	0123			1859
6. Ohio I	0171			1863
7. Ohio II	0172			1859
8. Ohio III	0173			1864
9. Ohio IV	0174			1864
10. Ohio V	0175			1859
11. Manhattan	0092			
12. Chicago	0085		1857	1862
13. St. Louis	0081			
14. Detroit	0098			
Other Areas				
15. England	0015[e]			1859
16. Glasgow	0004			1864
17. London	0009		<u>1856</u>	<u>1868</u>
18. Germany	0018			1866[f]
19. Hamburg	0030			
20. Berlin	0022	<u>1841</u>	<u>1851</u>	<u>1864</u>[g]
21. Stockholm	0039			
22. Victoria	0059			1866
23. Amsterdam	0052			
24. Paris	0035	1848		1868
25. New South Wales	0107			

NOTE: Underscore dates are for areas showing "inverted" timing; a date under a "peak" column marks a "trough" and vice versa.

a For a suggested "construction" chronology after 1861, see [1, pp. 105–107]. Abramovitz justifies extension of this reference chronology back to a trough at 1821 and peak

Peak, Early 1870's	Trough, Late 1870's	Peak, Late 1880's	Trough, Late 1890's	Peak, 1900's	Trough, 1910–21	Peak, Mid- 1920's	Trough, 1930's
1871	1878	1892	1898	1912	1918	1927	1932
1871	1878	1889	1896	1909	1918	1925	1933
1873	1878	1892	1898	1905	1910		
1868	1880	1888	1900				
1873	1878	1892	1902				
1873	1878	1891	1900	1907			
1874	1878	1887	1900	1906			
1868	1878	1892	1898	1907			
1868	1878	1892	1896	1912			
1872	1878	1889	1894	1903	1910		
1875	1880	1887	1898	1902	1910		
1871	1877	1887	1893	1905	1918	1926	1933
1872	1879	1892	1900	1911	1918	1926	1933
	1878^c	1892	1900	1908	1918	1925	1933
	1878	1892	1896	^d	^d	1926	1933
	1878	1886	1899	1914			
	1876	1883	1898	1912			
1873	1881	1892	1899	1914			
1874	1883	1890	1894	1904	1913		
1878	1883	1890	1897	1910			
1875	1880	1890	1900	1906			
		1885	1893	1903	1921	1930	1940
1874	1880	1889	1894				
1871	1881	1891		1905	1916	1924	1932
1870	1882	1886	1899	1908	1913		
1871		1885	1894				

at 1836. See particularly [198, p. 48; 200, pp. 24 ff.; 147, Tables 2, 3, 7-A, 10, 11]. The plausibility of the hypothesis that urban growth and building as far back as the 1820's developed a growth rhythm with a period between fifteen and twenty years has been reinforced by the work of Douglass North [207]. The outlines of a clear-

series of Ohio). None of the national building series exhibited specific cycles under ten years. The inference seems plain that the tendency of building fluctuations to drift into the mold of business-cycle fluctuations is confirmed both for large territorial aggregates and, in the long term, for local communities.

There was little consistency manifested in the distribution of durations, either local or national. Very long durations were found in the earliest phase of English capitalism up to the middle of the eighteenth century. Thereafter, and increasingly as the tempo of industrial revolution accelerated, the duration of English long swings shortened. At the apogee of this revolution—1830–40—the long swing in process coalesced with a well-researched major industrial cycle which ran its course between 1832 and 1843. After an interregnum of uncertain chronology, two distinct waves took shape with relatively slow tempos and long durations averaging twenty-eight years between 1857 and 1913. This return in the late nineteenth century to the pattern of long durations characteristic of the early eighteenth century seemed to spring from different conditions. The earlier pattern was markedly affected by the rhythm of the major wars, with their periodic diversion of labor force and loan capital from civilian use. In the later nineteenth century, the long duration seemed more closely related to the high degree of integration of the United Kingdom into the Atlantic and Empire economy, to

---

Notes to Table 1-1 (concluded)
cut expansion wave were cut between 1793 and 1808 (pp. 25 ff.). North indicates that the 1810's were a decade of relative stagnation in our foreign trade, urban population, and inland waterway traffic. Deflation followed the peace settlement, with prices falling from 1815 to 1823. North is, however, inclined to date the post-1815 long-term trough at 1823 rather than 1821 (p. 181, n. 11, and Chap. XIV). Regardless of this suggestion for timing, for a few of our series the reference chronology was extended back to 1821 and 1836.

[b] See [109, Table 15 and Chart 21].

[c] Derived from trough of our series number 0084.

[d] Skipped.

[e] Also series 0145.

[f] Though our series began in 1867, a variety of evidence indicated a trough in 1866. To derive specific cycle patterns, series 0018 was assumed to have a trough in 1867. To extend back our reference-cycle patterns for series 0019 and 0022 (building material prices and Berlin residential building), an additional pair of reference dates, 1850 (trough) and 1861 (peak), were utilized. These datings are tentative and provisional. The period of the 1850's was one of accelerated growth for Germany. See [240, p. 130; 232, pp. 80 ff.; 229, pp. 251 ff.; 49, p. 283]. The peak of 1861 is dubious but it was indicated by our Berlin and Bremen materials.

[g] Followed by an "extra" trough in 1870.

the marked tendency to invert long-swing rhythms of North America and Australia, and to an altered cyclical sensitivity of building to finance.

The pattern of other national durations exhibited no simple or clear-cut association with either secular growth rates or amplitudes. There were too few observations to throw into a regression, considering the wide range of variation of amplitude, growth, and duration, and the play of many influences on these variables. Consideration of the summary exhibit of our national series (see Chapter 7, Table 7-1) will indicate the crosscurrents which seemed to prevail. For seven of our series the duration range was intermediate—between fourteen and eighteen years—and yet for these series growth rate ranged between 124 and 295 cycle relatives. Slow growers have both long and short durations and high and low amplitudes. Thus, Germany has a duration and amplitude 85 and 83 per cent, respectively, of the American but a growth rate as high or higher.

There were many more observations of local building cycles to consider and a more definite pattern emerged (Chapter 3, pp. 59 ff.). Longer durations of local cycles are not associated with larger amplitude up to a critical amplitude boundary of 350 cycle relatives. Thereafter, per year amplitude rates are constant: whatever stretches out duration builds up total amplitude. There was no clear-cut pattern by which local or national duration was associated with growth rate or with time. In nineteen instances of successive long nationwide cycles, the distribution was not significantly different from random (Chapter 7, p. 200).

Amplitude and Conformity

The amplitude attained by building cycles over their full duration was measured for purposes of this investigation by taking what amounts to the sum of the differences, in terms of cycle relatives, between a cycle peak and the preceding and succeeding troughs. A beginning trough of 50, a peak of 200, and a terminal trough of 100 in terms of cycle relatives would thus result in a total amplitude of 250 cycle relatives, or a range of movement up and down that is two and a half times the average level over the entire cycle period. Specific amplitude for a given series means the rise and fall measured from the peaks and troughs of the given series; reference amplitude for the same series is measured by changes between peaks and troughs, which for any given area is usually represented for purposes of this investigation by the specific chronology of residential building activity. Differences between specific and reference amplitude are due to divergences in timing at turns between the given series and residential building, and thus constitute a crude measure of lack of perfect conformity of a given series with the cycle chronology of residential building activity.[15]

So measured, the amplitude cumulated by building cycles over their full duration was truly enormous. Specific total mean amplitude for 62 local building series was 303.4 ± 100.3 cycle relatives. The 30 local residential building series experienced a comparable distribution of amplitude and nearly the same mean value, 306.0 ± 92.4. The nationwide level of amplitude is understandably less, due to the imperfect coalescence of particular local cycles, the variety of local turns, and occasional "misses" or "extras." Thus the mean total specific amplitude for all our national series is 214.0, or 70 per cent of the corresponding local mean value (Chapter 7, Table 7-3). Mean specific amplitude for the state of Ohio was 131.3, or 64 per cent of the mean level for areas within the state. The corresponding ratio for eleven English urban series and for the nation was 67 per cent; for five major U.S. urban or regional areas and nationwide, 57 per cent; and for three major German cities, 54 per cent. This is the net measure of the degree of synchronization, or the lapses therefrom, emerging from the record of national and local long cycles (Chapter 7, pp. 206 ff.).

There was no clear-cut trend of amplitudes over time. For the nineteen recorded instances of *successive* long national cycles, the declines were only slightly more numerous than increases. The decade before and around World War I, America, Germany, and France experienced weak contractions and a less clear-cut form of long movement. But the English long cycle that reached a trough in 1911 was relatively clear-cut and of large amplitude. The high amplitude everywhere in the 1920's and 1930's gave little indication of a trend of declining severity. The two centuries of English building give little or no indication of a trend of amplitude. The total mean amplitude of the two long waves of the late nineteenth century was greater than that of the waves of the eighteenth or early nineteenth century but the difference is chiefly due to varied duration. Grouped in order of time, our measures for the English long cycle follow.

	No. of Cycles	Mean Duration, Years	Mean Specific Cycle, Amplitude		
			Total	Year	Per Year Fall
1711–81	3	23.3	133.9	5.74	−5.05
1785–1843	4	14.5	123.5	8.46	−8.15
1857–1914	2	28.0	191.6	6.84	−7.26

For the first two periods our statistical measures refer to over-all building activity. For the latest period only residential building is measured. The more inclusive aggregate of building will generally exhibit less amplitude; hence the figures for the latest period should be reduced by between 10 and 20 per cent to adjust to an all-building basis.

Long-cycle behavior of nonresidential building, either in the aggregate or in its various forms, was available for only a few of our larger aggregates—for the United States, Australia, Ohio—and on a local basis for our Ohio urban areas and for a few other cities. Everywhere nonresidential building as an aggregate conformed in its long-swing movements to residential building, with no indication of "missed" or "extra" or "special" cycles. This record of positive conformity is confirmed by the findings of other investigators.[16]

Conformity in pattern was, at least in the American case, associated with systematic variation in timing. Before the 1880's, nonresidential building series tended to lead by two to three years. Afterward a lag is prominent, especially at peaks (see Chapter 7). Nonresidential construction in Italy also lagged behind residential by between 1.5 and 1.9 years (see Appendix A, Table A-1, on microfiche).

This broad over-all conformity of movement of nonresidential to residential building, with variable timing, breaks down into special patterns for the different types of nonresidential building. Detail here was disclosed by Ohio average patterns for different types of building, as set forth in Chart 1-2. Measured long specific cycles in industrial building in Ohio (with a mean statewide duration of barely nine years) corresponded closely to

CHART 1-2
Patterns of Specific and Reference Long Cycle Averages, Ohio Statewide, Value of Building Activity

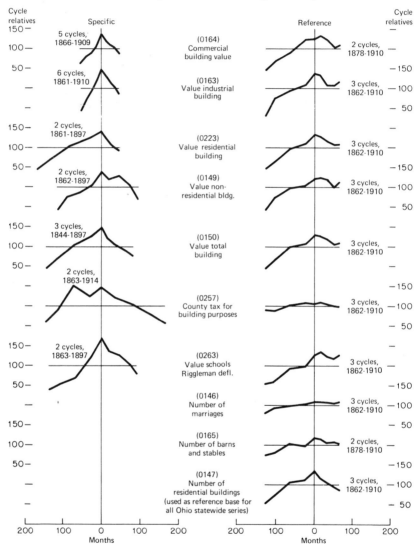

"major" business-cycle rhythms. The total specific amplitude exceeded that of residential building both in total movement and rate of change per year. This overt specific rhythm was overlapped by a longer oscillation period that showed up in our reference-cycle patterns and correlograms, with a tendency to lead residential building (Chapter 3).

Chart 1-2 shows that commercial building expansions tended to continue beyond residential peaks and led on residential upturns but with a much shorter lead than industrial building (see Chapter 3). As the chart indicates, public and quasi-public building exhibited the slowest and most uneven response to building rhythms. School-building rhythms conformed moderately to building cycles but with a long lag of more than two years. The lag may reflect slow decision making at governmental levels, the elaborate structure often involved, or lags in cycles of school populations (see Chapter 3). Another activity related to local public building—taxes levied for building purposes by county governments—exhibited a long specific rhythm which hardly reflected standard building rhythms in any way (Chapter 3). Street paving in at least two of three non-Ohio communities for which information was available exhibited clear-cut patterns with tendencies both to lag and to lead up to two or more years (Chapter 3, pp. 77 ff.).

Movement of farm building as such was not an object of investigation. However, our sources occasionally turned up information bearing on long swings in farm building. Two items of information indicated that at least between 1870 and 1914 long swings in agricultural growth were inverse to those of the nonfarm economy. For the United States this was directly indicated for capital formation and growth in cultivation for agriculture as a whole (Chapter 8, pp. 233 f.). The same tendency to inversion was exhibited by marriage rates in predominantly agricultural countries. On the other hand, Ohio agriculture exhibited two indications of building swings in a positive rather than an inverted form. One indication relates to farm mortgage credit recordings, which show clear-cut reference-cycle fluctuations in value (Chapter 4, pp. 104 ff.). A second indication is the clear-cut long reference-cycle behavior of barn and stable building shown in Chart 1-2. Perhaps extension of farm settlement in America and in other agricultural countries proceeded in contracyclical rhythms, and intensive building within settled farm communities developed in cyclical rhythms.

In the aggregate of nonresidential building, the tendencies of public building to lag behind turns in residential building is in part offset by a tendency of industrial building to lead. Hence, amplitude of fluctuation is scaled down, but the duration of expansions and contractions is sufficiently extended to bring all kinds of building eventually into a common movement. In Ohio, in America as a whole, in Italy, and wherever detail by types of building was found, the long-swing behavior of total building was so similar to that of residential building over comparable cycle periods that one pattern could frequently be substituted for the other with only slight variations in form or position. Long swings in urban building are thus a total, not a segmented, phenomenon and involve building as a whole.

Demographic Base

Since buildings are used by people, it is possible that long swings in urban building could mirror long swings in the growth of urban population and household formation. It was our initial hypothesis—and we believe our empirically confirmed conclusion—that long swings in demand for new building were grounded and sustained in good part on long swings in migration and household formation. An expansion of urban building characteristically occurs when people migrate from farm and village communities, where rates of natural increase are relatively high but marginal productivity of labor is low. Migrants go to cities where marginal productivity of labor is relatively high but where rates of natural increase are low. Rural migrants drift most easily to neighboring urban areas but, where opportunities are abundant, migrants will travel long distances and across national frontiers.

This rural-urban migration was often accompanied by a farm-to-farm migration, called for by settlement in the New World of fertile farmlands available at cheap prices. Currents of farm-to-farm migration, which played a role through most of the nineteenth century, do not necessarily flow at rhythms governed by building and real estate cycles. Hence, our reference-cycle patterns of international migration, which includes both farm-to-city and farm-to-farm components, have a specific source of irregularity built into them (Chapter 8, 237 ff.). Our local urban population or migration series for particular communities is free from this particular kind of irregularity, though the enumeration is more difficult to carry out and the statistics are correspondingly scarcer.

We surveyed three urban migration time series from which

were extracted eleven specific long cycles. These series uniformly exhibited, as expected, prominent and unambiguous specific long cycles with a total specific amplitude of 321, i.e., the same order of magnitude as for residential building. Turning points for migration series were varied in timing and magnitude of movement relative to that of building. Cyclical correspondence with residential building was loose. Only 28 per cent of the variability around the trend of building activity was "explained" by a linear regression against deviations from the trend of migration. The average deviation on twenty-five matched turning points was 2.3 years. Hence, total reference-cycle amplitude was reduced by 47 per cent from its specific level. Variation in timing did not obscure a clear tendency for migration to lead up to two years, particularly on upturns (Chapter 5, pp. 123 f.).

Our survey of nationwide migration experience was limited to the United States, England (and Wales), and Germany—the three countries most prominently represented in our local series. Fourteen long specific cycles were surveyed. The American experience was that of a net "receiving" country; the other two countries had a net emigration. As expected, American immigration up to the Civil War seemed appreciably affected by farm settlement. Likewise, during the earlier decades of the nineteenth century, emigrants attracted to farm settlement in the New World played an important role in English and German migration. By the end of the century this influence had nearly disappeared from the migration records of the three countries. However, migration patterns for all three countries were disturbed by a conflict of "push" and "pull," except when building and growth waves within England and Germany inverted the American experience. When this occurred, persons would become attracted abroad when least wanted at home and vice versa. We found that the tendency to inversion varied over time, with corresponding irregularity built into our national reference migration patterns. Nevertheless, it was highly significant that English and German emigration reference patterns in the nineteenth century were primarily inverted—with reference to their own patterns of residential building—while the American patterns were primarily positive. Mean specific amplitude was built up to 274 cycle relatives of which only 155 survived to the reference level. As in our local series, a primary tendency to lead shows up on the nationwide level for the three countries.

American amplitude was greatest and England and Wales after 1850 lowest.

The same force which attracts migrants—favorable opportunities for settlement or for gainful industrial employment—will encourage or discourage the formation by marriage of new mating households and hence increase the demand for additional shelter. Records for eight urban communities or groups of communities indicated that people married at a much steadier rate than they migrated. Amplitude for our marriage series ran to a sixth and seventh of that of migration. For many of our marriage series there were long stretches of time in which specific fluctuations were so muted or mild that they were not recognized apart from the short fluctuations in which they were embedded. Timing was more perfectly concurrent, with less variation at matched turning points. Some 39 per cent of the variation in building around its trend was explained by a simple regression of variations in marriages from their trend.

Rates of marriage on a nationwide basis do not as clearly exhibit long swings as corresponding rates for urban communities. Specific total mean amplitude for 10.5 specific long cycles of industrial countries averaged only 36.5 cycle relatives; and, due to timing variabilities, this was eroded to 16.7 on a reference basis (Chapter 8, Table 8-1).

This low amplitude in part reflects adjustment of our national marriage statistics to a per capita basis, thus eliminating upward trend. For the same reason turning points became advanced from two to four years. More important was the inclusion in national marriage statistics of marriages of farm populations. Marriage rates of agricultural populations will, of course, respond to changes in agricultural or crop conditions. For a number of countries, regression analysis traced out the decline of farm influence and the rise of industrial influence on nationwide marriage rates (Chapter 8, pp. 232 f.).

Vacancy Rates

Long swings in urban building are by no means entirely attributable to corresponding variations in labor force and urban investment. They were exaggerated by systematic tendencies to alternating states of over- and underbuilding, or—alternatively put—to changing rates of utilization of standing building stocks.

Direct evidence of long swings in rates of utilization of standing stocks—an unemployment of property rather than of people— is found in the vacancy rates, which fluctuated systematically over a specific total amplitude nearly matching that of residential building, 306 cycle relatives (Chapter 5). The cycle patterns of vacancy rates in different communities at different time periods were found to be sufficiently similar to warrant representation in terms of a single cycle pattern (see Chart 1-3). The chart graphically discloses the tendency of new residential building to lag behind but eventually outrun a fluctuating demand for additional shelter. Throughout the first half of the reference expansion, the demand for additional shelter outpaces new building, and vacancy rates decline. Throughout

CHART 1-3

Average Long Cycle Patterns, Specific Residential and Reference Vacancy, Six Cities, 1851–1940

Specific Residential composed of:			Reference Vacancy composed of:		
London	1856-1914	(3 cycles)	London	1873-1914	(2 cycles)
Glasgow	1864-1912	(2 cycles)	Glasgow	1864-1912	(2 cycles)
Berlin	1851-1900	(3 cycles)	Berlin	1851-1900	(3 cycles)
Hamburg	1878-1910	(2 cycles--I)	Hamburg	1878-1910	(2 cycles--I)
Stockholm	1870-1940	(3 cycles)	Stockholm	1893-1940	(2 cycles)
St. Louis	1892-1933	(2½ cycles--P.L.)	St. Louis	1892-1933	(2½ cycles--P.L.)

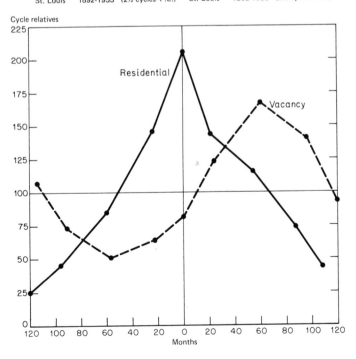

the second half of the expansion, new building outpaces additional demand, and continues to do so through the first half of the reference decline. Hence, vacancy rates reach their peak around the middle of the reference contraction.

A changed vacancy rate will generate changes in rent levels and in realty price levels, and all three affect the willingness of builders to build new dwellings. The relationship is inverted, i.e., a diminished rate of vacancies causes an increased rate of building and vice versa. But these changes in new building are induced directly and indirectly only over time. The lag of new building behind vacancies ranges from three to five years; it is consistent, with relatively small deviations (mean 2.25 years) on thirty-six matched individual turns, a mean correlation coefficient of −.77, and a ratio of reference to specific total amplitude of .78.

Vacancy fluctuations can be fruitfully expressed not only in terms of cycle relatives but as a percentage of the total stock of residential buildings. The mean reference vacancy rate for the communities involved was 2.6 per cent at the initial vacancy trough, 8.5 per cent at the vacancy peak, and 1.9 per cent at the terminal vacancy trough (see Table 5-2). Since the annual mean growth in nonfarm stocks of housing over the same stretch of years for the United States may be estimated at 2.6 per cent per year, the swing in urban vacancies on the rise amounted to 2.3 years of our mean annual increase in housing stock and 2.5 years on the fall.[17] The corresponding swing in Berlin building was on a somewhat reduced scale. But by either the American or Berlin magnitudes, the equivalent of a substantial amount of new building was added to or offset by the swings in vacancy rates.

Real Estate Market Activity and Values

The surging demand which generates long swings in building is not confined to new building alone; it also extends to demand for building sites. These sites are obtained by land development and subdivision into prepared lots. Both of these activities evince specific total amplitudes nearly double that of residential building, indicating a tendency to over- and underdevelopment of new sites as demand for shelter fluctuates. The primary phase of land development—procurement of land in urban environs—reaches its peak long after residential building has peaked and continues to decline until nearly midway through a building expansion. The work of lot preparation and subdivision is more promptly adjusted to building needs and conforms in its timing, with a lag of under six months, to movements of building activity proper.

Demand for new building not only affects land markets but also affects demand for old realty and for the mortgage credit used in financing both new and old realty purchases. The number of newly recorded deeds and mortgages—reflecting primarily transactions in used residential properties, in vacant lots, and in small business or consumer credit—exhibits clear-cut reference expansions and contractions. Turns in deeds lead turns in mortgage activity by up to two years. Amplitude of movements on a specific basis are considerable, ranging from one-half to two-thirds of amplitudes for residential building. The divergent rhythms of deed and mortgage activity may reflect a tendency towards accelerated nonfarm use of mortgage credit during reference contractions for activities not connected with real estate purchase, i.e., for personal credit or business financing. Such use of mortgage credit gives way to realty needs during reference expansions.

Comparable long swings in mortgage credit extended, when measured not by number of recordings but by the dollar consideration involved, were found for the American and German urban communities surveyed. But for larger areas American and German experience diverged. For Germany as a whole, long-swing fluctuations in the total flow of mortgage credit were almost as distinctive as for the city of Berlin. In Ohio all semblance of reference fluctuation in statewide value of mortgage recordings was rubbed out in the process of aggregating all uses of mortgage credit. Since the statistics of new building showed significant statewide long swings and since we may infer the existence of corresponding swings in statewide mortgage credit used to finance new construction, there must have been inverse long swings in the flow of credit for business or personal uses or to finance transfers in improved or unimproved property.

One set of market signals that would influence extension of mortgage credit to purchases of new or old realty is foreclosures. These play the role in realty credit markets that commercial failures play in commercial credit markets. Foreclosures develop a specific amplitude of the same order as residential building, with consistent timing, an inverse relationship, and a clear-cut tendency to lead. The pattern is similar to that of vacancy rates.

Building and real estate market activity result from choices made in a complex of markets, including those for rentals, sales of old buildings, urban sites, building materials, labor, and mortgage credit. Prices in these markets are linked in an equilibrium system. As demand for shelter, buildings, and realty investment rises and falls, sympathetic currents of fluctuation are propagated through the real estate and building markets. Price margins shift with the uneven response of the price system. Some of the principal measures of price response at different levels of building and realty markets are presented in Table 1-2. These summary measures vary in terms of accuracy, comprehensiveness, and comparability of the underlying statistics. We comment first on the price of undeveloped urban sites, go on to the various components of realty and building value, and finally discuss the value of improved realty.

Urban sites may be bought and sold as raw acreage or in the form of graded and cleared subdivided lots equipped with streets, sidewalks, and other improvements. Urban sites have tended to appreciate over time; they can be easily purchased on instalment terms at low interest rates; they are traded in organized realty markets; and they are subject to little or no upkeep and relatively modest property taxes. Hence investment in them has been cultivated in the quest for capital gains. These prospective capital gains depend upon expectations of the steady growth in value of the sites concerned. Expectations are grounded on hazy knowledge of the past qualified by vague allowances for the future. Hence land values, in terms of both price and volume of transactions, exhibit extreme instability and play an important role in mechanisms of amplification at the local level of realty and development swings.

Information on raw acreage sold in undeveloped form was available for study only in Ohio. The five and one-half long cycles in per acre values had a specific and reference mean amplitude of 336 and 188 cycle relatives, respectively, with a tendency to comparatively irregular timing, approaching full inversion.

Prices of urban site values for developed land were available for survey in only two cities, with a mean level of amplitude considerably below amplitude in the volume of subdivision

TABLE 1-2

Average Long Cycles in Price and Value Measures, Amplitude and Duration

	Number of Series	Number of Long Cycles	Predominant Lead or Lag Relative to Residential Building	Amplitude, in Cycle Relatives		
				Specific		Reference Total
				Total	Per Year	
1. Price per acre, under-developed land, Ohio	4	5.5	Inverted	336.0	16.2	188.0
2. Building material prices	3	12	Nearly concurrent	60.0	3.3	26.8
3. Hourly earnings, building trade differential over manufacturing, U.S.A.	1	4	Moderate lag	47.9	2.6	19.8
4. Cost of building	6	12	Moderate lag	50.6	2.9	34.1
5. Mortgage yield differential over bond yield, U.S. and Germany	3	8	Moderate lag	134.2	8.6	62.9
6. Dwelling rental						
Vacant	3	5	Strong lead	60.7	4.0	51.8
Occupied	2	5	Slight lag	37.2	2.3	22.6
7. Real estate prices, improved property	9	22.5	Nearly concurrent	103.2	6.4	62.4

SOURCE: Table 6-8.

activity itself. The mean specific amplitude for the price of subdivided vacant lots in Paris was 132 cycle relatives, while Chicago's record of improved urban site values over a comparable stretch of years was 193. In both cases, amplitudes receded as urban growth rates slowed down.

Some follow-through for urban site values is found in virtually all segments of the real estate market. Newly constructed properties will include, of course, an allowance for the cost of land on which the building is erected. Old properties will be appraised not only with reference to the usability of the improvements but with regard to the site's best potential use. But though important for new and old realty, urban site values in most urban communities play a lesser role in determining realty values than do the improvements worked into the site or placed on it in the form of a building.

The cost of improvements was resolved, for purposes of this investigation, into prices for building materials, building labor, and mortgage finance or the interest cost of loan capital. Since the three sets of prices are established in nationwide markets, with relatively small local differentials, nationwide price indexes were analyzed rather than those of particular urban communities.

Of the three cost components, only prices of building material exhibit clear-cut specific long cycles related to building cycles. These long cycles stood out prominently over the entire nineteenth century in the United States and Germany. Their amplitude is quite moderate, corresponding to the ease of expanding supply and the competitive nature of the product markets concerned. Mean specific amplitude, excluding the principal periods of wartime inflation, was only 60 (see line 2, Table 2). Because of wide variations in timing in England and in America, very little reference fluctuation showed up in measures for those two countries. In Germany, the process of reference fluctuation was more distinctive.

The long cyclical response of the other major direct component of building cost—hourly wages—was not as well marked. Our information on building-trade wages exhibits little direct indication of any long-wave movement with a rhythm resembling building cycles. There is ample indication, however, of tension in labor markets, generated by building cycles. Differentials between hourly earnings in the building trade and in manufacturing exhibit a clear-cut long-wave movement in America, with a tendency to lead residential building at earlier turning points, before building-trade unions were powerful, and to lag at the later ones. The mean specific amplitude of this percentage differential was only 48 cycle relatives, of which only 20 survived timing variabilities for inclusion in reference amplitude (see line 3, Table 2). Since both sets of hourly earnings were in a rising secular trend, shifts in the differential between them were probably accompanied by moderate accelerations and retardations in both set of rates.

As the wage differential rose and building-trade crews were enlarged, productivity probably slackened. The influence of this shift in labor cost is indicated in the cyclical behavior of our measures of total building costs, which chiefly cover expenditure for labor and materials (see line 4, Table 1-2). Specific amplitudes for twelve long cycles in unit building costs were 51 cycle relatives, and the reference amplitude was eroded to 34 cycle relatives. The sluggish timing of labor costs probably accounts for the tendency of building costs to lag one or two years behind building turning points. Long waves of building met a supply resistance which evoked a partial response in the cost of building. The latter fluctuates with an amplitude one-sixth that of building activity itself. It thus appears that building labor and materials are drawn from the economy and released in long swings with relative ease.

Mortgage interest rates share a common long-term movement with investment yields on high-grade securities of long maturities. This long-term movement typically spans two or three building cycles and overshadows any specific long rhythm of mortgage yields. A concealed or covert rhythm shows up, however, in mortgage-yield differentials relative to bond yield. Relative differentials in the United States, Germany, and Scotland exhibited clear-cut long cycles conforming in their general character to building cycles proper. Of eighteen potential reference turning points, all were matched, and the mean deviation from the mean lead-lag was only 1.44 years. Standard total specific and reference amplitude ran nearly three times the corresponding amplitude of wage differentials (see Table 1-2).

This amplitude of movement may be regarded as a measure of the capital market's resistance to shifting the pattern of its fund allocation to accommodate mortgage credit requirements entailed by long building swings. Thus regarded, resistance in the capital market is more tenacious than the resistance of the labor or industrial materials market to shifting the pattern of use of labor and industrial resources. Does the greater resistance in the capital market to financing long-swing building swings merely reflect the more competitive character of the loan fund market and the more precise adjustment of price to short-run market-clearing forces? Or again, does the greater resistance reflect the more crucial role of finance limitations in the mechanisms of generation and propagation of building cycles and long waves generally? These questions are raised but not answered in this volume.

The rise and fall of unit site value and building costs acts as a brake on long swings in building. But the effectiveness of this braking action may be offset by corresponding movements of rental levels and selling prices for improved properties. The variation in rental prices for vacant dwellings is considerable: a mean specific amplitude of 61 and a reference amplitude of 52 cycle relatives (see Table 1-2). Turns in vacant rental prices lead house building by a little over two years. These swings in turn induce swings in the rental prices for occupied dwellings, with turns delayed by two years and amplitude cut in half (Table 1-2). While the measured swings in building cost exceed occupied rental amplitudes, rental prices for newly erected structures may be supposed to fluctuate over a wider range. Hence, fluctuations in rental returns and building costs for newly erected properties partly offset each other so far as incentives to build, indicated by realty profit margins, are concerned (Chapter 6). However, since rental returns tend to lead and costs to lag, a cyclically shifting profit margin may generate swings in realty selling prices. Price swings for improved realty do have an amplitude of movement nearly double that of the cost of new building. This additional amplitude reflects a possible cyclical movement in rental profit margins and underlying shifts in urban site values. This movement may be generated in good measure by land speculation and land development activity, which, as we have seen, are very sensitive to long-swing movements. Here one of the sources can be seen for the fluctuation in financial inducements which helps to produce local amplification of long-run growth waves.

The following chapter presents a full statement and justification for the statistical methodology utilized in this investigation. In Chapter 3, we will consider long local swings in building activity as a whole and by type of building: residential, industrial, commercial, and public. In Chapter 4, the same local swings will be traced in real estate market, lending, and development activity. In Chapters 5 and 6, our center of interest shifts to more fundamental levels where causal influences will be encountered. These influences in Chapter 5 center on migration of labor force and formation of new households through marriage, and changes in vacancy and occupancy patterns. The influences dealt with in Chapter 6 involve a systematic survey of shifts in relationships between values and prices at various phases of building and real estate market activity: site values, lot values, real estate selling prices, rents, building costs, mortgage yields. In Chapters 7 and 8, certain crucial aspects of long national swings are reviewed.

NOTES

1. See [65, 149, 209, 242, 189, 159, 86, 188, 274, 81, 191, 220, 180, 219, 239, 179, 281, 283, 96, 79, 87, 80], a compilation of dissertations on Saarbrücken, Koblenz, Bonn, Aachen, München-Gladbach, Elberfelds, Barmens, Duisburg, Bremen, Kiel, Köln, Neuwied). For critical reviews of the Eberstadt position as developed in earlier works, see [273 and 282].

2. Thus Reich generally refers to ups and downs of building as a phase of general business cycles [219, pp. 1, 6 ff., 48 ff.]. Her chronology of peaks and troughs did not distinguish between long and short turning points, and her average cycle period for annual percentage change in residential building (Table III, pp. 126 ff.) is ten years. But her portrayal of the general course of a building cycle emphasizes its system of lagged reactions—in use of incomes, demand for shelter, reduced vacancies, higher rent, higher land values, etc. Spiethoff simply applies to residential building his standard chronology of phases and periods (averaging around eight or more years). See [239, pp. 17 ff.].

3. [179, Part I, particularly pp. 39 ff., 85 f.].

4. J. C. Spensley wrote about London [238] and Alexander Cairncross wrote about Glasgow [45]. North American investigators published studies about Chicago, St. Louis, Manhattan, Oakland, Pittsburgh, and Toronto [134, 224, 174, 186, 152, 37]. Paris was studied by L. Flaus [93]. Three investigators in the 1930's attempted to summarize American urban experience with building and real estate fluctuations: John R. Rigglemen [222], W. H. Newman [206], and C. D. Long, Jr. [173].

5. [280, pp. 97–153]. On these pages the results of an extensive collection of data were assembled and the results were graphically exhibited.

6. Allusion was there made to a "monograph on construction work which

will discuss in detail long cycles in building construction and related activities in the United States and foreign countries." This monograph has not appeared in published form.

7. See particularly Moses Abramovitz [1] and items cited in his bibliography (pp. 237 ff.) by himself; Blank; Easterlin; Gottlieb; Grebler, Blank, and Winnick; Guttentag; Kuznets; Ulmer; and Wickens. See also the work of Richard Easterlin [78], and Burnham O. Campbell [50].

8. The study and interpretation of long swings and business cycles in the United Kingdom have been converted, through the work of A. Cairncross and B. Thomas, into a study of long swings in the Atlantic economy. See Alexander Cairncross [46] and J. Parry Lewis [167] (London 1965), papers and studies by B. Weber [284], E. W. Cooney [66], John Habakkuk [116], and others. Recent American theoretical enquiry included three papers, by Bert Hickman, B. O. Campbell, and J. G. Williamson [126]. For recent discussions, see [168, 5, 246].

9. Alexander Cairncross very kindly sent us a copy of the original work-sheets of Bernard Weber, whose investigation of building activity in individual cities culminated in a new nationwide time series of English residential building from 1838 to 1950. See Appendix B, series 0001–0009. For the series borrowed from investigations of Parry Lewis, see Appendix B, series 0143–0145.

10. The character and composition of the sample are indicated in Chapter 2.

11. See publications by the author, Appendix B, series 0155, 0270-2.

12. See Appendix H, "Urban Residential Building Index, Germany, Series 0018."

13. See Appendix B, series 0037.

14. J. Parry Lewis' "descriptive work" on building cycles was incomplete because it lacked the "model" of an interacting network of fluctuating economies out of whose processes in a disturbed environment long swings are generated. See [167, pp. 2 f., 8, 211–232].

15. Two other simple measures of conformity often used in this study are the mean deviation expressed in units of a year between matching reference and specific turning points and the correlation coefficient.

16. Thus Abramovitz finds that Long's value of private nonresidential building permits (series 22) and his index of the value of public building permits (series 35) conformed perfectly during long swings between 1871 and 1935, though, in terms of annual change per year, two extra cycles characterized as "minor interruptions" (p. 105) were recognized and these reduced average durations to 12.56 years (series 22) and 10.36 years (series 35). See Abramovitz [1, Tables 13 and 15 and Chart 6].

17. See [109, p. 47]. The rise in vacancy rates from reference trough to peak of 5.9 per cent (8.5 minus 2.6) is equal to 2.3 years of new residential building at mean rates.

CHAPTER 2

Statistical Techniques and Procedures

A. SURVEY EXPERIENCE LIMITED

Our study of local building cycles encompassed all urban areas for which suitable time series were available, with at least two full long cycles of building activity unaffected by major war or extended governmental intervention. As a result, the series were affected primarily by forces generated by private decisions made in open markets. For most of Europe, this meant closing the books of our research at or near to 1914; for the U.S., at 1939. This limitation should be explained.

The practice of other investigators has varied, depending partly upon the time of writing and upon whether European or American experience was central to the story. The earliest continental European students of long building cycles derived their generalizations almost exclusively from pre-1914 local experience. To interwar analysts the catastrophic effects of the prolonged war and its aftermath of inflation and other disturbance made very questionable the projection into the postwar period of a process which required a considerable time period and "normal" conditions to come to fruition. Aggravated inflation continued in many European areas long after major hostilities ceased and in some cases was only overcome late in the 1920's. Fixed exchange rates and their concomitant financial stability were maintained for only about six years before their breakdown in the Great Depression. Price controls on housing and corresponding programs for public housing persisted through the thirties. As late as 1938, one-quarter of the English stock of housing remained under rent control, and a high proportion of newly erected homes were constructed only with governmental assistance [167, p. 230; 28]. Governmental controls over housing and building activities were extended during the period of World War II.[1]

Brinley Thomas expressly predicated "swings" of the "old"

Atlantic economy, distinguished from a "new" Atlantic economy, "born of the nineties and come to fruition after the second World War" and destined to "evolve its own conditions of equilibrium" for which "past experience is not always a reliable guide" [245]. And speaking still more plainly, the most recent British investigator characterized the swing that closed in 1913 as "the last building cycle of our uncontrolled economy" and noted that the growth of control made the "economic climate" prevailing in the postwar years "far different from any that has existed before" [167, pp. 209 and 233].

This use of a categoric 1914 boundary line has been absent from the work of more recent American investigators, who have primarily reviewed American experience.[2] American experience did involve a lesser degree of dependence upon outside terms of trade or access to capital. In America, World War I impacted on the economy chiefly as a dynamic of inflation and as a stimulus to industrial development. In the American view, the Great Depression, though affected by the "dislocations" produced by World War I and its aftermath, took on the character of a downswing phase of an American building cycle and was otherwise more readily accommodated to our tradition of heightened cyclical instability, extended contractions, and more recent experience with financial crisis. It was easier for American analysis to include the twenties and thirties in the long-swing chronology and we have done so in this work.

It is a different matter, however, to presuppose that the long-swing process continued on through the next three decades and is still at work. Here we meet the judgment of "comparability" pointed up by Simon Kuznets in his monumental *Capital in the American Economy*. We would not, says Kuznets, put in one time series trends of gross national products of American society in the sixteenth and nineteenth centuries because of our judgment "that the size, technological levels, social institutions, and international relations of the sixteenth century Indian society were vastly different from those of the United States economy during the last century and the latter cannot therefore be regarded as a continuation or later expression of the forces that molded the former." It was deemed proper to treat as a single period for study the stretch of years between the 1870's and the 1950's. There are many likenesses ranging from the political parties to political constitutions and there may be many differences "ranging from the income tax to the H-bomb." The judgment is then "necessarily a matter of weighing the like-nesses against the differences." This judgment must be made in relation to the purposes of inquiry, which for Kuznets concentrated upon characteristics of "underlying trend" and not the "long swings" which merely complicated "both our statistical analysis and our explanatory task." Given these purposes, Kuznets made the determination "that the balance is in favor of treating the 1870's and the 1950's in this country as belonging to the same historical epoch" [161, pp. 39 f., 200].

On the basis of similar reasoning but altered purposes, Moses Abramovitz in his main work on long swings made the same determination, assuming that the characteristics of long swings, and not their underlying trends, were common to both the 1870's and the 1950's. Abramovitz was prepared to recognize that many modifications in economic institutions and patterning—the sub-sidence of railway construction once so unruly, the emergence of public construction geared to nonmarket forces, the shift to owner-occupied construction carried on by merchant builders, altered conditions of finance, a much restrained elasticity of population growth, a restricted role of construction in aggregate construction expenditure, and altered susceptibility to deep depression—indicate that the whole interplay between construction and the rest of economic activity is altered "in ways we cannot now clearly see." Notwithstanding, Abramovitz con-cluded that the causes of long swings may be more deeply embedded "than we realize, causing the phenomenon to persist, even if in somewhat modified form, through many apparently radical alterations in our economic arrangements" [1, pp. 8f., 133–136]. For these reasons, presumably, Abramovitz added the three decades after 1933 to his stock of long-swing experience. Easterlin, who has followed Abramovitz in this decision, at-tempts to show that the essential features of long-swing analysis hold for the 1960's as much as for the 1860's. His book is an extended argument for the "similarities" between "recent and longer term experience" [78]. This same search for "similarities" dominated the discussion at the 1964 Christmas session of the American Economics Association, responding to the query, "The Postwar Retardation: Another Long Swing in the Rate of Growth?" Only much later has Abramovitz put a different interpretation on contemporary experience and in a cogently argued paper testified to the "passing of the Kuznets Cycle" from this experience.[3]

The similarities grow in part out of the basic fact that any slowdown in rate of growth, induced either by extended depression or short bursts of connected recessions, will in turn result in higher incidence of mass unemployment, which, since it is concentrated among the young, will in turn affect fertility and nuptiality and labor force participation rates. Easterlin has carefully traced the effects of a slowdown upon these demographic phenomena, which have persisted long enough to influence the character of American population projections for coming decades.

Similarities in "effect," however, are not at issue; concern rather is felt over similarity in causation. Was the slowdown in building and investment expenditure and the interplay between construction and over-all economic activity induced by the same process at work in previous long swings? Can it be seriously contended that the period of building expansion which took off in 1933 and was resumed after World War II lapsed into a period of slowdown in the later fifties and early sixties *for reasons which are comparable to those which played a role in earlier long-swing decline periods?* The very length of this period and the peculiar combination of forces which provided its driving power, the role of war and the institutional transformation which war spearheaded, the wholly altered international setting with world devastation set plumb in the middle of this "expansion period," all this and more argue against putting old labels on new facts.

And, if we turn to the contraction period or "slowdown" which set in during the middle 1950's, the unfitness of the old labels or formulas to illuminate the processes at work is obvious.

On balance our judgment—reached early in the sixties—held that the feedback process between construction and the total economy and between residential building and real estate markets had altered in so many fundamental respects that, given our purpose of isolating and illuminating this feedback process, it seemed worthwhile to drop out of review the thirty years after the Great Depression trough (1933) and thus put our American data on the same basis as data from other areas. It is conceded that we could have processed additional time series and have shown these alongside our series. The later series could have been excluded from the calculation of "average patterns." We did not wish, however, to complicate our presentation without at the same time being in a position to clarify its meaning and to evaluate its results. Because this was not possible, it seemed better to make that analysis when the period now in process can be reviewed with greater perspective. This does not exclude consideration of some aspects of recent American experience in a suitable context. We have, for example, compared the relation of recent American vacancy experience and residential building with earlier patterns. But we have excluded recent experience of processes which have in past periods connected up development booms, investment surging, and urban growth. This act of judgment is provisional and may at a later time be modified.

B. SURVEYED SERIES

Some thirty-one urban areas or closely related groups of areas with long-term building time series were available for study in Europe, Australia, and North America. In addition, we analyzed five American cities, for which only deed or lot development activity was available.

The thirty-one urban areas are distributed as follows:

Australia (2)	Melbourne (Victoria), Sydney (New South Wales)
North America (12)	Chicago, Cincinnati, Cleveland, Detroit, Manhattan (New York), Montreal, Ohio sample groups I, II, III, IV, V, St. Louis
Great Britain (11)	Birmingham, Bradford, Exeter, Glasgow, Hull, Liverpool, London, Manchester, Newport, South Wales, Swindon
Germany (3)	Berlin, Bremen, Hamburg
Other Europe (3)	Amsterdam, Paris, Stockholm

For eleven of the surveyed urban areas, only information on building activity was available. For nineteen of the areas, matching series were available for long time periods covering three or more phases of real estate market activity or building determinants. These areas, and the series covered by each, are shown in Table 2-1. The greatest detail on determinants of building activity for European cities is found in Berlin; of

TABLE 2-1
Local Time Series, Thirty Areas, by Activity

| | | | | | | | | | *Activity Covered by Time Series* | | | | | | | | |
	Period	No. of Series	Residential Building	Total Building	Nonresidential Building	Marriage	Population or Migration	Mortgage Lending	Lot Development	Selling Price Improved Realty	Building Costs	Volume of Real Estate Activity	Vacancy Rates	Rental Prices	Foreclosures	Street Construction	Other
Manhattan	1868–1940	9	x	x	x					x	x			x		x	x[a]
Chicago	1835–1931	8		x		x	x					x		x		x	x[b]
St. Louis	1890–1933	6	x	x									x	x	x		
Detroit	1830–1944	2		x					x								
Ohio-Cincinnati[c]	1857–1920	4	x	x		x		x		x							
Ohio-Cleveland[c]	1857–1920	7	x	x		x		x	x	x							
Ohio-Sample II	1857–1920	17	x	x		x		x	x			x					

		No. of series															
Ohio-Sample III	1857–1920	17	x	x	x	x		x	x	x		x	x			x	x
Ohio-Sample IV	1857–1920	17	x	x	x	x		x	x	x		x	x			x	x
Ohio-Sample V	1857–1920	17	x	x	x	x		x	x	x		x	x			x	x
Montreal	1867–1914	1	x	x				x									
London	1856–1914	3	x		x						x			x	x		
Glasgow	1864–1914	6	x	x	x	x	x				x			x	x		x
9 English Cities	varied	9	x														
Berlin	1840–1910	7	x	x			x	x		x				x	x	x	
Bremen	1855–1914	1	x				x										
Hamburg	1875–1913	5	x		x									x	x	x	
Paris	1833–1914	5		x		x				x				x	x		
Stockholm	1867–1948	4	x			x								x			
Amsterdam	1870–1935	3	x		x	x	x							x			
New South Wales	1861–1900	4	x	x	x						x			x			
Victoria	1861–1941	3		x							x			x			
Number of series of each type:		155	25	14	8	10	3	7	7	8	5	7	7	5	2	3	2

[a] Mortgage-yield differential.
[b] Manufacturing.
[c] Not shown when grouped together as Ohio-Sample I.

American urban areas, Chicago and Manhattan are liberally served with comparable measures.

A comprehensive set of measures for the State of Ohio was discovered and studied. The counties containing two of the larger cities of the state—Cleveland and Cincinnati—were analyzed individually and are so represented in Table 2-1. Eight additional counties out of the eighty-five available were selected for detailed study as moderately urbanized counties with central cities exceeding 24,000 in population by 1900. Returns for these ten counties were tabulated in three subgroups: large metropolitan, containing Cleveland and Cincinnati (sample group I); large urban, containing three major urban areas (sample group II); and small urban, containing five smaller urban centers (sample group III).

Ten additional counties selected for detailed scrutiny were combined in two groups of five counties each. One group with some industrial development was drawn from the southeastern part of the state along the Ohio River. These counties have a modest degree of urbanization, with city size classes by 1900 under 24,000 persons. The other group was drawn from rural counties of northwestern Ohio, with no city in 1900 over 10,000 persons. These two sample groups together with the three mentioned above thus represent areas spanning the spectrum of urbanization, industry, and city size. A detailed report on the makeup of the Ohio group samples and procedures used is provided in Appendix C.

C. SELECTING SPECIFIC CHRONOLOGIES

Time series for the local communities under survey can tell their story of long swings only if these long swings can be accurately identified and measured.

To this end, our first objective was to select chronologies, that is, sequences of dates corresponding to our best judgment of peaks and troughs or turning points for both short and long cyclical movements [41]. Our short-cycle chronologies were selected mechanically, by counting every reversal of direction as a specific turning point. These chronologies were used chiefly as a means of smoothing the time series by eliminating the influence of overt short cyclical and irregular influences. Out of the smoothed series, measures for average annual rate of growth were computed from cycle to cycle or phase to phase, as well as averages of these rates which approximate satisfactorily to a long-term secular growth rate of an underlying trend value.

Our procedure for long-term chronologies was formally similar but substantively more difficult. Series were graphed in their annual values or, if the data were very irregular, with a three- or five-year moving average. By inspection, selection was then made of turning points in the quest for recognition of periods of sustained contraction. Since virtually all of the series exhibited secular growth, processes of expansion did not require special identification. A period of sustained contraction was recognized, if it extended, with a few exceptions, for three or more years of continuous or intermittent decline, making up in depth for narrowness of breadth. For series with a steady upward trend but with little movement around trend, a clear-cut shift in trend of growth was recognized as a turning point. Most turning points involved reversals of clear-cut movements in the original data. Hence, though our methods, like those of Burns and Mitchell, "make no pretensions to elegance" [41, p. 64], we feel the results are trustworthy. The patterns of cycle behavior will give their own evidence of this, for short and shallow long-swing contractions appear dubious when depicted in the form of a cycle pattern.

While most of our series possessed very plausible turning points, this was not true of all. For thirty-seven of them—nearly all of which were in Ohio—no specific cycles could be traced. These series measured sluggish activities, such as marriages, number of deeds, or relationships not systematically affected by long movements. In a few cases, specialized types of building for schools or public purposes responded to no distinctive specific long-wave pattern.

The work of judgment in the selection of turning points was troublesome in the case of our four Paris series. Market forces were paramount, but the stress of the past and storms of the future marked out their own chronology on the building and real estate life of that city. This is rather clearly indicated in Chart 2-1, which reproduces the various time series of building real estate and demographic activity in Paris. Comparison of the behavior of the building series, represented by building materials utilized, with other more direct measures of building available for certain decades indicates close and dependable covariation.

CHART 2-1

Real Estate, Building, and Other Activity, Paris, France, 1834–1939

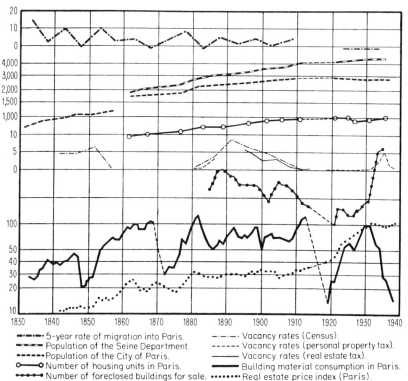

- ▬·▬·▬ 5-year rate of migration into Paris.
- ▬▭▬ Population of the Seine Department.
- ▬▬▬ Population of the City of Paris.
- ○———○ Number of housing units in Paris.
- •———• Number of foreclosed buildings for sale.
- —·—·— Vacancy rates (Census).
- ------ Vacancy rates (personal property tax).
- ——— Vacancy rates (real estate tax).
- ▬▬▬ Building material consumption in Paris.
- •••••••• Real estate price index (Paris).

Building activity until the 1870's exhibited a strong upward trend punctuated by sharp two-year declines around 1848 and 1870. These declines attest to the bursts of street fighting and political commotion which have made those years red-letter dates in French political history. The second drop in building associated with the Paris Commune in 1870 was sharper, corresponding to the greater intensity and more prolonged character of the political struggle during that year. World War I understandably left an even greater imprint on annual aggregates of building, partly because its effects were cumulative.

However, between 1870 and 1914 the rhythm of long swings is apparent. The long wave of 1870–86 was marked, and that of 1886–1908 is observable. And even if the contraction phases of 1848 and 1870 are excluded, a plausible average cyclical pattern emerges. There are many indications that the resulting pattern of long-wave movement (excluding the declines of 1848 and 1870) may be traced during the earlier swings. Thus the two real estate price series reached clear peaks not in 1870 but in 1863 and in 1867.

These peaks marked the culmination of a classical building boom, reflecting in part the release of economic energies and the adventure in creative real estate finance for which the second Napoleonic Empire was distinguished.[4] The standard NBER reference cycle chronology for France follows conventional business cycle history in dating annual peaks at 1847 and 1869.[5]

We concluded that building and real estate activity in Paris exhibited clear-cut long waves which were sometimes reinforced and sometimes disturbed by political events.

The Ohio series on industrial building was also difficult to accommodate to long-wave chronology. Chart 2-2 shows Ohio industrial building in three-year moving averages. The annual data exhibit a conventional short-cycle movement with tendencies to a clear-cut decennial (major or Juglar) movement. The smoothed series exhibits this major decennial rhythm with peaks in the early 1880's, 1890's, and 1900's. The prominent character of this rhythm indicates the close connection of industrial building with industrial investment generally, and the correspondingly close connection of both with business cycles.

Using contracts data on industrial building for later years, Arthur Burns noted that "the enormous cyclical amplitudes and high degree of conformity of each series on industrial contracts, together with the close similarity in timing between the specific cycles in total industrial contracts and business cycles, indicate that industrial building has exceptionally strong causal ties with business cycles—more so than any other branch of building" [39, p. 57]. Accordingly, we marked out a set of conventional short-cycle and long-cycle chronologies which result in the unusually short duration for long cycles of eight years (on a statewide basis) and somewhat longer for the sample groups (mean: eleven years).

D. REFERENCE CHRONOLOGIES

Analysis of our time series by their specific chronologies yields measurements showing the distinctive characteristics of wave movements for each of the series. In the terminology of the National Bureau, these characteristics are "specific" to a par-

CHART 2-2
Industrial Building, Ohio, Annually and 3-Year Moving Averages,
Statewide, 1859–1912

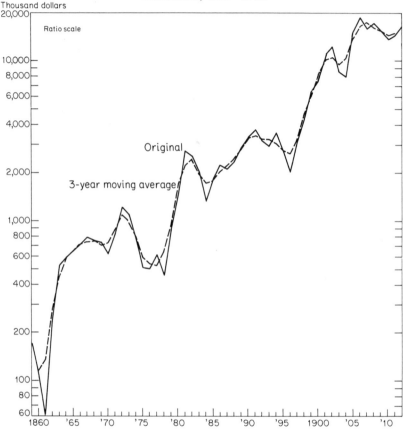

ticular series. Our interests, however, go beyond knowledge about such characteristics. We also want to know how the various activities in a given area relate to each other and to any more diffused patterns of movement. Specific cycles in each series could have been related to each other, but when the analysis covers hundreds of series, as Burns and Mitchell noted, "It is clumsy and wasteful to compare the timing of each series with every other." Much clearer results "can be attained by adopting some common denominator, i.e., by setting up a reference scale on which every series can be laid out in a strictly uniform fashion" [41, p. 70].

The search for a common denominator or reference chronology clearly pointed to residential building, which has, at least in terms of volume, outweighed other kinds of building. For the United States and for England, residential building ran to between 49 and 65 per cent of total building, and between 21 and 56 per cent of total construction (see Table 2-2). A substantial part of nonresidential building is of a complementary type (shops, offices, utility connections, places of worship or play). It has been estimated that the volume of such complementary building in recent years is about 75 per cent of the volume of residential building [185, pp. 465–473]. Most of the major influences at work in building cycles relate directly to residential markets. Mortgage markets chiefly apply to residential building; the used market in realty is most active with regard to residential properties.

It is recognized, however, that there is variation in the relative importance of the activities that shape the course of building

TABLE 2-2
Residential Building as Per Cent of Total Building or Total
Construction[a]

Country	Years	Residential Building as Per Cent of:	
		Total Building	*Total Construction*
U.S.	1850–1910	49.0	
	1910–1940	53.8	
Italy	1870–1898		46.6
	1898–1918		56.1
Australia	1861–1895		31.5
	1895–1918		21.3
	1918–1932		21.6
Canada	1901–1910		32.6
	1911–1920		30.1
	1920–1930		33.4
Sweden	1925–1930		42.9
England	1907	62.9[b]	35.9[c]

Source: U.S. [110]; Italy [143, pp. 266–267]; Australia [44, pp. 391, 397, 403]; Canada [35, p. 38]; Sweden [171, pp. 177, 237]; England [46, p. 110].

[a] The specification of "construction" as contrasted with "building" varies with different sources, but generally "construction" series include all building plus road building, canal and railroad building, and related types of heavy construction.

[b] New residential construction to new building.

[c] New residential construction to total new construction.

cycles—rents, land value, development, vacancies, cost of building, real estate market. Nonresidential building occasionally becomes dominant, as during 1917–19, so that real estate markets for such periods are quite poorly measured by residential building alone. But these times have been exceptional and allowance may readily be made for them. The relationship of residential to total building has varied within a narrow range over long periods; and the role of rental markets in real estate market behavior has been surprisingly uniform. There are obvious advantages to settling on a reference scale that can be objectively determined and easily measured. Hence, in this work "reference" chronologies for analysis of interrelated long swings of different time series were obtained, with few exceptions, from the chronology of turning points of residential building.

In each region or area specific chronologies for residential building were matched to other types of building, real estate market, or demographic activity. Local residential building series were in turn analyzed against the national reference chronology, fixed in relation to turns in aggregate residential building, thus yielding a measure of synchronization of local cycles with each other. For some American series of building material prices and costs, a reference chronology related to turns in aggregate construction was used. This chronology was developed in the work paralleling our own by Moses Abramovitz.[6]

We were not able to compose a satisfactory reference chronology for Sweden, for reasons that are worth noting. In Chart 2-3 available measures of construction, building, and related activities are presented for Sweden. Gross deflated construction exhibits no clear long-wave pattern though smoothed first differences or annual rates of change would show a low in 1896, a peak around 1912, a trough around 1922, and a peak in 1930. Residential building could be read to show a peak in 1905–6, a trough in 1918–20, and a peak in 1930. Alternatively, we could find three major movements in 1900–1909, 1909–20 and 1920 on. Information before 1900 was unreliable except for urban population change. A three-year moving average of increments in town population exhibits clear-cut major cycles of a mean duration of nine years, with an overlapping longer pattern (peaks in 1884 and 1915) averaging 27.5 years. The composite of village added to town increments changes the pattern somewhat.

CHART 2-3

New Rooms Added, Gross Value Total Construction Deflated and
Annual Increments, Urban Population, Sweden, 1863–1930

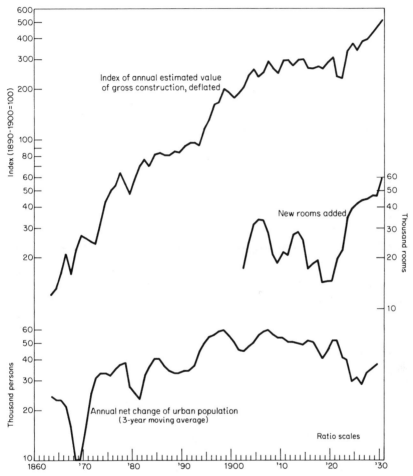

The major cycle is thinned out after 1904 and the longer-wave
pattern has nearly disappeared. At best, a whole spectrum of
vaguely outlined long swings including a suggestion of a long
sixty-year movement from 1870 to 1930 is indicated, none of it
however very readily apparent or solidly established.[7]

E. LONG-SWING PATTERNS

Selection of long-swing chronologies was only the first step in
a procedure designed to achieve the statistical isolation, mea-

surement, and representation of long swings. The chronologies establish the *duration* of long swings and the *proportion of expansion to contraction* but little else. We knew that long-term secular trends were at work in our series along with short-term fluctuations of the business cycle. These would weave an irregular course during long-swing movements, which would tend to be tilted upward by secular growth trends.

The isolation of cyclical components from time series, or time series decomposition, is a field of professional expertise cultivated in the 1920's when statistical business-cycle analysis became practically a specialized field.[8] Adjustment for trend has been called the "fundamental logical problem of time series decomposition" [94, p. 8]. Debates over trend adjustment and its effect on cyclical measures have long divided cycle practitioners into two basic camps: those who do and those who don't. Those "who do" take the trends out of the time series by many means ranging from fixed term moving averages, freehand drawing, imposition of mathematical equations devised to achieve a close "fit," conversion to smoothed link relatives or to percentage rates of change for overlapping periods. Common to all methods of trend elimination is the presupposition that the force of growth is separate from fluctuation and that the economic system tends to grow by a smooth, continuous movement and then to oscillate around that movement.[9] In all these ways upward trend is converted into a level plane around which cyclical fluctuations occur.

Conversely, the school "that doesn't," believes with Schumpeter that economic development has a mixed dynamic of *creation* and innovation, and that "evolution is essentially a process which moves in cycles," so that the trend "is nothing but the result of the cyclical process or a property of it . . ." [229, I, p. 206]. Those who accept this in itself unprovable hypothesis necessarily oppose trend elimination from cyclical contours so that these contours can "reproduce *the form of development* common to the industrial activities of nations whose economic life has been organized on a business basis."[10] To this fundamental objection in principle there is joined a lesser objection arising from the distorting effects of trend adjustment on measures of cyclical behavior, causing cycles to be multiplied or reduced in number and modified in form, amplitude, and timing.

Neither the case for or against trend elimination can be proven in any conclusive way. Each investigator must reach his own judgment as to whether the advantages of trend elimination—by way of facilitating a more clear depiction of the long-swing process in hazy or borderline cases—is worth the cost in distortion of cyclical measures and its tendency to obscure the idea that the trend itself is affected by the surging movements of long swings. My judgment follows that of Schumpeter, and Burns and Mitchell; and that is why in this work we do not follow the lead of Kuznets, Abramovitz, and Easterlin in using and relying upon trend-adjusted measures for generalized representation of and analysis of long swings. This judgment need not rule out trend adjustment in all instances, and some use of it will be found in this volume.[11]

This decision to include, as a general rule, the effects of trend growth on long-swing contours leaves unresolved a related question: how to separate from the long-swing contours the influence of short-term cyclical fluctuations. The need for such adjustment grows out of the fact that during most long building swings many complete business fluctuations will have run an irregular course. These fluctuations tend to obscure the slower long-swing rhythms, hampering visual comparison of many long swings with each other. Without some form of purification of long swings from these shorter fluctuations, we will have trouble identifying the very phenomenon we hope to explain.

To achieve this purification, two major types of adjusting methods have been practiced. The first, and most popular, involves a fixed-term moving average, a form of which, contrived by Simon Kuznets, involves a five-year moving average or aggregate reduced to a link relative over a ten-year span.[12]

A second type, designed by Moses Abramovitz, involves use of a chronology of peaks and troughs representing turning points of national business cycles ranging up to ten years, with an average period of about four years. Average annual values centered for the cycle period are entered on an overlapping basis, peak to peak and trough to trough. The resulting figures "may be regarded as approximations to series from which the influence of business cycles of ordinary duration and amplitude have been eliminated" [1, p. 22]. For most reference periods this scheme of adjustment would smooth out the larger portion of short cyclical fluctuation. But some phases of national business cycles involving prolonged and severe contractions, such as occurred in 1873–79 and 1929–33, overlap with phases of a long-swing movement. These severe contractions embody a coalescence of the two movements or a single movement with multiple impulses or determinants. Application of the national reference schema with their prolonged contraction periods to such phases tends to dampen the amplitude of those particular long swings unduly and thus tends to give to long-swing patterns an undeserved and misleading kind of homogeneity.

The fact that long-swing and cycle movements may coalesce—and always do to some extent—suggests use of a smoothing technique which minimizes transformation of data and which is designed to avoid alteration of the shape and character of the long swings of recorded experience. We should remember that a good deal of smoothing is indirectly accomplished because much of our statistical information comes to us in the form of annual figures. Annual summation alone, in comparison with quarterly or monthly data, effects a significant degree of smoothing, which, as Burns and Mitchell showed, "hides many of the cycles revealed by monthly data, sometimes introduces spurious cycles and influences the amplitude, pattern, and other features of all cyclical movements" [41, p. 204]. The harmful effects of this smoothing are, perhaps, reduced for measures of simple construction work, which involves a concentration of "new starts" in early spring months and "completions" in fall or early winter. But many of our other activities—migration, marriage, buying a home, buying land, entering a mortgage loan—are spread out over the year and are significantly smoothed by yearly aggregation.

Because of the significant degree of smoothing already incorporated into our data, it was decided to use the mildest of the existing smoothing schemes devised for cyclical analysis. This scheme is that developed by the National Bureau of Economic Research for allocation of the stretch of experience between long-swing peaks and troughs into three segments of about equal length. Smoothing is effected by computation of a simple annual average for the segment, centered as a segment or stage "standing." A long-swing expansion phase of twelve years would involve two segments of three and one segment of four years duration, for each of which a smoothed (average) annual "standing" would be prepared. A typical contraction phase would also be allocated into thirds, each of which would rarely extend over two years. As phase periods shorten, smoothing thus becomes reduced. But even for long phase periods *the effect of smoothing is basically felt only within a segment of experience.* Disturbance in a segment is not "spread" over behavior patterns for a broader period. A tendency for expansion or contraction to become accelerated or retarded will show up faithfully in the segment of experience where the tendency was felt. Experimentation with this form of smoothing, when extended over a finer set of intervals, showed little or no gain in fidelity of representation, though it is conceded that a certain tendency toward "angularity" for the nine-stage cycle pattern may result if peak or trough values are specially exaggerated [41, pp. 144–160].

Nine-stage annual standings were thus computed for the three turning point years and for the six intervening "cycle stages," yielding a smoothed contour line of a long swing.

Can these long swings thus purified of cyclical disturbance be detached from their time series progression, i.e., from the context of development and succession, and be grouped together, with similar long swings occurring earlier or later *or elsewhere* and transformed into some *average type* or *representative long swing*? Are the bonds of historical context so weak and is the homogeneity of process so great as to legitimize this procedure? Opinion differs here too, and most long-swing investigators are loath to take this final step, which cuts the umbilical cord between the long swing and its historical context. Swings have been presented chiefly in their time series connection, or as isolated historical experiences, but not as a generalized process.

We took this step, designed to make possible the preparation of some average or representative long-swing pattern, partly because cogent grounds could be given for believing that the process of long-swing fluctuation in urban development—and it is this phase of long-swing fluctuations which is here under review—was even more homogeneous than are the fluctuations in building activity associated with business cycles, and hence is possibly more suitably treated by the smoothing and averaging process which is now contemplated. Burns found evidence (see Table 2-3) that, so far as amplitude and duration were concerned, long cycles in American building activity were more homogeneous than the short ones associated with business

TABLE 2-3

Coefficients of Variation for Duration and Amplitude, Specific Full
Cycles, Long and Short, Selected American Series, 1878–1933

	Coefficients of Variation for Full Cycles			
	Duration		*Amplitude*	
Area	*Long*	*Short*	*Long*	*Short*
Per capita permits,"All Cities"	13	48	31	64
Adjusted indexes of permits, "All Cities"	13	48	26	42
New England cities	41	36	16	47
Middle Atlantic cities	13	36	26	47
South Atlantic cities	11	43	17	36
East North Central cities	13	35	13	29
West North Central cities	16	34	11	45
South Central cities	12	32	31	45
Western cities	15	37	11	40
Total or new building permits				
Manhattan	19	36	24	62
Brooklyn	15	48	22	33
Chicago	11	41	21	42
Detroit	35	44	59	51
St. Louis	13	30	10	42
Subdivision activity				
Chicago	17	57	11	37
Pittsburgh area	16	33	18	21

SOURCE: Burns [39, Table 20].

cycles, as attested to by lower coefficients of variation. The forms of behavior assumed by the real estate market over the years of our survey, which exclude the period when governmental controls over residential building or housing markets were predominant, were in all probability widely diffused among the growing cities in North America, England, France, and Sweden. The distinction between owner-occupancy and rental submarkets, the relatively slow response of housing supply to changes in demand, the tendency of ultimate site values to appreciate, the dependence of house buying on long-term mortgage finance, the immobility of structures, the uncertainty in forecasting future market conditions, the psychology of land speculation, the sticky behavior of rents and building costs, the recruiting of a labor force from young migrants enticed from villages and farms—all these were structural features of urban market behavior, whether located in the new or the old world, or in the later eighteenth, nineteenth, and early twentieth centuries.

The requirement of homogeneity to give meaning to our statistical procedure does not specify complete uniformity in structure or process. Differences among cycle patterns or duration and amplitude show up in the measures of dispersion or in the individual cycle patterns themselves. Analysis can differentiate as well as reconcile. Such analysis is only valid if reasonable homogeneity is assumed, and this assumption is itself a hypothesis to be explored in our investigation.

On this working assumption of homogeneity, for each analyzed time series an average cycle pattern was computed *by averaging* the cycle relatives for the stage standing and the length of the interval between the stages. The sense of growth through *successive* swings has been eliminated in this measure, but *process of development or growth occurring during swings* has been retained in the relatively prolonged expansion and upward tilt of the cycle pattern. Where the form of movement of the individual cycles has been markedly discrepant, an average cycle pattern is always presented in this work, together with measures of deviation or the component patterns themselves.

Average patterns have been prepared, with few exceptions, only for a given area or region. With only one exception, we have not gone beyond this, because our surveyed areas were geographically scattered and were subjected to different environmental influences. The averaging of consecutive swings for a given area, but not between areas, implies belief that continuity within a community or area is greater than comparability with other communities. This belief is, of course, only a hypothesis to be supported or rejected according to the evidence.

These "average" patterns, as indicated earlier, take two forms: specific and reference. A specific pattern is one for which the peaks and troughs are those of a given series; a reference pattern uses a chronology of peaks and troughs which is usually that of residential building in the same area or, for a local residential building series, residential building for the region in which the area is located, and with which, presumably, it is integrated. Comparison between specific and reference cycle patterns throws light on the degree and nature of conformity of fluctuations in the surveyed activity to parallel fluctuations in residential building proper. Comparison between specific and reference patterns for residential building activity throws light on the degree and nature of local conformity in building fluctuation to the course of fluctuation in the larger region.

Comparison of cycle patterns for different activities in the same area throws light on the different degrees of their participation in long-swing fluctuations and the rhythm of that participation. All of these graphic comparisons are facilitated by uniform scaling of graphs in terms of cycle duration, usually represented in months to and from a peak (in the case of a trough-to-trough version of a "positive" cycle) or from a trough (in the case of a peak-to-peak version of an "inverted" cycle). With duration measured on the horizontal axis, cycle amplitude is represented on the vertical axis in the form of index relatives of cycle standings around a "cycle base" represented by the standing of one hundred. One per cent on the amplitude scale thus equals one month of cycle duration, so that on all charts, unless otherwise noted, a slope of 45 degrees represents a change at the monthly rate of 1 per cent per month or a doubling of the level of value over approximately eight years.

Successive cycle patterns for each series on a specific and reference base have been graphed and, where helpful, these graphs are introduced into the chapters following. Average patterns for each series have been grouped together in two different ways: (a) relating the same or similar activities in *different* areas, or (b) relating *different activities* in a *given area*. The activity patterns in different areas are shown in the chapters to follow, when the particular activity is described and analyzed. The area profiles—collections of average patterns for an area—were consulted in the analysis wherever the reference was appropriate, but in the main these area profiles are unpublished.

These cycle pattern charts, of course, speak a special language best understood after training or experience with them. Readers for whom this language is obscure or unfamiliar are advised to read over the relevant chapters of the standard monograph on cyclical patterns [41] or a later summary presentation by Mitchell

[193]. As Mitchell observed when he introduced a corresponding collection of cycle patterns, "the nature of the activities represented and thinking of reasons why these activities differ from or resemble one another in cyclical behavior, should make up an 'interesting' exercise and should whet the appetite for the analytic chapters to follow" [193, p. 31].

F. OTHER MEASURES

The statistical measures of long swings are not exhausted with preparation of graphic cycle patterns. The strength of the graphic presentation is its suggestion of influences too subtle to show up in simple numerical measurements. But these influences need an undergirding of fact reduced to appropriate measures of dispersion, amplitude, secular change, duration, and timing. From the original series or the cycle patterns these were all computed and are presented in later chapters when the activities concerned are reviewed. Only with regard to measures of timing or determination of lead and lag were special difficulties encountered; accordingly, a variety of timing measures was used. One method resorts to a simple comparison of the difference, if any, between corresponding turns of matching reference and specific chronologies. We would thus relate reference turns in residential building in Chicago with the corresponding turns in a Chicago marriage or real estate activity series. But a bias in locating either set of turning points will affect the result unduly, since comparatively few turning points are available even in very long time series. The other standard method measures timing of characteristic lead or lag by behavior of reference series with leads or lags calculated in "stages" of a cycle. These "stage" leads and lags may be converted into years by use of measures of average cycle stage duration. We found that in building activity, reference cycle patterns come out with somewhat longer lags (of two or more months) than were exhibited by direct comparison of turning points. With nonbuilding series the position of the two measures was reversed. A good deal of variation was indicated in particular cases.

In view of this divergence, a third measure of lead-lag was utilized by use of correlation analysis. If the reference and the specific time series, smoothed of short cyclical fluctuations by a moving average, are correlated with a variety of leads and lags serially arranged, the resulting series of correlation coefficients graphically laid out in a "correlogram" will exhibit timing characteristics of the correlated series. A formula was devised by which the schedule of correlation coefficients could be corrected for secular trend running through the correlated series. The correlogram takes account of all paired experience, including stretches of years that run beyond our initial and terminal turning points. The form of movement and level of the correlogram will indicate the closeness of the association and affords another measure of duration. A full study of the results of the three methods is provided in Appendix F. We concluded that an unambiguous and correct measure of lead and lag is not to be had with any available measure, and that various techniques were to be considered and utilized in the light of the particular circumstances.

NOTES

1. For a general survey see [285].

2. Insularity arises from a tendency to regard the American economy as essentially self-contained and as the primary generator of long-swing rhythms. See [78, Ch. 2; 289, pp. 205, 215 f.].

3. ". . . the specific set of relations and response mechanisms which were characteristic of pre-1914 'long swings' in growth are unlikely to be characteristic of future long swings" [3, p. 350]. The relations and mechanisms only in part overlap with those stressed in this work and presuppose a far-reaching set of empirical findings regarding the phasing of rates of growth of employment, labor force, capital formation, and demand for output. There is also presupposed "as a general rule and in a rough way" an inversion of "European" and "American" waves of industrial growth (p. 354). Brinley Thomas who spawned the inversion hypothesis for the pre-1914 period applied it only to the United Kingdom and a limited set of "overseas developing countries" (U.S., Canada, Argentina, Australia), a contention he has sought to reaffirm in the light of recent research [246, Ch. 4]. Application of the inversion concept to Europe "as a whole" runs into difficulties in the light of our empirical findings as set forth in Chapters 7 and 8 below. With arguments more closely related to those developed here, Homer Hoyt argued that "a fundamental change in the structure of our national economy" has mitigated the severity or eliminated both major business cycles and also "major real estate cycles" [135, p. 7].

4. An immense program of public works which pivoted on the creation of a new network of Paris boulevards reached a clear-cut peak in 1866. "The number of expropriations for public works, which reached a peak of more than 800 in 1866, fell to 8 in 1870" [211, p. 61]. For a broad sketch of this boom in its larger aspects, see [48].

5. [41, p. 78 ff.]. On the 1847 peak and for a treatment of its French origins and greater severity, see [74, pp. 81 ff. 366 ff.]. and [163]. These studies go a long way to confirm the contemporary observations of Marx regarding the sharpness of the conjunctural movement of 1846–47 and its political consequences.

6. See Table 1-1, note *a*.

7. For a contrary interpretation of this data, see [287, pp. 17–38].

8. A very useful and judicious summary of this literature through the middle twenties was presented by Wesley Clair Mitchell [192, Ch. 3]. For a recent summary by a participant in the early debate, see Oscar Lange [164, pp. 19–65]. For a comprehensive early survey, see Altschul [7, pp. 60–90] and a monograph supervised by Altschul [215].

9. "Trend adjustment," declared Joseph Schumpeter, in [229, Vol. I, p. 203], assumes that "our material reflects, as a matter of economic fact, first a smooth and a steady movement, and second fluctuations around it which are due to random shocks or disturbances that behave as if they were random shocks . . . this implies a definite theory of economic evolution . . . the Marshall-Moore theory of organic growth" (see the entire Chapter 5, "Time Series and Their Growth"). This concept of organic growth has been given concrete form by Simon Kuznets, who has in a recent work recognized "that forces that mold and determine the long-term trend resist, as it were, any counterforces that tend to alter the trend" [161, p. 44]. This "resistance" of the trend follows from a supposed tendency to negative correlation of disturbances. "If by some accident, the output of a commodity rises steeply above its secular level, we would expect . . . a relative decline in prices of that commodity," a subsequent fall in output in response to the price decline, "and offsetting of the original 'disturbance' " [161, p. 363]. Kuznets applies this familiar logic of "partial equilibrium" to aggregate output and demand so that a "severe depression" is thus bound to be offset by a "strong expansion" with a kind of "negative serial correlation" or a "cancelling reaction" [161, pp. 365, 424]. His argument is the more startling since the long swings are in good measure grounded on swings in overseas immigration which can by no means be regarded as a *predestined quantity*, especially since the *direction of emigration* between *countries* or *areas* of settlement is surely open to modification and for most rural Europeans seeking to move there was a plausible choice between movement to growing urban centers on the Continent and overseas. The metaphysic of the Kuznets position rules out extended stagnations or slowdowns of a Keynesian variety.

10. "It is fairly common for statisticians to assume that the elimination of the secular trend from a time series indicates what the course of the series would have been in the absence of secular movements, and that the graduation of a time series, whether in original or trend-adjusted form, indicates what the course of the series would have been in the absence of random movement. There is no warrant for such simple interpretations. . . . When a continuous 'trend factor' is eliminated from the data, it is therefore difficult to say what influences impinging on the activity have been removed and what influences have been left in the series" [41, pp. 38, 39].

11. The technique of trend adjustment practiced by this school involves

transformation of original series, often aggregated and averaged over stretches of years, into link relatives which converts *trend* into a *level plane* around which cyclical fluctuations occur. Kuznets, Abramovitz, and Easterlin vary in the degree of reliance upon trend adjustment in the actual course of analysis and degree of smoothing involved. Kuznets is boldest in use of smoothing with calculation of link relatives over decade intervals. Abramovitz employs smoothing only over relatively short (reference cycle) periods to supplement use of unadjusted annual data for purposes of selecting chronologies. Conversions to link relatives (growth rates) are smoothed only over the same short periods; and these conversions are analyzed primarily to resolve doubts raised by behavior over periods where evidence for long swings is questionable. Easterlin, who has dedicated his work to Kuznets, follows him more closely in this regard.

12. Kuznets [161]. It has been shown that use of such a radical smoothing device with averaging terms which do not conform to short cyclical rhythms will convert any form of disturbance into a wavelike form, and will generate special long rhythms arising out of shifting periods or amplitudes. See the incisive criticism in [20].

CHAPTER 3

Building Activities in Local Long Cycles

A. DURATION AND AMPLITUDE

Buildings of different types are complementary to each other, and an increase in demand for one type of building cannot long be extended without involving other types. We will thus, at the outset, review the findings of our survey of 62 building series and 162 specific buildings long cycles without distinction to the type of building involved. In later sections of this chapter the characteristics of long swing fluctuations for each type of building are separately reviewed. Findings with regard to amplitude and duration are presented separately, by cycle phases and with breakdowns between Ohio and non-Ohio building in Table 3-1.

Nearly 54 per cent of our recorded cycles are from Ohio data. An exact parallel between types of building within and outside Ohio does not, of course, occur. The distribution patterns emerging from our tables will reflect to some degree these differences in the raw data. At the same time, the sample of cycles is broad enough to permit certain of their structural features to emerge.

The most prominent feature of our distribution is the wide range of recorded durations. At the lower end of the range the count is inherently arbitrary, for cycles with total durations under seven to eight years or with contractions of less than three years were not distinguishable from (short) business cycles. Even so, some 14 per cent of all long building cycles recognized in this work had a duration under ten years. At the other end of the array, some 20 per cent of recorded cycles had a duration exceeding twenty-two years, with a broad distribution in between. Ohio building had modal durations between thirteen and twenty-one years, while for non-Ohio areas the mode is between thirteen and eighteen years. As measured by the coefficient of variation, relative dispersion around the two mean durations was nearly the same (36.7, and 35.4). The Ohio distribution pattern

TABLE 3-1
Number and Percentage Distribution of 162 Long Local Specific
Cycles, Ohio and Non-Ohio, by Duration and Cycle Phase

	Building					
	Ohio		Non-Ohio		Total	
Years	No.	Per Cent	No.	Per Cent	No.	Per Cent
			Expansion			
2 & under	1	1.1	0	0	1	.6
3–4	17	18.9	6	8.0	23	13.9
5–6	19	21.1	10	13.3	29	17.6
7–8	8	8.9	17	22.7	25	15.2
9–10	19	21.1	10	13.3	29	17.6
11–12	10	11.1	10	13.3	20	12.1
13–14	7	7.8	10	13.3	17	10.3
15 & over	9	10.0	12	16.0	21	12.7
Total	90		75		165	
Mean	8.5	(4.08)	10.7	(5.01)	9.5	(4.64)
			Contraction			
2–3	11	12.5	6	7.6	17	10.2
4–5	28	31.8	18	22.8	46	27.5
6–7	18	20.5	16	20.2	34	20.4
8–9	14	15.9	16	20.2	30	18.0
10–11	13	14.8	13	16.4	26	15.6
12 & over	4	4.5	10	12.7	14	8.4
Total	88		79		167	
Mean	6.6	(2.76)	7.8	(3.38)	7.2	(3.29)
			Full Cycle			
Under 10	16	18.4	6	8.0	22	13.6
10–12	11	12.6	5	6.7	16	9.9
13–15	19	21.8	16	21.3	35	21.6
16–18	16	18.4	15	20.0	31	19.1
19–21	16	18.4	8	10.7	24	14.8
22–24	7	8.0	11	14.7	18	11.1
25–27	2	2.3	7	9.3	9	5.6
28 & over	0	0	7	9.3	7	4.3
Total	87		75		162	
Mean	15.0	(5.5)	18.6	(6.6)	16.6	(6.2)

NOTE: Figures in parentheses are standard deviations.

for the longer durations thinned out. In consequence the mean duration of Ohio building cycles at 15.0 years was considerably lower than mean duration of non-Ohio building cycles at 18.6 years.

The tendency to shorter duration in Ohio is characteristic both of expansion and contraction phases. The mean building expansion in Ohio was 8.5 ± 4.1 years or 79.4 per cent of the mean expansion elsewhere; the mean contraction in Ohio was 6.6 ± 2.76 years, or 84.6 per cent of the mean contraction elsewhere.

Another feature exhibited in Table 3-1 is the comparative length of contraction phases. Over 19 per cent of Ohio and 24 per cent of non-Ohio long building contractions were ten years or over in duration, and the mean contraction comprised between 42 and 44 per cent of the total span of building cycles. A statistical record of the relative proportion of contractions in business cycles and in short specific cycles in production and building is presented in Table 3-2. Over the same years the short business cycle reference chronologies of the four countries from which most of our measures are taken had a mean contraction share of 43.9 per cent.

Duration of building cycles will vary slightly when considered by class of building. Thus, our thirty residential building series, spanning some eighty-one specific cycles, had a mean duration of 19.7 years, or nearly two years longer than that of cycles in all types of building. Our seven series of total nonresidential building covering 15.5 specific long cycles had a mean duration of 17.5 years, considerably less than those for total building. Both Ohio and non-Ohio territories exhibit the same characteristic of a mean residential duration in excess of all building durations—in Ohio by 11 per cent, outside Ohio by 2 per cent. In part this arises because of a tendency for a special rhythm to occur in nonresidential building, which produces "extra cycles" and hence shorter durations. Thus, our five Ohio industrial building series experienced an altogether shorter rhythm, with a mean duration of 11.2 years.

Average amplitudes of the series have been studied in terms of total rise and fall during reference and specific cycles, rise and fall per year during specific cycles, and ratio of reference to specific amplitude. Since central tendencies for these measures are affected by the composition of the groups of series, caution will be needed in drawing conclusions. Table 3-3 presents

TABLE 3-2

Contraction Expressed as a Per Cent of Total Duration—Building
and Business Cycles

I. Building cycles	
A. Building activity	
1. Ohio mean duration	44.0
2. Non-Ohio mean duration	41.9
B. Nonbuilding activity	
3. Ohio mean duration	37.1
4. Non-Ohio mean duration	41.1
II. Business cycles[a]	
C. Reference cycles, national	
5. U.S. 1854–1933	46.8
6. Great Britain 1854–1932	42.8
7. France 1865–1932	43.1
8. Germany 1879–1932	42.9
D. U.S. production activity	
9. Deflated clearings 1878–1933	26.3
10. Pig iron production 1879–1923	35.6
11. Riggleman's per capita index:	
building permits 1830–1878	47.2
building permits 1878–1932	47.0
12. Manhattan value plans for new building 1870–1933	46.8
13. Chicago value of total building permits 1862–1933	46.0
14. St. Louis value of total building permits 1878–1932	55.0
15. Long's monthly index of building permits 1882–1916	44.1
16. Value building permits (20 to 120 cities) 1908–1933	60.5
17. Business annals—U.S. 1790–1925	40.0[b]
18. Business annals—England 1790–1925	47.4[b]
19. Seventeen countries 1890–1925	36.8[b]

[a] NBER files, Business Cycle Unit.

[b] Ratio of years of "depression" to years of "prosperity" as defined by Thorp in [251] and summarized in Mitchell [192, p. 408 ff.].

summary measures of amplitude with distributions of certain characteristics.

The dominant fact that emerges about the amplitudes of our surveyed activities is that they are, relative to those of business

TABLE 3-3
Mean Amplitude Measures, All Building Series

Mean Total Amplitude	Per Cent Distribution of Series	
	Specific	Reference
400 and over	17.7	2.0
300.0–399.9	27.4	14.3
200.0–299.9	41.9	34.7
150.0–199.9	11.3	36.7
100.0–149.9	1.6	12.2
Number of series	62	49
Mean amplitude, all series	303.4 (100.3)	221.4 (81.8)
Mean amplitude, Ohio	285.8 (99.5)	202.2 (85.9)
Mean amplitude, non-Ohio	324.8 (96.9)	245.0 (69.5)

NOTE: Figures in parentheses are standard deviations.

cycles, "enormous" [41, p. 418]. The mean total reference amplitude or range of fluctuation of a series about its own average reference business cycle level was reported by Mitchell to equal 55.5 for production series and 40.0 for 794 series covering a wide variety of types of economic activity [193, pp. 102–107]. The corresponding mean reference total amplitude for our building series averaged 202 (±86) for Ohio and 245 (±69) for non-Ohio. Mitchell's business cycle amplitudes mainly pertain to nationwide series on a monthly basis; our building cycle amplitudes are for local series on an annual basis. Series which are aggregated differently are smoothed to different degrees, annually more than monthly. Therefore, we cannot tell by how much building cycle reference amplitude exceeds business cycle amplitude, but the difference must be considerable.

In specific form, a long building series will typically rise to peak values three or four times the initial trough over a sweep of ten years and then fall halfway back to the origin over a seven-year period of decline. By contrast, business-cycle movements in total production typically undulate much more gently about their mean level.

The summary table of amplitudes indicates that long cycles tended to be both longer and more severe outside of Ohio. This applies both for building activity proper and, as we shall see later, for the behavior of real estate, prices, and population movements.

The greater amplitude of cycles outside of Ohio is due partly to the somewhat greater intensity in rate of fall and to the somewhat greater relative role of contraction phases. It is probably also attributable to the greater role of smaller towns in our records of Ohio experience and to the presentation of Ohio urban experience for groups of urban communities rather than for these communities separately.

The gap between reference amplitude of building activity and specific amplitude is a wide one. Reference amplitudes are 73.0 per cent of specific amplitudes for all building series. The reference scale for local nonresidential building was the local residential building series; a local residential series was analyzed on a national or regional reference frame.

The disparity between specific and reference amplitudes reflects a tendency for imperfect synchronization in timing and pattern among urban areas of an economy and among the varied types of local building activities.

B. RESIDENTIAL BUILDING

Within building, residential building predominates and has long been regarded as a generating force making for distinct long-wave movements. Altogether, thirty long residential series were analyzed. Table 3-4 presents a summary of cyclical measures covering duration, amplitude, timing, and growth.

The measures point to a basic divergence between Ohio and non-Ohio residential cycle patterns in growth rates, amplitude, and duration. Ohio residential building grew more rapidly, 4.01 per cent per year compared with 1.84 per cent per year elsewhere. At the same time, Ohio mean durations were shorter and amplitudes were less—by 12 and 30 per cent respectively—than for the non-Ohio areas. Long cycles of residential building in Ohio thus conform to the finding of Borts that "rapid growth and cyclical instability do not necessarily grow together" [27, p. 152]. This same finding is confirmed by the results of regression analysis of our residential building series presented in Appendix G. Although rates of secular growth do not appear to affect amplitudes of fluctuation, our records show that long fluctuations typically occur on a rising secular trend of building. The

TABLE 3-4

Summary Measures for Residential Building: Local Specific Long Cycles[a]

Measures	Ohio[a]				Non-Ohio[b]				Total	
	Mean	Median	High	Low	Mean	Median	High	Low	Mean	Median
Full specific duration (annual)	17.38 (1.96)	16.5	20.5	15.3	20.27 (5.25)	18.4	33.0	10.7	19.67 (5.00)	18.45
Specific cycle amplitude (in cycle relatives)										
Full	227.3 (38.1)	215.4	284.1	181.2	325.7 (91.4)	309.6	482.0	191.9	306.0 (92.4)	287.5
Full per year	13.14 (2.17)	13.32	16.95	10.08	16.88 (5.22)	16.9	33.36	9.25	16.13 (5.04)	15.95
Fall per year	−12.93 (1.98)	−13.06	−15.46	−9.71	−20.25 (8.15)	−18.3	−41.31	−9.06	−18.79 (7.89)	−17.22
Secular weighted average growth per year (per cent)	4.017 (1.11)	4.195	5.557	1.745	1.840 (2.71)	1.235	9.489	−2.790	2.275 (2.62)	1.688

NOTE: Mean values are presented plus or minus standard deviations.

[a] Includes the six series 0110. 0123, 0172–0175, covering fifteen specific long cycles.

[b] Includes the twenty-four series 0001–0009, 0022, 0030, 0034, 0035, 0039, 0048, 0052, 0075, 0079, 0081, 0085, 0092, 0098, 0143, 0144, covering sixty-six specific long cycles.

trend on a per year basis was rising at a mean rate of 2.3 per cent per year for all of our series, and only two communities had a declining annual level of building through two or more long swings. Even in these instances the stock of building was increasing, though at a diminishing linear rate.

The measures exhibit the diversity of duration and amplitude of fluctuation previously noted. Duration ranges from 10.7 to 33.0 years, while amplitudes range between 192 and 482. Smaller amplitudes tend to be associated with shorter durations, so that the range of amplitude per year is less than that of total amplitude (for details see Appendix G).

C. INDUSTRIAL AND COMMERCIAL BUILDING

Statistical series on industrial and commercial building are available as distinct types only for Ohio. The results are set forth in Table 3-5 and the average cycle patterns are in Charts 3-1 and 3-2.

The relatively short duration of industrial cycles, noted earlier, stands out prominently, as does the high secular growth rate. Specific industrial cycles have both higher growth and higher specific amplitudes—total and per year—than commercial building cycles; and the degree of cyclical conformity as measured by the ratio of reference to specific amplitude is higher. It is not clear, however, whether this set of results is due to the very short durations of Ohio patterns of industrial building or, more precisely, to a greater influence of standard business-cycle rhythms within observed long movements. The high amplitude of industrial building relative to residential or commercial building is characteristic of short as well as long building cycles in the United States.[1] Only the ranking of American commercial and residential amplitudes for building cycles is different. The building cycle ranking runs: industrial, commercial and residential; the business cycle ranking runs: industrial, residential, commercial.

The higher amplitude of industrial building is accompanied by earlier timing. The mean lead of industrial over commercial building ranges from a low of 3.6 months at turning points to 12 months pointed to by correlograms.[2] The respective correlograms of industrial and commercial building indicate a tendency of industrial building to lead considerably relative to commercial building, particularly in the rural Ohio groups.

Summary Measures for Industrial and Commercial Building: Local Long Cycles; Ohio Sample Groups

Measures	Industrial Building[a]				Commercial Building[b]			
	Mean	Median	High	Low	Mean	Median	High	Low
Full specific duration (years)	11.2	11.7	14.6	7.5	14.2	11.7	21.0	10.8
Specific cycle amplitude (cycle relatives)								
Full	383.9	330.6	625.6	262.6	272.1	252.8	348.0	194.8
Full per year	34.82	32.99	53.99	22.54	20.19	18.12	29.76	16.31
Fall per year	−34.66	−32.15	−47.83	−23.02	−20.71	−16.66	−28.57	−16.10
Full reference amplitude (cycle relatives)[c]	338.4	292.6	560.3	206.3	196.5	197.8	232.8	158.8
Secular weighted average growth per year (per cent)	5.952	5.999	8.614	4.169	4.589	5.674	6.779	1.708
Lead-lag turning points (years)[d]	.09	.57	3.50	−2.83	.39	.29	4.67	−2.20
Average deviation (years)	2.04	2.17	2.70	1.30	1.90	1.89	2.41	1.36
Lead-lag reference pattern (years)[c]	.13	−.85	4.30	−2.10	.70	1.40	3.10	−2.40
Optimal serial correlation, trend adjusted								
Lead-lag (years)	−1.6	−1.0	−.5	−2.0	−.60	0	2.0	−3.0
Correlation coefficient (r)	.674	.671	.921	.369	.696	.676	.962	.343

[a] Includes series 0191 through 0195, which had nineteen specific long cycles in which twenty-nine turning points were matched and sixteen were unmatched.
[b] Includes series 0187 through 0190 and 0227, which had fourteen specific long cycles in which twenty-nine turning points were matched and three were unmatched.
[c] Excludes series 0190, 0227 for commercial and series 0193 for industrial.
[d] Excludes series 0193 for industrial.

CHART 3-1
Patterns of Average Specific and Reference Long Cycles, Ohio
Statewide and Samples, Value Industrial Building

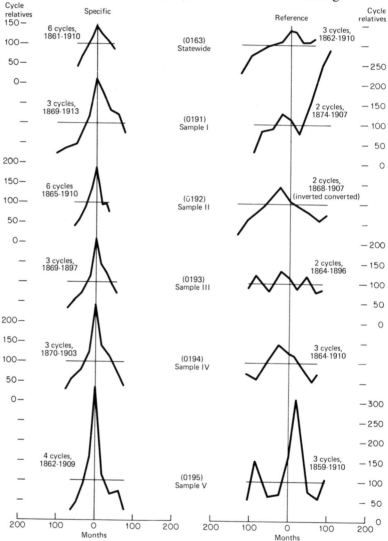

There is more uncertainty regarding the timing relation of industrial to residential building. So far as means go, reference phase analysis points to a slight lag of industrial building by about five weeks; in turning point analysis, a lag of seven weeks occurs. But extreme lag values have affected these means. Three

CHART 3-2
Patterns of Average Specific and Reference Long Cycles, Ohio Statewide and Samples, Commercial Building

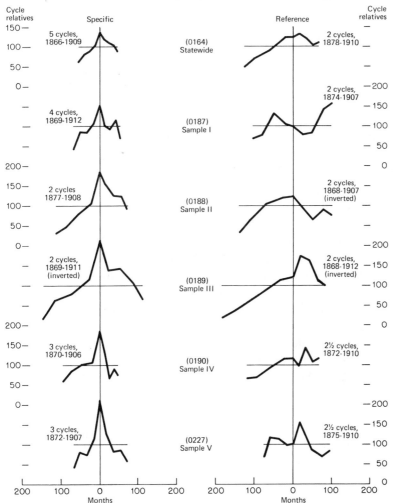

of the five sample groups exhibited leads of between eight and ten months by both types of analysis. The median reading for the sample groups is confirmed by correlation analysis, which points to a mean lead of 19.2 months. The tendency to lead in correlograms prevailed among all of the Ohio sample groups, though more strongly and with least variability among the medium urbanized groups III and IV. Correlation analysis takes account of all recorded values and correlated series were smoothed to scale down the unusually strong short cyclical influences. These influences unavoidably affected judgments on turning point analysis based upon unsmoothed data. These same influences show up in the reference cycle patterns and dominate the pattern for group III. It thus seems likely that, while on recorded turning points a highly variable relationship existed, industrial building generally responded more quickly to influences of expansion and contraction than residential building. Reference cycle patterns (see Chart 3-1) indicate that the tendency of industrial building to lead was marked and most uniform on upturns and was most variable and irregular at peaks.

A tendency for industrial building to lead local long cycles on upturns may readily be rationalized. Industrial building provides the facilities which expand local jobs and production and thus generates local commercial and residential expansion. This pattern was clear for Ohio groups I, II, and IV, but more erratic for groups III and V.

Since the course of industrial building responds to influences running through product and investment markets on a nation-wide scale, it is consistent with our hypothesis that local industrial building should exhibit some indication of the inter-mediate rhythm of eight to ten years which some observers have found in so-called major cycles. This is quite clearly the case. The smoother time series charts of industrial building (see Chart 2-2) exhibit the major decennial rhythm characteristic of the seventy years before 1914. Because of these "extra" cycles, the mean long specific cycle duration for industrial building is only 11.2 years, compared with 14.2 for commercial and 17.4 years for residential. For the same reason, the annual rate of change of industrial building is greater, 34.82 cycle relatives per year, while commercial building fluctuates at a yearly rate of only 20.2 and residential building at a rate of 13.1 cycle relatives.

D. CHICAGO MANUFACTURING EXPERIENCE

Long swings in industrial building should generate long swings in industrial capacity; and it would be strange if these swings would fail to become associated with long swings in the flow of industrial output. For well-known reasons, amplitude of fluctuation of output from durable facilities will be considerably less than for the flow of new facilities themselves. It is, of course, entirely possible that swings in new facilities or standing stocks should be matched on the output side by swings in the rate of plant-utilization so that output flows would be free from any tendency to long swings. It is of interest to know if this were the case, i.e., if there were no feedback effects of long swings in building activity upon the flow of industrial output.

We cannot find the answer to this question for the state of Ohio where our information on industrial building is most detailed, due to lack of suitable annual measures in Ohio for industrial output. We have such measures however, over an extended time period, covering three long building cycles, for the city of Chicago where our information on building and demographic movements points to sizable long swings which in all probability were associated with corresponding movements of industrial building in Chicago. Because of radical price shifting in several of the decades it was necessary to deflate the manufacturing output series with a wholesale price index, which probably overstates both deflation during the 1870's and inflation during World War I. The successive specific and reference cycle patterns are shown in Chart 3-3. The successive reference cycle patterns are shown in inverted form; the average pattern is shown both in inverted and positive form.

The upward trend of growth is so strong that characteristic reference contractions are difficult to identify in the naked series or cycle relatives. Reference contractions become more discernible, however, when expressed in terms of rates of change. These rate patterns, which are not reproduced, also show that manufacturing activity clearly leads at upturns and lags at peaks with a net lead over the entire period of from one to one and a half years. We recall that industrial building in Ohio also exhibited a net timing lead compared with residential building, with a tendency to lag at peaks. The scale of the timing leads seems to correspond. If we join timing evidence from Chicago and Ohio, we can say industrial firms apparently expand or slacken building as their long-term demand for output expands or slackens in its rate of growth.

E. SCHOOL BUILDING

Summary results for school construction are presented for the five Ohio sample groups in Table 3-6. The respective cycle

CHART 3-3

Patterns of Successive Long Cycles and Their Average, Specific and Reference, Deflated Value Manufactures, Chicago, 1872–1929

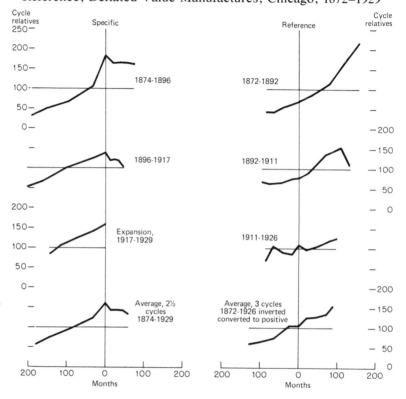

patterns are found in Chart 3-4. Mean specific durations are fairly close to those of residential building. Reference cycle patterns all indicate that local school building responds to the influences which govern residential building and with a considerable amplitude. All our measures for timing indicate a considerable lag—1.6 years at matched turning points, 1.79 years on reference cycle phase turns, and a full 2.5 years by correlation analysis. The correlograms, considering the strong trends running through the series, give unambiguous testimony of the lag. Disturbance in the relationship is considerable, as indicated by the mean reference cycle amplitude, which is only 57.3 per cent of specific cycle amplitude.

The reasons for the lag are perhaps related to the greater formality of decision making in public construction. Any growth in demand for new residential building would be reflected in a

TABLE 3-6
Summary Measures for School Building: Local Long Cycles;
Ohio Sample Groups[a]

Measures	Mean	Median	High	Low
Full specific duration (years)	15.8	16.0	18.0	12.3
Specific cycle amplitude (cycle relatives)				
Full	323.7	334.5	392.3	265.8
Full per year	20.58	18.80	24.52	18.47
Fall per year	−20.81	−22.45	−29.64	−11.63
Full reference amplitude (cycle relatives)[b]	196.8	185.0	278.7	138.5
Secular weighted average growth per year (per cent)	4.257	4.520	5.865	2.666
Lead-lag turning points (years)	1.61	1.83	4.40	−.67
Average deviation (years)	2.56	2.33	4.33	1.11
Lead-lag reference pattern (years)[b]	1.79	1.30	3.80	.75
Optimal serial correlation, trend adjusted[c]				
Lead-lag (years)	2.5	2.0	3.0	2.0
Correlation coefficient (*r*)	.681	.726	.748	.524

[a] Includes series 0258 through 0262, which contain 13.5 specific long cycles, twenty-six matched turning points and seven unmatched turning points.
[b] Excludes series 0258.
[c] Excludes series 0260.

need for additional school facilities. However, the decision to build a dwelling is taken with a minimum of formality. The decision to build a public school involves the decision to build, the search for adequate sites, and the drawing up of building plans, all of which take more time than is usually required for a private dwelling or apartment house. Our computed mean lag, which ranges between 1.6 and 2.5 years, may measure this more cumbersome procedure.

F. TOTAL NONRESIDENTIAL BUILDING

Summary results for seven nonresidential building series are found in Table 3-7 and specific and reference cycle patterns are

CHART 3-4

Patterns of Average Specific and Reference Long Cycles, Ohio Statewide and Samples, Cost of Schools, Riggleman Deflated

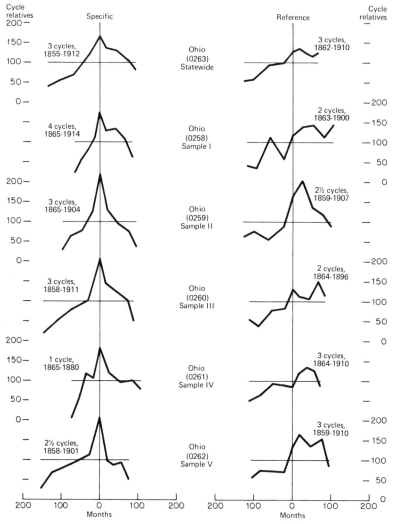

presented in Chart 3-5. Our Ohio graphs are on a statewide basis. Four series are of non-Ohio origin and in three instances relate to number rather than value of nonresidential building. Since per-unit values of nonresidential building have high rates of secular growth, the non-Ohio mean growth rate (at 1.3 per cent per year) would understandably be lower than the Ohio rate (8.9 per cent per year). Amplitude measures should also be higher for

TABLE 3-7
Summary Measures for Nonresidential Building: Local Long Cycles

Measures	Ohio[a] Mean	Non-Ohio[b] Mean	Non-Ohio[b] Median	Total Mean	Total Median
Full specific duration (years)	14.2	19.9	19.8	17.5	16.5
Specific cycle amplitude (cycle relatives)					
Full	329.2	315.1	357.7	321.2	347.3
Full per year	23.31	15.74	16.89	18.98	18.69
Fall per year	−25.18	−18.45	−19.98	−21.33	−20.59
Full reference amplitude (cycle relatives)[c]	202.9	239.2	248.6	227.1	231.5
Secular weighted average growth per year (per cent)	8.958	1.276	1.065	4.568	7.940
Lead-lag turning points (years)	−.10	−.11	.05	−.11	−.60
Average deviation (years)	2.19	1.96	1.81	2.06	1.87
Lead-lag reference pattern (years)[c]	.58	1.21	1.33	1.00	1.15
Optimal serial correlation, trend adjusted[d]					
Lead-lag (years)	n.a.	.5	.5		
Correlation coefficient (r)	n.a.	.778	.856		

n.a.—not available.

[a] Series 0111, 0116, 0124, which include 7.5 specific long cycles with fourteen matched and nine unmatched turning points.

[b] Series 0093, 0053, 0033, 0011, which includes 8 specific long cycles with nineteen matched and two unmatched turning points.

[c] Excluding series 0111 from Ohio and total columns.

[d] Includes a nonresidential building series subjected to correlation analysis only.

CHART 3-5
Patterns of Average Specific and Reference Long Cycles, Nonresidential Building

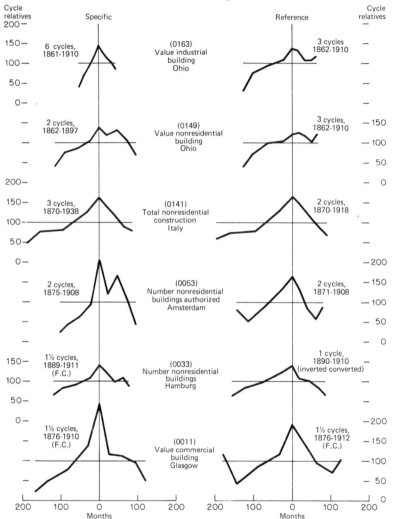

Ohio than non-Ohio series, though the per-year rates of movement are close together.

Our nonresidential series, partly because they are expressed on a numbers basis for non-Ohio areas, yield a divergent pattern of lead-lag. Turning points exhibit a lead; reference cycle and correlation analysis, a lag. This irregularity of pattern may be due to the shifting course of public building, which is least integrated into the mechanism of local building movements. As we have just seen, Ohio school building lags strongly, as did Ohio commercial building. Long's studies of median dates for various cities showed that public building as a whole exhibited lags in two of three long cycles averaging nearly three years. An even more clear-cut and longer lag of public building, approximating inversion of timing on short cycles, is indicated by a fifteen-year span of building in Germany before 1914. This same tendency to inversion is indicated in our more comprehensive study of building in Ohio between 1853 and 1912, which showed between long cycle phases a regular alteration in the proportions of private (taxable) and public (exempt) building. The ratio of net exempt to net taxable building increments of standing stock, as evaluated in periodic statewide tax appraisals, is as follows:[3]

Period	Per Cent
1853–59	41.2
1859–70	16.9
1870–80	42.9
1880–90	9.7
1890–1900	27.3
1904–12	6.1

The long lags and a tendency to inversion in public building may be related partly to the formal process of decision making applicable to school construction as noted above but also to the character of construction and financing. C. D. Long attributes the lag primarily to the large average size of public structures built only upon order and according to precise specifications with long lead times [173, pp. 141–142]. He mentions as a supporting consideration what Hunscha considered primarily, namely, that local building expansions generate realized surpluses over revenue forecasts and thus stimulate in the following years a more or less favorable adjustment of building plans [136, pp. 43–44].

G. STREET PAVING

A form of construction activity, street paving, is reported for three cities for which we have building data and the forms of cycle patterns are worth noting (see Table 3-8 and Chart 3-6). The small sample hinders drawing reliable conclusions. Only some 8.5 long cycles were covered. Street paving conforms as closely to building cycles as nonresidential building does: the mean ratio of total reference to specific amplitude is .66. It is higher for Glasgow and Chicago than for Manhattan.

The cyclical rhythm of street-paving activity may be affected by whether the streets are newly constructed or are being resurfaced and whether innovations in technology are involved. Resurfacing of old streets should lag behind residential building; new street development should lead building; and innovations in traffic design or street construction should vary at random. For the three urban areas, a mixture of these tendencies is indicated with a net tendency to lag.

TABLE 3-8

Summary Measures for Street Paving, Local Long Cycles for Three Urban Areas[a]

Measures	Mean	High	Low
Full specific duration (years)	22.73	31.00	17.8
Specific cycle amplitude (cycle relatives)			
Full	370.7	513.3	282.6
Full per year	16.33	17.81	14.61
Fall per year	−28.75	−31.87	−24.63
Full reference amplitude (cycle relatives)	253.3	411.7	166.4
Secular weighted average growth per year (per cent)	1.608	6.216	−2.708
Lead-lag turning points (years)	.523	2.87	−.75
Average deviation (years)	2.56	2.87	2.05
Lead-lag reference pattern (years)	.433	2.30	−1.0
Optimal serial correlation, trend adjusted			
Lead-lag (years)	0	1.0	−1.0
Correlation coefficient (r)[b]	.918	.923	.913

[a] Includes series 0012, 0087, 0094, which cover nine specific long cycles, having twenty-one matched, and no unmatched, turning points. The three areas are Manhattan, Glasgow, and Chicago.

[b] Excluding series 0094.

CHART 3-6
Patterns of Average Specific and Reference Long Cycles,
New Streets Laid

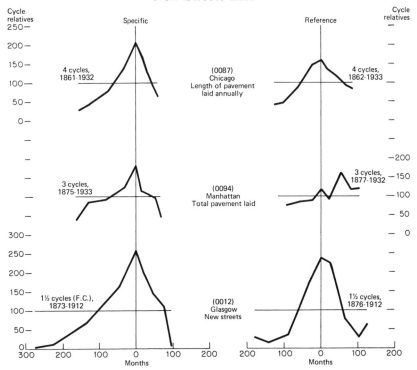

H. SUMMARY

Our survey supports the judgment that urban building fluctuated in waves which were impressively regular. These waves
develop amplitudes which are enormous relative to ordinary
business cycles. Our sample of thirty urban communities experienced eighty-one long waves marked out in our chronologies.
These waves had a mean duration of 19.7 ± 5.0 years. Total
specific amplitude fluctuated in a high-low range of 181–482 and
experienced a mean value of 306 ± 92 cycle relatives. Yearly
rates of movement averaged 16.1 ± 5.0 cycle relatives. The
implicit monthly rate of movement falls well within the range of
rates characteristic of industrial production during business
cycles. But whereas an upward movement of industrial production will reverse itself after cumulating for a few years, a
comparable upward movement of building will endure for a

decade or more, while all building contractions alone have a mean duration of 7.3 ± 3.0 years.

Our survey shows that residential building fluctuates with other types of building. With residential construction goes the work of site preparation and development. Any newly established residential neighborhood will require schools, service facilities, churches, and public buildings which provide important neighborhood services. Moreover, this whole residential development will in turn be complementary to new industrial or service facilities. New industrial and residential facilities will in turn require or grow out of improved or extended facilities of transportation. In short, all new extensive construction appears to be complementary in character, demanded and supplied as a whole.

But the process of growth spreads and works unevenly. For industrial building, specific long local cycle rhythms are decennial in duration (mean duration 11.2 years) and thus correspond to the "major" or Juglar rhythm of the business cycle. The total specific amplitude is relatively large, 384 cycle relatives, and is reflected in high rates of monthly variability (2.9 per cent per month) on both rise and fall, and a very high secular growth rate (5.95 per cent annually). Side by side with this overt rhythm is a longer oscillation which showed up in our reference cycle patterns and correlograms. If our median correlogram and reference pattern values can be trusted, industrial building tended generally to lead residential building by a year, though on twenty-nine matched turning points the lead was reversed and turned into a lag. Probably this reflects no more than the arbitrariness in matching turning points in series with different basic periodicities.

Commercial building was clearly subject to the longer building rhythm: though both total specific and reference amplitudes were nearly a third less than with industrial building, the conformity to residential building rhythms was closer. Commercial building perceptibly lagged behind industrial from a half to a full year, though with variable timing.

Perhaps public and quasi-public building responds most slowly and unevenly to the rhythm of building cycles. School building exhibited a long specific rhythm which corresponded moderately to the rhythm of residential building, but with a lag of two or more years. The lag in public construction probably reflects slower decision making at governmental levels and more elaborate structures which take longer to build. In two of our three communities surveyed for street paving, there was a clear-cut reference pattern of fluctuation, with tendencies both to lag and to lead up to two or more years.

In general, tendencies of public and commercial building to lag are offset by tendencies to lead in industrial building. Amplitude of fluctuation is somewhat scaled down to that approximating the residential, while on balance a moderate lag up to one year tends to prevail. Thus well within the long span of years needed for a completed building cycle, accumulated shortages or surpluses will have aligned building operations of different types into a common movement.

NOTES

1. Four short cycles between 1919 and 1933 in series on the dollar value of American building contracts had mean amplitudes of 258, 176, and 130 for industrial, commercial, and residential building, respectively (see [39]). Comparable German amplitudes, computed on the basis of trend-adjusted data for the fourteen years before 1910, for the three categories of building were 36.3, 57.6, and 33.4 per cent, respectively (see [136, p. 37]).

2. The different methods yield the following mean lead of industrial over commercial building: correlation analysis, 12 months; turning point analysis, 3.6 months; reference cycle phase, 6.8 months. German short cycles in industrial and commercial building for seventeen years before 1914 showed a variable relationship for four short cyclical turning points, with an average mean industrial lead of three months (see [136, p. 35]).

3. See [108, p. 249].

CHAPTER 4

The Behavior of the Real Estate Market
in Long Local Cycles

A. INTRODUCTION

The shifts in demand which generate building cycles are by no means confined to new building alone. The preparation of building sites and the development and subdivision of land are necessarily involved.

The demand for building on new sites is rarely isolated from demand for old realty, which is competitive with the new. Ownership of parcels of old realty is continuously changing; in terms of volume and value these transfers will outnumber sales of newly built property. Do improved realty sales as a whole rise or fall with building cycles? Is an increase in demand for new building a spillover from a surging tide of demand for improved realty? Or does the demand for new realty alternate with that for the old and run inversely to it? These questions will concern us in this chapter.

Both new and old realty are subject to common financial constraints. Realty sales are rarely financed solely out of equity capital; a mortgage loan is usually required also. The equity-loan ratio is highest with industrial and commercial and lowest with public and residential construction. All equity capital is saved out of the proceeds of past income and is managed predominantly by owners. Loan capital can be shifted more readily from where it is accumulated to where it is needed; it will usually be advanced and managed by thrift intermediaries; and it may be created by commercial banks through credit expansion.

A high proportion of capital invested in new residential construction—up to 80 to 90 per cent in pre-1914 Europe and somewhat less in the United States—was borrowed.[1] Much of this loan capital could be drawn from loan repayments and hence would not constitute a charge on outside capital flows.[2] But to individual realty buyers access to mortgage funds was crucial.

Mortgage funds drawn from the capital market are applied with near impartiality to new and old realty purchases and to business, farming, residential, and miscellaneous personal uses. Thus, to determine the effect on building cycles of long-wave movements in mortgage markets, the different uses of mortgage credit must be distinguished.

Mortgage credit is extended at relatively low interest rates on the assumption that prospects of default and loss are relatively low. The risk of foreclosure is difficult to gauge, and lenders will generally be influenced unduly by recent experience with fore-closures in the community or elsewhere. A rise in foreclosure rates will thus render lenders more cautious and tend to divert loan capital to nonmortgage uses or slow up investment activity generally. We cannot adequately trace the rise and fall of new building and realty and mortgage movements without extending our survey to include a canvass of foreclosure experience.

The purpose of this chapter is to throw light on the character and scope of fluctuations in land development and subdivision, realty sales, uses made of mortgage credit, and foreclosure experience.

B. LAND DEVELOPMENT

Our information on land development is drawn wholly from American records, reflecting perhaps its more fateful role in American experience. The phase of land development for which our statistical information is fullest is subdivision activity, that is, the number of lots added or acres subdivided for use in building. Two of the available time series cover Ohio cities; six additional surveyed cities are located in the Middle West or Far West. Average specific and reference cycle patterns for these series are shown in Chart 4-1; and summary tabular measures are presented in Table 4-1.

The high specific amplitude of subdivision activity has often been noted and stands out prominently in our records. Mean total specific amplitude for the eight series is 681.5, or approximately double that of residential building itself. Equally significant is the relatively high proportion of this variability which was coordinated with, and which shows up on, reference chronologies. For the four cities for which reference measures are available, participation—as gauged by the ratios of total

CHART 4-1

Long Cycle Activity Profile of Town Lots—Chicago, Grand Rapids, Milwaukee, San Francisco, Alameda, Detroit, Ann Arbor, Ohio Statewide, Toledo, Cleveland—Specific and Reference

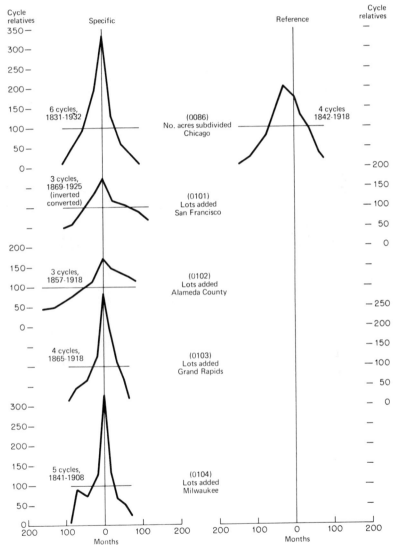

reference amplitude to total specific amplitude—ranged between .583 and .718 (with a mean of .661), indicating that even reference amplitudes of subdivision activity exceeded that of residential building by nearly a third.

CHART 4-1
(Concluded)

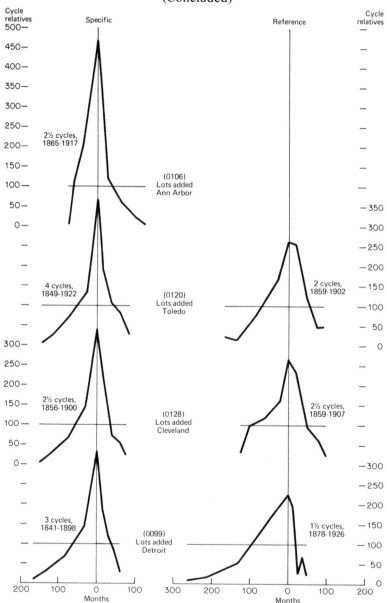

In part this greater amplitude reflects the accelerator relationship between vacant lots and building. An upward wave of new building will excite an even faster rate of growth in subdivision. The equilibrium stock of vacant lots varies in rough proportion

TABLE 4-1
Summary Measures, Local Long Cycles, Subdivision Activity

Measures	Ohio[a] Mean	Non-Ohio[b] Mean	Non-Ohio[b] Median	All
Full specific duration (years)	18.6	17.0	16.7	17.38 (2.9)
Specific cycle amplitude (cycle relatives)				
Full	681.5	644.0	626.4	653.6 (122.4)
Full per year	36.81	38.35	39.77	37.98 (4.9)
Fall per year	−52.44	−45.25	−45.26	−47.07 (9.5)
Full reference amplitude (cycle relatives)	472.3	398.6		435.5 (40.0)
Lead-lag turning points (years)	.10	.01[c]		.055 (.23)
Average deviation (years)	1.24	1.38[c]		1.31 (.15)
Lead-lag reference pattern (years)	.63	.60[c]		.61 (.61)

NOTE: Figures in parentheses are standard deviations.

[a] Includes series 0120, 0128, which had 6.5 specific long cycles, ten matched turning points, and one unmatched turning point.

[b] Series 0086, 0103, 0104,0106, 0099, which had 26.5 specific long cycles. Series 0086 and 0099 had fifteen matched, and no unmatched turning points. Series include Pittsburgh, "Net Increase in Building Lots" 1831–1932, with six long specific cycles, having a mean duration of 202 months ± 46.0.

[c] Includes only series 0086, 0099.

with the stock of housing and with the volume of new building.[3] Hence, on an upward trend, each new building erected must be accompanied by more than one lot produced.

Timing is nearly synchronous. The four subdivision series for which a reference comparison was available exhibit, on twenty-five matched turning points, a mean slight lead of a month or so; reference cycle patterns indicate a short mean lag of six months. While considerable variability is indicated, this points to substantial synchronization. Building and subdivision turn at or near the same time and tend to move together.

The act of subdividing breaks up land originally acquired on an acreage basis into smaller lots prepared more or less for building. Transactions in acreage at the wholesale level should also reflect the wavelike process of subdivision activity. These transactions transfer land from farmers to speculative investors or would-be developers. Developers could buy either from farmers or from speculative investors, and the latter can, of course, sell to each other.

We were unable to sort out the total mass of wholesale transactions by transactor group or purpose. But fortunately Ohio conveyance statistics shed light on sales of acreage at the wholesale level. Statistics were collected from records of transactions in land located within municipal corporate limits but unimproved and unplatted, i.e., not built upon or divided into lots. These transactions included deed transfers and the mortgage loans which usually accompanied them. Deeds on which information on consideration or sales price was recorded are labeled "bona fide"; other deeds are labeled "nominal." A record was made of the number of acres involved. The three statewide series—value of consideration in bona fide deeds, number of acres sold, and dollar value of mortgage loans—were tabulated on a statewide basis. Individual and average patterns are presented in Chart 4-2. Though the mortgage series misses half a long cycle, and though the deed value has a definite downward bias (see Appendix E), the three sets of patterns all exhibit clear-cut neutral timing. On a statewide level, wholesale transactions in acreage respond with a long lag to the variations in housing demand which generate the long-wave process. Throughout the first half of the expansion, wholesale demand for land is still falling, possibly in response to the previous cyclical decline of realty values. By the fourth or fifth year speculative or

CHART 4-2
Successive and Average Reference Cycle Patterns, Statewide Ohio
Sales and Mortgages of Acreage Land, 1878–1910

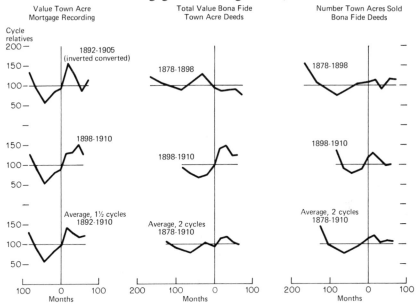

developmental interest in raw land commences to become stronger. As the building expansion reaches its climax, sale and purchase of land are accelerated; and not until a variable period has elapsed—from ten to fifty months—will the boom in land reach its climax.

On the local level these movements seem to develop extreme amplitudes and considerable irregularity, due possibly to the placing of a few large transactions and to special features of value which bring high- and low-valued land into the same field of development. Our two local measures are subject to different limitations. The most reliable measure, funds borrowed on mortgage recordings for town acres, is only available from 1885 onward and hence covers only one pre-1914 long reference cycle (1890's to 1910). The local reference cycle patterns and the statewide aggregate are shown in Chart 4-3.

The other local measure, that of number of town acres sold in bona fide deeds of record, is available back to 1878 and hence covers two full pre-1914 reference cycle periods. Moreover, the number of acres is a comparatively simple statistic to compute and to record. The yearly returns were irregular, however,

CHART 4-3
Patterns of Average Reference Long Cycles, Ohio and Samples, Value Town Acre Mortgages

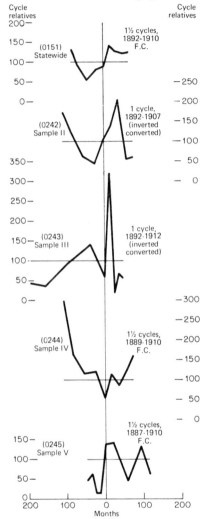

partly because of variations in reporting either total sales and/or the fraction of sales which were recorded for nominal consideration only. Since the practice of recording deeds on a nominal consideration basis gradually increased during the period under review, our results are subject to a downward bias difficult to erase, though some irregularities were smoothed by a three-year moving average (Chart 4-4). For only two of the groups (IV and

CHART 4-4
Individual Reference Cycle Patterns, Number of Town Acres Sold,
Ohio Groups II–V, 1878–1912

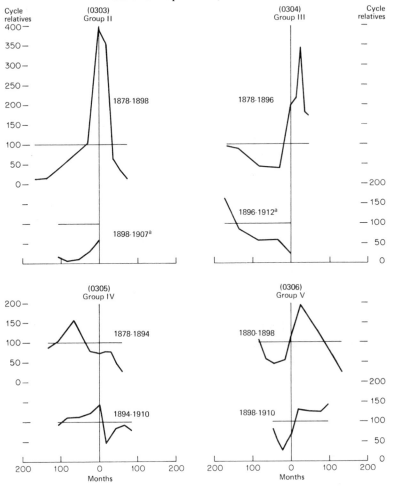

[a] Taken from inverted base.

V) were two reference periods available; for the other two groups, only one and one-half cycles are available.

On an acres sold basis, the tendency to neutral timing in a disturbed field shows up more clearly. Of the seven reference patterns graphed in Chart 4-4, five and one-half either lead or lag. Only one pattern is clearly positive; the remaining half-phase is inverted. Group V, which was ambiguous on the mortgage recordings, exhibits a tendency to neutral timing on the acreage basis, while group II, which was clearly neutral in the mortgage value, shows up as positive in the acreage. Considering the statistical imperfections of the material, the tendency toward neutral timing, both leading and lagging, seems clearly indicated. As Table 4-2 indicates, on matching turning points lags dominated, with a mean lag of 4.83; on reference cycle bases, a mean lag of 2.99 prevailed. As expected, the specific amplitudes of acreage sales and mortgage loan cycles are enormous, averaging 602.9 for 8.5 long specific cycles. The corresponding mean amplitude on six series with reference cycles is 409.9. Of the eight series, three were ranked as inverted and three positive; two were ranked as irregular.

C. REALTY SALES

Some reflection of new building activity should be found in realty sales, because a significant proportion of new structures are erected by operative or speculative builders and are then sold. The 1956 and 1961 surveys of realty sales disclosed that 36 to 40 per cent of residential property sales involved properties not previously occupied [261, 1957, Table 13; 1962, Table 14]. Even when new buildings are erected without conveyance, a chain of realty transfers may be generated, i.e., a builder may have to sell an old property before moving into a new one, and buyers may likewise make a purchase contingent upon a sale.

A change in realty sales will be reflected in the number of real estate transfers recorded as warranty deeds in local records. This presupposes that the relative number of warranty deeds which do not accompany bona fide sales, arising out of gifts, intrafamily transfers and bequests (recent surveys indicate that 33 to 34 per cent are of this character) does not fluctuate to an appreciable degree in long swings [261, 1959, p. 18].

Though deed records are available nearly everywhere in America, few long time series met our requirements for pre-1914 coverage. Altogether eight such series were available, five for Ohio groups and three for other urban communities, plus a series for the entire state of Ohio. Summary measures are presented in Table 4-3 and average reference patterns are presented in Chart 4-5. Between 1862 and 1910, three clear-cut specific cycles are exhibited and, with only minor variations in datings, three reference cycles.

TABLE 4-2
Summary Measures, Local Long Cycles, Town Acreage Sold or Mortgaged[a]

Item	Units	Mean or Total	Median	High	Low
A. Totals					
1. Number of series		8			
2. Number of specific long cycles		8.5			
3. Number of turning points (TP)					
a. Matched		19			
b. Unmatched		4			
B. Mean or other values					
4. Full specific duration	Years	21.5	17.5	31.0	12.5
5. Specific cycle amplitude					
a. Full	Cycle relatives	602.9	589.8	831.5	352.7
b. Full per year	Cycle relatives	30.75	26.82	47.18	17.99
c. Fall per year	Cycle relatives	−28.11	−21.42	−46.11	−18.29
6. Full reference amplitude	Cycle relatives	409.9	400.0	721.6	134.3
7. Overlapping short cycle change per year[b]	%	5.39	5.98	11.84	−2.25
8. Lead-lag (LL) TP:[c]					
a. LL	Years	4.83	3.25	13.30	1.25
b. Average deviation	Years	2.32	1.56	5.25	.80
9. LL reference pattern[c]	Years	2.99	3.35	7.50	−2.25

[a] Including series 0242-5, 0306; series 0242 included only in items 6, 7, 9; 0244 included in items 6 and 7 only.
[b] Includes only series 0242-5.
[c] Using 0242, 0304 on positive rather than inverted basis to allow for uniform timing analysis.

TABLE 4-3
Summary Measures, Local Long Cycles, Number of Deed Instruments Recorded

Measures	Ohio[a]		Non-Ohio[b]
Full specific duration (years)	n.a.		18.97
Specific cycle amplitude (cycle relatives)			
Full			185.7
Full per year	2.62	(1.00)	9.77
Fall per year	−1.09	(1.68)	−7.89
Full reference amplitude (cycle relatives)	58.6	(15.8)	124.0[c]
Secular weighted average growth per year (per cent)	2.459	(1.13)	3.53
Lead-lag reference pattern (years)	.57	(.94)	n.a.
Optimal serial correlation, trend adjusted			
Lead-lag (years)	.50	(.45)	n.a.
Correlation coefficient (r)	.671	(.17)	n.a.

NOTE: n.a.—not available. Figures in parentheses are standard deviations.

[a] Including series 0216–0220, which had 12.5 reference long cycles (specific cycles were not analyzed). The number of turning points was not available.

[b] Including series 0089, 0101, 0102, which had nine specific long cycles. Series 0089 had eight matched turning points and no unmatched turning points; data on turning points for the other series were not available.

[c] Computed from mean specific amplitude by applying the Chicago relation of specific to reference amplitude.

The data indicate that deed turnover varies systematically with long swings in building, though with a much dampened amplitude. The three non-Ohio communities—Chicago, Alameda County, and San Francisco—exhibited considerably more amplitude than the Ohio communities, with San Francisco leading (a mean specific amplitude of 226.2) and Chicago lowest (146.7). Mean amplitudes of Ohio communities are only about half those of Chicago. This divergence may be partly a function of secular growth rates, since Ohio's are about a third under those of the other areas, and the more rapidly growing Ohio sample groups tend to have higher amplitudes. Other unknown influences, however, predominate in the outcome.

The Ohio and Chicago patterns of deed activity exhibit greatly

CHART 4-5
Patterns of Average Reference Long Cycles, Ohio Statewide, Sample Groups, and Chicago, Number of Deeds[a]

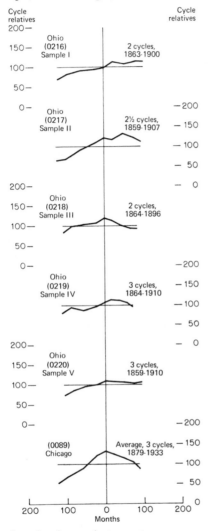

[a]For Chicago, number of real estate instruments.

dampened amplitude of fluctuation as compared with the pattern of residential building. For the Ohio areas, total mean amplitude of deed activity was barely 26 per cent of the corresponding amplitude for residential building. For Chicago and for Ohio as a whole, corresponding percentages are 36 and 31. Since part of deed amplitude is attributable to turnover of properties in transactions linked to new building, it is apparent that the true amplitude of transfers of old property in long swings is not very considerable, except in cases where a strong boom occurs. In those cases timing at turns, as in the case of Chicago, is coincident; but in three out of five Ohio sample groups a building contraction has been under way from ten to fifty months before a turn in deed activity begins.

D. MORTGAGE CREDIT AND FUND USES

The relative intensity of the different uses made of mortgage credit in the course of long swings is more difficult to sort out than the tracing of deed activity. Outside of Ohio our statistical record of mortgage flows is confined to Berlin, where a series of new mortgage recordings was developed, and to Germany as a whole, where we have a series showing annual growth in institutional mortgage portfolio holdings. The record of information from Ohio is more detailed. It includes mortgage recordings for the state as a whole and for its sample groups, by number and by the amount of mortgage credit extended. From 1857 to 1879 no distinction was made between farm and nonfarm mortgages. From 1880 onward, or for substantially two of these cycles, we have separate series for nonfarm and farm mortgages, by number and by value.

New mortgage instruments can be recorded either by number or by value of consideration involved. Variation in the number of nonfarm mortgage recordings will result primarily from variation in mortgage loans growing out of sales of residential property and lots. In the 1880's this was indicated by the relatively small unit value of the great bulk of nonfarm mortgage loans; only 4.05 per cent of them were in excess of $5,000, and over two-thirds were under $1,000 in amount. The 1965 survey of real estate nonfarm sales showed that 97.1 per cent involved residential properties or vacant lots, and in roughly a 3-to-1 proportion [270, p. 1005; 261, 1957, Tables 7, 9, 10, and 13]. The proportion of vacant lot transactions was probably greater in earlier decades and more use was made of mortgage loans to raise funds for purposes other than the purchase or improvement of realty. Some 19 per cent of mortgages on owner-occupied homes in 1890 raised funds for business purposes or for other nonhousing needs.[4]

Any value series of mortgage loans will be only slightly affected by transactions on vacant lots. The major influences on the series are mortgage recordings for new houses, with their relatively larger unit values, and mortgage loans on business properties. In the 1956 real estate sales survey, sales of business property accounted for 2.2 per cent of the number, but for 9.2 per cent of the value, of all sales. The relative proportion of nonfarm mortgage recordings for business use is somewhat greater, 17.5 per cent. In earlier decades the percentage of both nonfarm sales and of mortgage funds for business use was larger. The share of nonfarm mortgage funds for business purposes in 1890 is estimated at 40 per cent. Mortgage loans contracted in the 1880's with an individual amount in excess of $5,000 accounted for some 40 per cent of funds borrowed, while loans in excess of $25,000 accounted for 15 per cent of funds borrowed [270, p. 1005; 114, Appendix L]. The value of mortgage loans must therefore reflect a mixture of residential and business use of credit.

The Ohio patterns of mortgage fund flows between 1857 and 1914 ran their course amidst powerful price movements which pulled down values between 1880–97 and pushed them up thereafter. The deflated value series exhibits two bursts of growth, between 1866 and 1877 and between 1900 and 1914. These patterns demonstrate that while mortgage lending experienced a definite specific cycle with duration and amplitude characteristics similar to building cycles, the timing of this movement varied so widely and randomly from reference chronologies that all cyclical characteristics were eliminated from reference cycle behavior, creating a nearly straight-line trend. Since divergent price trends partly offset each other, the average cycle patterns of the undeflated totals (Chart 4-6) have the same cyclical and trend characteristics as the deflated series. Because of this, and to avoid problems of bias in deflation, we have used the undeflated value series for the more detailed analysis which follows.

The comparative stability of average mortgage lending flows on a statewide level indicated that total mortgage borrowing in Ohio as a whole did not systematically vary with the building cycle. However, *local* mortgage recordings exhibit clear-cut reference as well as specific cycles with distinct phases of reference contraction. Summary measures are presented for Ohio local groups and for Berlin in Table 4-4 and Chart 4-7. Unlike those for

CHART 4-6

Value Total Mortgages, Ohio, With and Without Riggleman
Adjustment, Specific and Reference Cycle Patterns

------ Specific
———— Reference

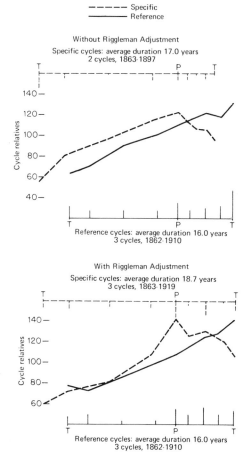

Without Riggleman Adjustment
Specific cycles: average duration 17.0 years
2 cycles, 1863-1897

Reference cycles: average duration 16.0 years
3 cycles, 1862-1910

With Riggleman Adjustment
Specific cycles: average duration 18.7 years
3 cycles, 1863-1919

Reference cycles: average duration 16.0 years
3 cycles, 1862-1910

Berlin, the local Ohio reference patterns show a delayed peak, with a mean lag at all turns of nearly two years and an average lag at peaks of nearly four years. Reference amplitudes of local Ohio cycles are nearly half their Berlin counterpart. The all-German movement had a specific total amplitude which was more than double that of residential building and a reference cycle amplitude some 96 per cent of national residential building (see App. H). In the United States over the same stretch of years, the distinct impress of a long cycle was rubbed out in the process of aggregating at the regional level. This indicated that the over-all flow of mortgage credit was steady in the United States, at least

TABLE 4-4
Summary Measures, Local Long Cycles, Value of Mortgage Lending

Measures	Ohio[a]			Berlin[b]
	Mean		Median	
Full specific duration (years)	19.4	(4.6)	17.7	17.0
Specific cycle amplitude (cycle relatives)				
Full	260.9	(139.1)	177.0	277.0
Full per year	12.75	(4.74)	10.41	16.28
Fall per year	−17.92	(9.12)	−14.14	−14.94
Full reference amplitude (cycle relatives)[c]	110.4	(46.3)	93.9	189.5
Secular weighted average growth per year (per cent)	5.25	(1.40)	4.94	6.39
Lead-lag turning points (years)	1.88	(.73)	1.33	−1.12
Average deviation (years)	1.99	(1.26)	2.17	.42
Lead-lag reference pattern (years)	1.86	(.89)	1.75	−.75
Optimal serial correlation, trend adjusted				
Lead-lag (years)	1.0	(.8[d])	1.0	−1.0
Correlation coefficient (r)	.685	(.134[d])	.735	.873

NOTE: Figures in parentheses are standard deviations.

[a] Including series 0119, 0127, and 0207 through 0209. These series had twelve specific long cycles with twenty-six matched and four unmatched turning points.

[b] Series 0027, with three specific long cycles, eight matched and no unmatched turning points.

[c] Excludes series 0127.

[d] Excludes series 0119 and 0127.

99

CHART 4-7
Patterns of Average Specific and Reference Long Cyles, Value,
Mortgage Lending, Eight Areas

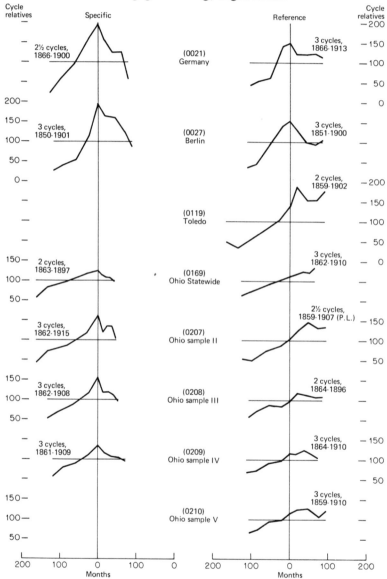

on a statewide basis, though in its local applications or in its various uses mortgage credit had a cyclical movement. It will be worthwhile to attempt to trace out the pattern of offsetting movements which developed either in local applications or in divergent uses.

Mortgage borrowing to finance new building must have declined in reference contractions. The number series shows a clear-cut tendency for reference declines, which, as previously indicated, would reflect personal loans and turnover in residential properties and in vacant lots. The cycle patterns set forth in Chart 4-8 show three clear-cut reference declines which are still recognizable in the average cycle pattern. The mild character of these declines indicate that the increase in the number of old residential properties or vacant lots traded has partly offset the decline in mortgage loans on new residential building. The onset of decline is delayed, and long lags are indicated. With greater amplitude of movement but equally extended lags, the same distinctive cyclical movement of mortgage numbers shows up in the local average cycle patterns for Ohio sample groups (Chart 4-9 and Table 4-5).

In the light of this behavior of number of mortgages series, a direct comparison of these series with those for deeds may be

CHART 4-8

Patterns of Successive Long Cycles and Their Average, Number Total Mortgages, Ohio, 1862–1910

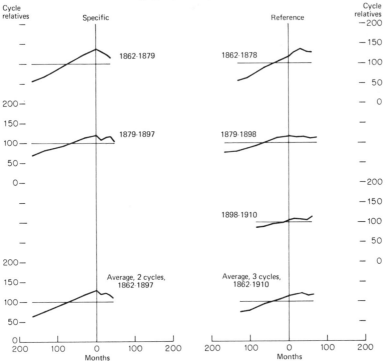

CHART 4-9
Reference Cycle Patterns, Ohio Statewide and Samples, Number of Mortgages and Deeds

TABLE 4-5

Summary Measures, Local Long Cycles, Ohio Mortgages

| | Number of Mortgages | |
Measures	Mean, Total Mortgages[a]	Mean, Nonfarm Mortgages[b]
Full specific duration (years)[c]	17.14 (1.72)	n.a.
Specific cycle amplitude (cycle relatives)[c]		
Full	130.0 (31.9)	n.a.
Full per year	7.51 (1.39)	5.18 (3.59)
Fall per year	−8.62 (2.55)	−8.98 (12.04)
Full reference amplitude (cycle relatives)	78.5 (28.4)	87.7 (9.6)
Secular weighted average growth per year (per cent)	3.261 (1.15)	2.923 (1.94)
Lead-lag turning points (years)[c]	2.03 (.56)	n.a.
Average deviation (years)	2.04 (.30)	n.a.
Lead-lag reference pattern (years)	1.52 (1.04)	.45 (1.93)
Optimal serial correlation, trend adjusted[d]		
Lead-lag (years)	1.38 (.4)	n.a.
Correlation coefficient (r)	.722 (.17)	n.a.

NOTE: n.a.—not available. Figures in parentheses are standard deviations.

[a] Series 0113, 0126, 0202 through 0205. These had fourteen specific long cycles, twenty-nine matched and three unmatched turning points.

[b] Series 0230 through 0233. These had seven long reference cycles (specific cycles not analyzed). The number of turning points was not available.

[c] Series 0205 excluded.

[d] Includes only series 0202 through 0205.

helpful. If the proportion of realty sales involving a mortgage loan behaves as a constant for long cyclical purposes, the differential behavior between deed and mortgage numbers should indicate the relative movement of nonrealty borrowing, which includes distress borrowing for personal and business needs. This differential behavior is exhibited in Chart 4-9, which shows average statewide and local reference patterns of the number of deed and mortgage recordings. The divergences are systematic and cumulative. In reference expansions, deeds accelerate and reach an early peak which leads the peak of residential building by twenty months. The number of mortgage loan recordings continues to rise and reaches its peak only some thirty-two months after the reference peak. In part the difference in timing reflects the stronger trend growth in number of mortgage loans (3.3 per cent) over deeds (2.5 per cent). But the number of mortgage loans in reference contractions increases, though realty sales are declining. This is because mortgage funds are used for purposes not correlated with real estate purchase or improvement. In the expansion phase of the building cycle, mortgage loans would appear to be used primarily to finance realty transfers; in the contraction phase the role of other borrowing increases.

Until now we have attempted to trace out the mortgage fund flows in relation to movements of building and real estate sales. During this entire period, however, agricultural mortgages played an important role in mortgage finance.[5] It may be presumed that some, perhaps many, farm mortgages were negotiated in connection with family succession or quasi-partnership arrangements which have little direct bearing on, or competition with, fund flows in capital markets.[6] Hence, it may be deceptive to use mortgage data aggregating farm and nonfarm recordings.

In Chart 4-10 the behavior of farm and nonfarm mortgage patterns is contrasted. The number of farm loans exhibits a cycle pattern with essentially random variation, without the strong upward growth trend characteristic of numbers of nonfarm loans. The pattern for nonfarm mortgages evinces a cyclical character because during reference contractions loan activity levels off or declines, reflecting in part the decline in sales of used and newly built houses and vacant lots.

The average value cycle patterns for town lot mortgages (shown in Chart 4-11) shifts this relationship. The mean value of a nonfarm mortgage evinces a distinct acceleration or rise in the

CHART 4-10
Average Long Reference Cycle Patterns, Ohio Statewide, Number and
Value of Mortgages, Farm and Nonfarm, 1878–1910

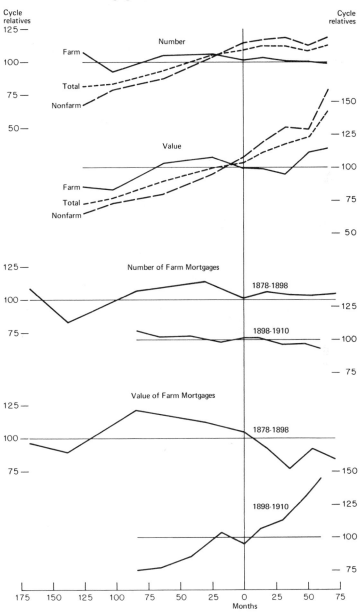

CHART 4-11
Reference Cycle Patterns, Ohio Statewide, Average Value Town Lot Deeds and Average Value Town Lot Mortgages

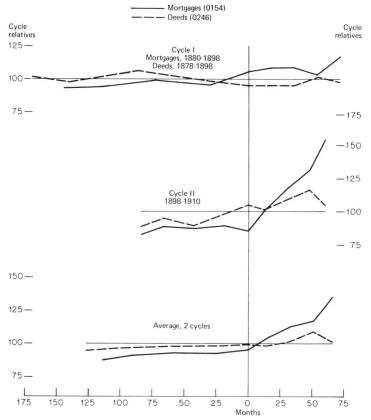

reference contraction. Since new building and mortgage lending associated therewith have declined during reference contractions, we infer the existence of an increased demand for mortgage credit for other uses. This is indeed indicated in the contrast of nonfarm deed and mortgage value behavior (see Chart 4-11). These patterns cover the two pre-1914 reference cycle movements which began in the late 1870's. The same element of price movements—downward to 1897, upward to 1910—runs through both series. Both deed and mortgage values per unit are relatively stationary or are subject to a very moderate upward drift during the reference expansions. Reference contractions are conspicuous for a lift in these values, reflecting a relative increase in higher-valued transactions and a widening differential in favor of per-unit mortgage over per-unit deed values. This differential increases in the last phase of the reference contraction, indicating that nonrealty mortgage transactions have become especially prominent. This statewide outcome was doubtless subject to local variation depending upon the demand for different credit uses.

E. FORECLOSURES

One ground for cyclical variation grows out of foreclosure experience. Mortgage credit is extended on the assumption that such loans are comparatively safe investments. A foreclosure weakens this assumption; a wave of foreclosures should dampen willingness to extend mortgage credit.

Unfortunately our Ohio data do not include tabulations on mortgage foreclosures. However, this information is available from two other cities—Berlin and St. Louis.

Our two series on foreclosure have the same logical form as our development series. They should reach peaks at building troughs and vice versa. This clear-cut inversion is found in our cycle patterns for Berlin and St. Louis, as shown in Chart 4-12. Amplitude even exceeds that of residential building and suffers very little erosion in reference chronology (see Table 4-6). The

CHART 4-12

Patterns of Average Specific and Reference Long Cycles, Foreclosures, Two Cities

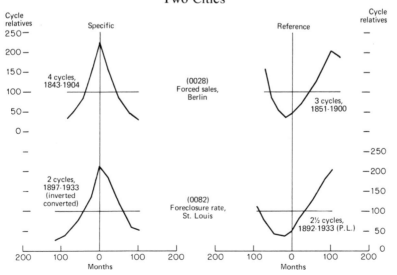

TABLE 4-6

Summary Measures, Local Long Cycles, Foreclosures

Measures	St. Louis[a] Mean	Berlin[b] Mean
Full specific duration (years)	18.0	15.2
Specific cycle amplitude (cycle relatives)		
Full	344.4	386.9
Full per year	19.13	25.37
Fall per year	-18.92	-23.58
Full reference amplitude (cycle relatives)	239.4	275.9
Secular weighted average growth per year (per cent)	-2.695	1.902
Lead-lag turning points (years)	-1.60	-1.67
Average deviation (years)	1.28	1.33
Lead-lag reference pattern (years)	-.75	-1.65
Optimal serial correlation, trend adjusted		
Lead-lag (years)	-3	-3
Correlation coefficient (r)	-1.000	-.428

[a] Series 0082, which had two specific long cycles, with five turning points matched and none unmatched.

[b] Series 0028, which had four specific long cycles with nine matched turning points and none unmatched.

definite tendency to lead on reference downturns in both Berlin and St. Louis and on reference upturns in Berlin only—with a mean lead of about seventeen months—could not fail to exert a psychological influence. The correlograms clearly point to an over-all lead of some three years. Foreclosures are even more visible than vacancies; and the increase in the foreclosures rate should tend to reduce willingness to invest in building ventures or willingness of bankers to lend on them. Interpreting them in this way, as a distress signal, Roos [224, pp. 69–110] found through multiple correlation analysis that foreclosures were highly influential. The influence was nonlinear. At a very low foreclosure rate (under 250 per year), the influence of a change in the foreclosure rate is potent, and capital flows freely to satisfy demand for building. At relatively high foreclosure rates, credit flows are slower and are not directly sensitive to small variation in rates. An increase in foreclosure rates over (say) 1,000 per year has little additional inhibitive effect. Thus, within a limited range of values the relationship is sensitive. But these results describe only a limited experience in one city and have not been tested in other areas or in the same city for later time periods.

While detailed data have been analyzed for only two cities here, a shorter series of foreclosures for Paris exhibited the same characteristics. The series was clearly inverted with a mean lag of one year on three matched turning points (mean deviation of 2.66 years). Correlation with building activity produced a mean negative correlation of -40.2. Amplitude of Paris foreclosures is less than amplitude of variation of building activity—as in Berlin and St. Louis—but exceeds amplitude of real estate selling price as was the case elsewhere.[7]

F. SUMMARY

Since the demands for new and old building compete, the market behavior for realty vitally influences demand for new building. This rival demand, in turn, translates into a joint demand for long-term mortgage capital required to finance most purchases of realty. Not all realty transactions use mortgage capital, and mortgage loans can be used to spread purchase payments over time or to raise funds for purposes other than realty purchase or improvement. And of course, our mortgage data include farm as well as nonfarm transactions. Variations in demand for mortgage funds generated by new building are measured by our reference chronologies and amplitudes. Variation in mortgage use for farm and nonfarm purposes can be directly determined. Variations in business use of nonfarm mortgage loans are reflected chiefly in movements in the value of mortgage recordings. Variations in used and new residential realty and vacant lots transactions are more fully reflected in number of mortgages series. Comparative analysis of mortgage, deed, and building behavior indicated that the total value of mortgage recordings between 1858 and 1914 in Ohio shows no long-term reference cycle contraction and only faint traces of a relative reference slowdown in growth rates. Hence, a cyclical impulse was not imparted from the "funds" or supply side to capital flows in any sector; demand influences in a given sector are indicated to be dominant. Oddly enough, farm mortgage recordings by value exhibited a clear-cut reference contraction (IV–VII), so that nonfarm mortgage credit accelerated in its rise during reference contractions. In Germany, mortgage recordings and institutional portfolios for the nation as a whole and for Berlin showed clear-cut and relatively high amplitude reference swings, indicating possible supply pressure at work in mortgage credit markets during reference contractions.

Deeds and number of mortgages series exhibit reference expansions and contractions of comparable amplitude, allowance being made for divergent trends, but with a clear-cut lead at reference peaks for deeds and a lag for number of mortgages. Nonrealty use of mortgage funds is accelerated in reference contractions, while realty use is accelerated in reference expansions.

If mortgage credit activity as a whole only weakly reflected building cycles, land development reflected them to an exaggerated degree. At the wholesale level in sales or mortgage recordings on town acreage, extremely high mean specific total amplitudes, 602.9 ± 157.3, are exhibited, nearly double that of residential building itself. These exhibit a clear-cut tendency to disturbed neutral timing, showing up as a collection of leads and lags which tend to offset each other in the aggregates. Moderate regularity is indicated by a relatively low-valued mean turning point deviation (1.56 years) and a relatively high ratio of reference to specific amplitude (.674).

Once acreage is prepared for a building site it must be graded, dedicated for public use, improved, and subdivided into lots. This work of subdivision also develops extremely high specific total amplitudes (654.0 cycle relatives) of the order of magnitude exhibited by developers at the wholesale level. These amplitudes also show up on the reference scale with fair regularity, having a reference-specific ratio of .661 and a low mean deviation (1.31 years) at matched turning points. As would be expected, at the retail level, timing tends to be concurrent, with a slight tendency to lag from one to six months. The high amplitudes on development activity testify to the speculative impulse, which will overstate the rise but will promptly adjust new supply to changing currents of demand.

Foreclosures are to realty markets what failures are to commercial markets. Foreclosures signal distress; they frighten institutional suppliers of long-term funds and speculative builders. Hence, though our recorded total amplitude—in the 300's—does not reach the intensity of development amplitudes, the consequences of the fluctuation may be significant. As expected, behavior is inverted and with a clear-cut lead from .75 to 1.7 years. Our two sampled foreclosure series were consistent in their timing, with relatively low mean deviations and a high ratio of reference to specific total amplitude.

NOTES

1. Pre-1914 German loan-shares were 80 to 90 per cent. See [33, pp. 167 ff.]. In the English capital market of the late nineteenth century, British builders could borrow 70 per cent on a first mortgage loan at a rate of 1 per cent above Consols, while a second mortgage loan was obtainable at 6 per cent [28; 165]. German second mortgage financing was more difficult and expensive, as was true elsewhere. See [166, XXIII ff.]. The American share of equity capital has been reported at higher levels: 50 to 55 per cent was typically covered by a first mortgage loan, 20 to 25 per cent was often covered by a second, and between 4 and 22 per cent of all purchases were without loan financing. See [13, I, 347 ff.; 91, pp. 357 ff.].

2. Grebler et al. [114, pp. 184 ff.] estimate that on a sector basis between 1911 and 1920, 51.5 per cent of total new housing expenditures was covered by equity funds and for 1948–52, some 27.3 per cent. They term "an optical illusion" the assumption that "investment in new residential construction has been generally and uniformly characterized by extremely low proportions of equity capital." The assumption is not an illusion for the individual builder or investor, only for financial institutions. Thus, higher rates of amortization of mortgage loans would not reduce the dependence of home buyers on mortgage finance but would reduce the dependence of mortgage institutions on fresh savings or "outside funds." Goldsmith's survey of the capital market in the postwar period

shows that about three-fifths of new mortgage recordings are offset by mortgage repayments, of which again three-fifths were full prepayments of the mortgage indebtedness outstanding on properties at the time of sale [104, Table 101].

3. See discussion in Chapter 5.

4. [270, p. 1075]. The loans raised were some 17.89 per cent by number and 18.78 per cent by value of all mortgage loans on encumbered owner-occupied nonfarm homes in 1890.

5. Some 40.5 per cent of mortgage funds raised in the 1880's in the United States involved mortgages on farm lands [270, p. 995]. Comments by both Goldsmith and Kuznets indicate awareness that their summary statistical measures may underrate the role of agriculture in financial markets of the late nineteenth century [161, pp. 236 ff.; 105, Vol. II, pp. 409 ff.].

6. Goldsmith [105, Vol. I, p. 749] estimated that in 1896–97 financial institutions held only 12 per cent of outstanding farm mortgages. When detailed comprehensive statistics on holders of farm mortgage debt recordings first became available in 1910, they showed that financial institutions were making from 25 to 29 per cent of farm mortgage loans. See [255, pp. 156 ff.].

7. Measuring amplitude by the coefficient of variation, we have for the entire 1860–1935 period: building activity, 7.1; foreclosure, 5.6; real estate selling prices, 2.7. These and related measures for Paris were derived from [93, Fig. 1, Table V and text]. It is interesting to note that the coefficient of correlation of foreclosures with real estate price level was somewhat higher than that with building. The two sets of coefficients are as follows:

	Correlation of Foreclosures with	
	Building	*Real Estate Prices*
1886–96	−.25	−.08
1895–1903	.31	−.88
1902–09	−.50	−.67
1908–13	−.95	−.78
1927–35	−.62	.10
Mean	.402	−.462

CHAPTER 5

Marriage, Migration, and Vacancies in Long Local Cycles

A. INTRODUCTION

Fluctuations in real estate and urban building are commonly believed to be accompanied by, and to a certain extent grounded in, corresponding fluctuations in the growth of urban population. Housing and building are, after all, designed to serve the needs of people. That there is a "constant proportion" between people and building was classically argued nearly three centuries ago and has been reiterated by a long train of investigators who have pointed out the close relations between building swings and migration swings.[1]

Urban population growth has in the first instance derived from inflows of migrants from farms and villages seeking work opportunities in urban communities undergoing industrialization. But a growing labor force through in-migration must involve at some stage the forming of new households by acts of marriage which have been cogently held to be, "as a voluntary and controlled action, the most important factor in population growth as it can be related to economic development" [83, p. 45]. The activity of both migration and marriage grows out of decisions which involve appraisal of economic conditions, the search for better opportunities, and the quest for personal maturity. Hence we will in this chapter seek to trace out the mutual interrelations between migration and marriage activity and long swings in building, real estate market activity, and urban development.

These interrelations are many sided and complex but so far as housing markets are concerned they will involve shifts in rates of utilization of dwelling stocks or, the inverse of these rates, in vacancy rates. As we shall see in the next chapter, this sensitive market indicator exerts a potent influence on valuation and price making in real estate and building markets and tends to guide the activity of new building and land development. Hence the study of vacancies and of rates of building utilization is pursued in this chapter together with related demographic processes.

B. DEMOGRAPHIC ACTIVITIES

The demographic activities of migration and marriage have their similarities and differences with regard to economic fluctuations. Migration is, for example, both a responsive and determining force. The changing state of the business cycle and employment opportunities will induce changes in migration, and a migratory shift will exert a reflex influence on the business cycle by increasing the capacity to produce. With marriage rates, the short-term relationship is more one-sided. Changes in business conditions over the short cycle regularly induce changes in marriage rates. However, no reflex influence of marriage rates on business cycles is ordinarily envisaged. This is not so in long waves of building. The demand for shelter will be significantly influenced by changes in the rates of marriage, and by resultant delayed changes in the rates of birth. Changes in the demand for shelter will play an important determining role in building waves. Thus, in short cyclical analysis, marriage rates appear primarily in the character of a determined series; in long building swings, marriage rates appear more in the character of a determinant. In both cases, the influence is reciprocal.

Demographic data—like our other time series—may be recorded and analyzed by a direct count of events, e.g., marriages performed, or passengers going overseas, or by taking the rate of enumerated events to the population of total possible events.[2]

For marriages this population constitutes a class of persons normally eligible for marriage or an aggregate of the age-generation cohorts within given eligibility-class bounds (i.e., 18 to 45 years), inclusive of all age-eligible persons not living in institutions or in a married state. The class is steadily dissipated by emigration, by new marriages, by death, by institutionalization, and by retirement of eligible persons out of the age bounds. The class is augmented by immigration, by separation of marriages of eligible persons, and by maturation of youngsters into the eligible age categories. The sustainable magnitude of this class will vary proportionately with total population. But over short-term or transition periods, total population can be an unreliable guide to the population of marriageable adults. With a constant total population the composition of the marriage class can become unfavorable, e.g., by shift to older-age distribution or by dispersion in localities with unequal sex composition or sex-eligibility matching.

Major wars and waves of migration exert profound effects on marriage potential and may change its course for an extended time period. The ratio of marriages performed to an appropriate measure of marriage potential constitutes net marriage rates; gross marriage rates are marriages reduced to a per capita basis.

Changes in the rate of marriage would probably exert little influence in long swings if they were accompanied by parallel changes in the rate of marriage dissolution (through divorce or death or rejoining with another family) so that the total number of mated pairs occupying households remained constant. If, however, population is growing, so that both the employed labor force and total number of households are growing, new marriages in excess of marriage dissolutions will, within the span of time covered by building cycles, lead to an expansion of births and to an increase in the number of families with young children seeking shelter. If the rate of marriage dissolution is more stable than the rate of new marriages, then the impulse of fluctuation imparted by the marriage rate will be amplified as it affects new household formation.

Even with constant marriage rates, demand for shelter would be affected by altered headship rates or tendencies to form independent households. In the recent phase of building expansion in post-1946 America, these alterations played an appreciable role in generating demand for housing.[3] In past building cycles, their relative weight was minor compared with changes induced by new marriages in excess of marriage dissolutions.

C. MARRIAGE AND MIGRATION SWINGS

Although consideration of demographic processes is thus of special interest, it was hard to find actual data applicable to our surveyed local communities. A population count is difficult and expensive to administer; few communities outside of Sweden have maintained detailed housing registries which would keep track of annual movements of population arising out of internal migration or birth or death. Since the event of marriage usually involves some form of public recording, the count of marriages in local communities is more frequently encountered and is more accurate than the enumeration of population. We have analyzed marriage series for eight of our surveyed local areas: the five Ohio sample groups, Chicago, Stockholm, and Paris. Population or migration series are available only for Berlin, Amsterdam, and Chicago. Two series measure net population change, a third measures net migration, which should vary in close correspondence to it. Since natural population growth will have an amplitude of movement much less than growth induced by migration, the Berlin migration series, as expected, behaves more sensitively than the other two series. We have also included in our charts population patterns for some Swedish towns and for a composite of seventeen American cities.

Local marriage and migration series were analyzed in unadjusted form, i.e., without conversion into rates of utilization of marriage potential, because data measuring the potential was not available. Our resulting patterns thus have growth trends incorporated within them. A decline in rates of utilization of marriage potential may, in our series, assume the form of plateaus in absolute numbers. If allowance is made for this possibility, the unadjusted data may be serviceable.

Charts 5-1 and 5-2 present the average cycle patterns, both specific and reference, for our surveyed areas.

Table 5-1 shows our standard summary measures for long-cycle behavior, covering duration, amplitude, growth, and timing. Since few series are available for survey, the measures of central tendency will need to be interpreted with regard to the range of dispersion of the surveyed activity.

No trace of reference long-swing rhythm was found in Stockholm marriage activity, as is clearly indicated in Chart 5-1, possibly due to the unusually high average age of marriage and proportion unmarried and the tendency for the marriage ceremony to be "less valued" than in other countries.[4] As expected, population growth and migration patterns apparently have a much wider range of amplitude than marriage patterns. This is vividly indicated by inspection of our charts and it is brought home in the mean amplitude, both on a total and per-year basis. Mean amplitude for the former patterns is 321 and total movements per year are 18.07, i.e., at a level of variation of the same order of magnitude as was experienced for building operations. It is not

CHART 5-1

Patterns of Average Reference Long Cycles, Marriages for Chicago
(Cook County), Stockholm, Paris, Ohio Statewide and Five Samples

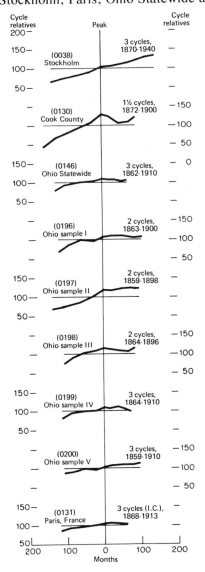

easy to make similar comparisons for marriage patterns, since it
was found possible to ascribe specific cycle behavior to only three
of the eight marriage series. Using these three as a basis for
comparison, the total specific amplitude for the marriage series is
estimated at 87.4, or only one-fourth of population amplitudes.

CHART 5-2

Patterns of Average Specific and Reference Long Cycles, Population Factors, Five Urban Areas, 1839–1933

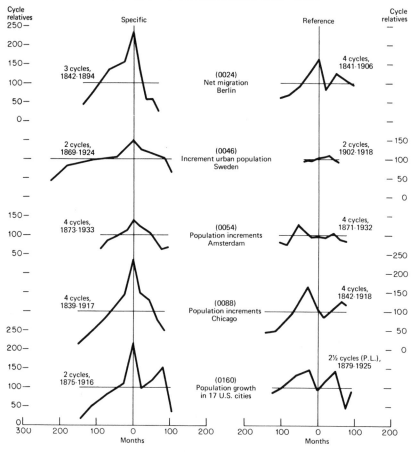

The rate of annual fall of the population series is formidable, but barely perceptible in our marriage series, though in terms of rates of change the slowdown is clear.

A similar order of variation is found in respective amplitudes of short cycles. Thus, the mean amplitude of British marriage rates over the nineteenth century was from 15 to 17 per cent of the corresponding amplitude for British migration.[5] German marriage patterns experienced an amplitude of fluctuation only 7 per cent that of migration.[6]

Similar relationships show up in the Paris time series available for the same period in the form of five-year totals. Chart 5-3 shows building, migration, and per capita rate of marriage. The use of a per capita rate eliminated the influence of the strong upward growth trend of marriages (nearly threefold between 1851 and 1911), and brings out variation in the rates of utilization of marriage potential. The migration series are smoothed with a three-term moving average because of erratic behavior. The absolute magnitudes of migration and marriages over the period are comparable: net migration to Paris amounted to 80 per cent of the number of marriages between 1851 and 1911; yet unsmoothed migration is extremely volatile compared with either building or marriages. In terms of standard deviations, when marriage rates are equal to 1.0, building activity fluctuates at a rate of 2.65 and migration at a rate of 9.97.[7]

Delayed timing seems to go with dampened amplitudes or, conversely, high amplitudes are here associated with a lead. On turning points, all three of our population series led by a reasonably stable mean of 1.22 years. Two of the three sets of reference cycle patterns exhibited leads, with an over-all mean value close to turning points. Berlin reference patterns point to synchronous timing, but this is belied both by the form of the time series and by the correlogram. Timing patterns in Berlin, as in the other areas, were complicated by the clear tendency of reference-cycle patterns to separate into eight- to twelve-year segments. These segments reflect the rhythm of the "major" or so-called Juglar process previously noticed in our cycle patterns of industrial building (see Chapter 2). Making allowance for disturbed timing relationships, it seems clear that population "leads" from one to two years.

Marriage volumes, however, seem to be characterized by a tendency to lead on long upturns and to lag at peaks. Turning-point and reference-cycle analyses do not clearly point to a statistically significant net lead or lag because of sampling variability. Correlograms exhibit the same divergence, with perhaps the tendency to lag predominant. Thus, the mean correlation coefficient (trend unadjusted) for all Ohio sample-group lag periods is 0.8372 and for lead periods 0.8036. However, the extreme leads exhibited by the Stockholm and Paris correlograms are not significant, and probably reflect the strong trends running through the series.

The general conclusion pointed to by these results—that population and migration significantly lead and marriages either synchronize on balance or tend to a short lag—are confirmed by correlation analysis performed on the Paris five-year aggregates

TABLE 5-1
Summary Measures, Local Long Cycles, Demographic Activity

| Item | Units | Marriage Activity[a] | | | | Population Growth Non-Ohio[b] | | |
		Ohio[c] Mean or Total	Non-Ohio[d] Mean or Total	All Mean or Total	All Median or Total	Mean or Total	High	Low
A. Totals								
1. Number of series		6	2	8		3		
2. Number of specific long cycles		15	4.5	19.5		11		
3. Number of turning points (TP):								
a. Matched		10[f]	n.a.	14[g]		25		
b. Unmatched		2[f]	n.a.	2[g]		2		
B. Means or other values								
4. Full specific duration	Years	2.26	2.67	2.36±1.25	2.23	17.3	19.5	15.0
5. Specific cycle amplitude:								
a. Full	Cycle Relatives					321.1	414.9	144.9
b. Full per year[h]	"					18.07	23.27	9.66

c. Fall per year[h]	"	−.005	.005	−.003±.97	.19	−24.42	−36.98	−9.33
6. Full reference amplitude	"	54.5[k]	56.9	55.2±25.1	43.7	218.4[l]	244.5	192.3
7. Secular weighted average growth per year	%	2.659[f]	2.619	2.084±2.05	2.62	2.296	5.643	.583
8. Lead-lag (LL) TP:	Years							
a. LL	"	.21[f]	n.a.	−.11[g]		−1.22	−.56	−1.80
b. Average deviation	"	1.34[f]	n.a.	1.47[g]		2.29	3.34	1.24
9. LL reference pattern	"	.02[k]	−.075	−.007±.52	0	−1.90[l]	0	−3.80
10. Optimal serial correlation, trend adjusted:								
a. LL	"	.63	−1.33[j]	−.21±1.1[j]	0[j]	−2.0[l]	0	−4.0
b. Correlation coefficient	r	.650	.805[i]	.716±.170[j]	.682[j]	.508[l]	.622	.394

n.a.—not available.

[a] For all marriage series reference cycle measures for lines 2, 5b, c are substituted for specific.

[b] Series nos. 0024, 0054, 0088.

[c] Series nos. 0197, 0198, 0199, 0200, 0117, 0112.

[d] Series nos. 0130, 0131.

[e] Mean values are presented plus or minus standard deviations.

[f] For only series 0117, 0112.

[g] For only series 0117, 0112, 0130.

[h] Using I–V reference timing for marriage activity.

[i] Based on 0130, a St. Louis and a Berlin marriage series.

[j] Excluding 0117, 0112, but including 0130, a St. Louis and a Berlin marriage series.

[k] Excluding 0200.

[l] Excludes series 0054.

CHART 5-3
Marriage Rates, Migration (Net), and Building Activity, Paris, France, 1851–1911, Quinquennially

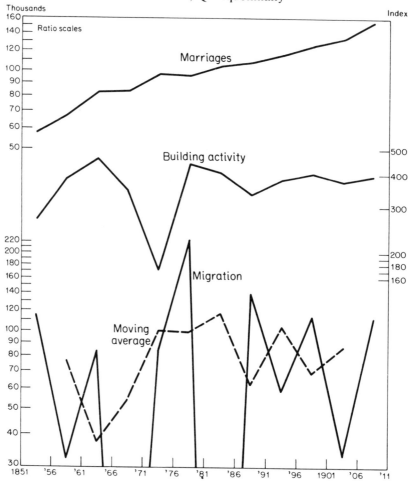

SOURCE: L. Flaus [93] and letters.

for marriage rates, building, and migration (see Chart 5-3) between 1851 and 1911. On the lead of a five-year period, both marriage rates and migration show a high total correlation with building. A converse high, inverted correlation is shown with the lag. The partial coefficients and cross-correlation indicate a tendency for migration and marriage rates to influence each other at a ten-year lag.

With twelve observations, the linear multiple regression equations yielded normalized correlation coefficients (adjusted for degrees of freedom) significantly above zero only for a one-period lead and lag (out of five lead-lag pairs computed). With X_1 as building, X_2 as migration and X_3 as marriage rates per capita, we obtained (with $\bar{X}_1 = 364.3$, $\bar{X}_2 = 83.3$, $\bar{X}_3 = 49.4$):

$$X_{t-1} = 781.7 - .7451X_2 - 7.352X_3$$

R1.23 = − .64
R12.3 = − .66
R13.2 = − .46

$$X_{t-1} = -220.2 + .396X_2 + 11.47X_3$$

R1.23 = .59
R12.3 = .43
R13.2 = .62

Equally significant is the pattern of correlation coefficients for different lags:

Correlated Variables	Correlation Coefficients Lead-Lag of First Correlated Variable				
	$t - 2$	$t - 1$	t	$t + 1$	$t + 2$
$X_1/X_2, X_3$ (normalized)	0	.64	0	.59	0
X_1/X_3	.10	.26	0	.53	0
X_1/X_2	0	.63	0	.23	0
X_2/X_3	−.33	−.07	−.12	−.07	−.07

Since marriage rates would lead marriage volumes, the Paris experience with both migration and marriage data confirms our tentative finding. The Paris lead on marriage *rates* would probably characterize our long marriage series generally and, as we have shown elsewhere, it characterizes national rates for five out of six surveyed countries. This would be consistent with synchronous timing on *actual marriages*, as disclosed by our local time series. There is a notable contrast, in this regard, with marriage-rate behavior during short cycles. As is well known, many tests both on an annual and on a monthly basis have found that marriage *rates* exhibited synchronous timing in short cycles.[8]

Migratory flow will tend to generate a counterpart flow of marriages over time. Like marriage, migration is concentrated in the young adult population [259, pp. 290 ff.; 235, Chap. 24; 247, pp. 40, 49, 75, 78]. Although the marital state of emigrants has not generally been recorded, it predominantly appears that the young adult migrated unattached and sought to get married only after becoming settled.[9] Sex disparities among migrant groups would stretch out the lag and reduce the number of marriages.[10] However diluted or lagged, any migratory flow which is large relative to the marriage potential of the emigrant and immigrant countries, will generate fluctuations in crude marriage volumes and, to a lesser degree, in per capita and net rates. The American experience, since the restriction of immigration, shows that a considerable range of variation in net marriage rates remains to be explained by changes in economic conditions [77].

Does the pattern of movement in our marriage series reflect a composite of influences affecting migration and levels of per capita income? A tendency for a strong lead in marriage volume in long-wave reference upturns could grow out of the improvement of job opportunities that simultaneously elicits the recorded upward wave of migration. Conversely, the tendency of marriage-volume reference peaks that occur synchronously with building or that show a lag long after migration has turned downward may reflect the delayed marriages contracted by migrants who have become settled and whose incomes hold up, even though the growth of job opportunities has declined.

D. VACANCY RATES

The expansion of the labor force through migration and the formation of households through marriage will obviously affect the demand and supply for building in many ways. The most immediate impact of both the influx of additional workers and their formation into new households will be on the margin of vacant housing. To some extent the inflowing migrants will fill up the rooming houses and hotels or private households which, to a greater degree in the past than currently, provided shelter for hire.[11] In the contemporary American world, the number of married couples "doubled up" with another household probably reached its normal level by 1960.[12] Increased demand for shelter, generated by immigration or new marriages, tends to step up housing densities at the same time that it reduces the number of vacant dwellings.

The relative proportion of vacant dwellings will normally vary directly with the mobility of population in and out of dwellings. Modern industrialized populations have been characterized "as truly nomadic, shifting about almost incessantly from locality to locality" [234, p. 407]. Some of this mobility springs from change in business life. Thus, about 10 per cent of retail service and small business establishments are discontinued each year. From 3 to 4 per cent of the employees in manufacturing industries will be "separated" and hired monthly [236, pp. 48 f.; 14, p. 398; 103, pp. 171 ff.; 226, pp. 9 ff.]. Many changes run their course within a city; others involve migration. Any given migratory impulse will induce adaptive migrations from adjacent areas. This high state of social mobility is not purely or even predominantly an American characteristic. There was the same need elsewhere for the continual sorting out of persons between town and country, from job to job, and through the personal life cycle. The lesser role of home ownership in European cities and a relatively short term rental contract for smaller dwellings facilitated the continuous movement of persons [258, pp. 472 f.; 8, pp. 164 f., 171 f.].

These shiftings and migrations give rise to an extensive movement in and out of urban residential dwellings. It has been estimated that the average term of occupancy of an American urban owner-occupant ranges from fourteen to twenty-four years. The average term of property ownership elsewhere seems to be of the same order of magnitude. One out of three tenants in America and in London before rent control, but two or three out of five Berliners, moved each year [106, Vol. 1, p. 316; 219, pp. 34, 59; 90, p. 141; 91, p. 240].

Both in rental and sale property, incoming occupants may or may not follow quickly on the heels of the outgoing. Thus, the vacancy needs of an area in the first instance will be proportional with its characteristic rates of turnover: "the more mobile people are, the greater is likely to be the demand for house-room [and] there will be on the average a larger number of houses standing empty" [46, p. 216].

However, given the rate of turnover, there will also be an independent tendency for vacancy to depend upon the average age of structure. A city with a higher mean age of structures will have relatively more properties in a deteriorating or dilapidated condition. When vacancies tend to concentrate in older buildings, the greater the proportion of these buildings, the higher the vacancy rates. Thus, the relatively higher average rate of vacancy in Glasgow (1870–1914), 6.29 per cent, is due in part to the carry-over of a reserve of dilapidation maintained partly because vacant dwellings in Great Britain were generally exempt from local property taxation [98]. So also the nationwide British decennial record of vacancies between 1801 and 1911 showed a rising trend, which nearly doubled in absolute level.[13]

Since average age or dilapidation of dwellings, mobility of persons or turnover of property, and relative composition of home-owners and tenants—as well as still more underlying forces, such as average family age, marital condition, and pattern of industry—vary among urban areas, so normal vacancy rates will vary. In 1950, Miami, Wichita, and Los Angeles had net vacancy rates of 8.1 per cent, 4.0 per cent, and 3.0 per cent, respectively, while the national average for all metropolitan areas was 1.6 per cent. Similarly, by size of dwelling unit there appears to be a tendency for vacancy rates to vary inversely with size, but directly with age of structure [91]. There are many reports indicating an unusually low range of vacancy rates for many European cities in the pre-1914 period and persistent reference to a standard 3 per cent rate in Europe and a 5 per cent American "norm."[14] It can only be said that these "norms" lie within the range of realized statistical vacancy time series and near some measure of central tendency.

E. SURVEY RESULTS

Long series were available for seven cities: Stockholm, Glasgow, London, Hamburg, Berlin, St. Louis, and Paris. Supplementary data on other experience with vacancies will be presented when relevant. The respective average specific and reference patterns are individually presented in Chart 5-4. Tabular data are presented in Table 5-2. The tabulated series all refer to vacancy rates, except for Berlin. For that city, the number of vacant units, with a mean average growth per year of 1.319 per cent, was analyzed. Consequently, Berlin cycle patterns have a slight upward tilt because of the lack of trend adjustment. No specific allowance for this was made because trend rates were slight and widely divergent. The correlogram of absolute numbers rather than rates takes on a different form, though it discloses the same periodicity.

Observations of both the correlograms and reference cycle patterns indicate a common structural form for six of our series. Paris stands out as a deviant on reference cycle patterns. Whether

CHART 5-4
Average Specific and Reference Vacancy Patterns Seven Cities,
1841–1945

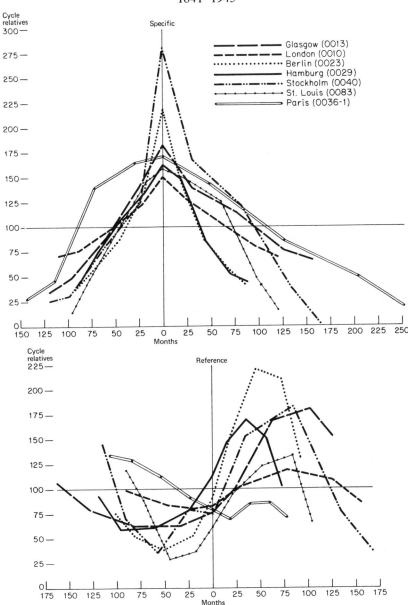

TABLE 5-2
Summary Measures, Local Long Cycles, Vacancy Rates[a]

Measures	Mean		Median	High	Low
Full specific duration (years)	21.0	(5.62)	19.0	33.0	14.7
Specific cycle amplitude (cycle relatives)					
Full	305.6	(108.2)	288.0	533.3	161.6
Full per year	15.31	(5.65)	16.00	23.92	8.50
Fall per year	-14.06	(6.01)	-13.60	-24.41	-7.25
Full reference amplitude (cycle relatives)[b]	242.9	(95.8)	238.5	402.8	91.9
Secular weighted average growth per year (per cent)	.311	(1.52)	0	3.169	-2.151
Lead-lag turning points (years)	-3.83	(2.01)	-3.75	.33	-8.0
Average deviation (years)	2.25	(.75)	1.76	3.60	1.56
Lead-lag reference pattern (years)[b]	-3.93	(1.16)	-4.00	-2.40	-5.90
Optimal serial correlation, trend adjusted					
Lead-lag (years)	-3.0	(1.19)	-3.25	-.5	-4.0
Correlation coefficient (r)	-.769	(.127)	-.752	-.956	-.589

NOTE: Figures in parentheses are standard deviations.
[a] Series 0013, 0010, 0023, 0029, 0040, 0080, 0036-1. All series are for rates except 0023 which is expressed in dwelling units. Timing analysis matched reference against specific series on an inverted basis, with regard to turning points, reference cycle timing, and negative or positive optimal coefficient used. There were 15.5 specific long cycles, with thirty-six matched and two unmatched turning points.
[b] Excludes Paris.

this is related to the shorter span of cyclical time available for the Paris average (only 1.5 reference cycles), to the statistical imperfections of our Paris series eked out from three primary sets of vacancy data, or to structural peculiarities of the Paris real estate market, cannot be determined. It seemed desirable to consider the Paris patterns a special case and to combine the other six patterns into a common average. The mean value of this average is graphed, though median values were very close to it and could have been used. For the same cities a specific mean residential building pattern was also computed; the two patterns appear in Chart 1-3.

In smoothed form the timing of our vacancy pattern is perfectly neutral, with peaks and troughs nearly midway in the reference phase. The five-year gap somewhat exceeds the mean lead at turning points (4.45 years), indicating the possibility that vacancy rates responded more quickly to the movement of an expansion and contraction than to residential building itself. It is believed that if the correlograms had been extended to the higher serial orders, smoothing nearer to a five-year lead-lag would have resulted. In any case, the true lead-lag would fall in the range of four to five years.

Since timing is perfectly neutral, vacancies can be said either to lead or to lag. They lag behind building in the sense that an increase in the rate of building, if sustained over time at a rate exceeding change in demand, will induce a rise of vacancies. But a high or low level of vacancies in turn will stimulate or restrain decisions to build. In this context, vacancy leads.

The distinctive form and regularity of movement of vacancies, as disclosed in Charts 5-4 and 1-3 is arresting. Formally, too, the smoothness of our average pattern reflects the fact that our vacancy series have experienced less variability than has generally been indicated in our surveyed series. Thus, the mean deviation from the mean lead was only 2.25 years or 1.6 years less than the mean lead itself. This performance put the series in the top decile of all our series ranked for variability by this measure. Restrained variability is also exhibited in the comparatively high fractions of specific cycle amplitude, which carries over into reference amplitude. The mean ratio of reference to specific total amplitude, 0.740, exceeds the mean ratio of all surveyed nonbuilding series (0.651). Optimal correlation coefficients adjusted for trend are high.

To conclude: the variability that exists in vacancy behavior should not be allowed to dim our view of a structural mechanism, which apparently operated in the nineteenth and in the twentieth centuries with great uniformity in many different cities, located in four different countries.

Both structural mechanism, with its long lead-lags and nearly neutral timing, and variability, reflective of other influences, are also indicated by our few available nationwide measures of vacancy rates and residential building. The national time series for England (1900–1914), for Germany (1890–1913), and for the United States (1945–62), are shown in Charts 5-5, 5-6, and 5-7. The results both confirm expectations and raise questions. The English vacancy rates are completely in step, with an inverted lead of some five years.[15] The American peak on vacancies is true to form in coming five or more years after a long-term building peak in 1955. The German movement is more irregular and indicates, after 1900, a greater variety of influences at work. Vacancies shift from a synchronized inverted status, as in the early period (1890–97), to a synchronized positive relationship, and keep cyclical step with residential building, faintly suggesting a lead (1900–1913). In this period builders are apparently overresponding to demand signals without appreciable lag on both the rise and fall.

F. SUMMARY

Both the data, though meager, and the expert judgment expressed in the literature concur in the finding that the building cycle is, in the words of Cairncross, "little more than a migration cycle in disguise." More urban building was undertaken to meet the needs of more people, and these additional people were primarily migrants from rural and farm communities. Our migration and population growth series exhibited powerful and specific cycles, with a total long specific amplitude of the same order of magnitude and range as urban residential building. However, correspondence with residential building cycles was relatively loose. The mean trend-adjusted correlation coefficient for optimum lead-lag was 0.51, reference cycle amplitudes were only some 53 per cent of specific cycle amplitudes, and the average turning-point deviation on twenty-five matched turning points was 2.3 years. This variation in timing occurred around a

CHART 5-5

Annual Rental Vacant Dwellings for 1900–1914 and Value of Residential Buildings for 1899–1914, England and Wales

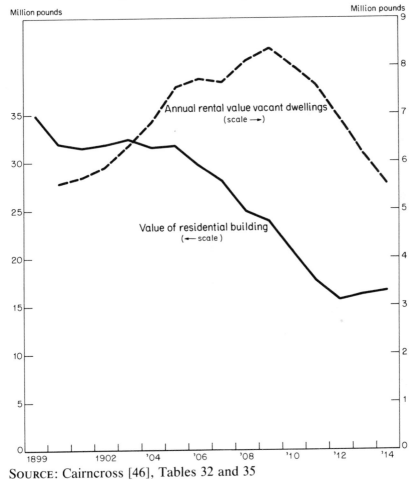

SOURCE: Cairncross [46], Tables 32 and 35

clear-cut tendency to lead, between 1.2 and 2.0 years, particularly on upturns.

Some of this variability in the relationship between new residential building and population growth may have been due to an underlying variability between population growth and marriages. Buildings are used by people but homes are chiefly lived in by families, and the rate at which new families are formed —minus the rate at which old families are dissolved—would exert some specific influence on the course of residential build-

CHART 5-6
Metropolitan Vacancy Rates for Five Cities and Urban Building Index,
Germany, 1810–1913 (1890–1900= 100)

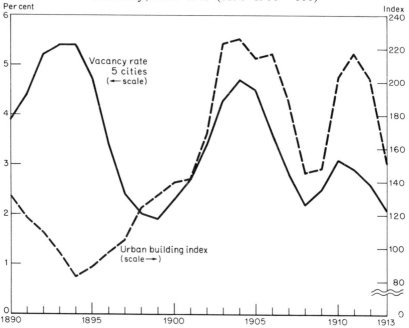

ing. Our analyzed records for eight marriage series showed that people married at a much more steady rate over time than they migrated. The amplitude for our marriage series ran to one-sixth and one-seventh of that of our population series. Accordingly, total marriages fluctuated nearly concurrently with building cycles, with a relatively low measure of variability at matched turning points (mean deviation of 1.03 ± 0.77 years) and a trend-adjusted correlation coefficient of 0.65 ± 0.05. Most of the single people who migrate ultimately marry, but they marry over a long distributed time lag. The distribution steadies the annual rate and scales down amplitude of fluctuation.

Both migrations and marriages directly add to the demand for housing. Augmented demand, in the first instance, reduces available vacancies and serves to signal changing conditions in the shelter market. Vacancy rates fluctuate systematically over a specific total amplitude, nearly matching that of residential building, 305.6 cycle relatives. There is an equilibrium stock of vacancies, adjusted to turnover or movement rates of tenants and owner-occupants, the age distribution of dwelling stocks,

CHART 5-7
U.S. Dwelling Production, 1945–1964 (Annually) and Vacancies,
1950–1962 (Quarterly)

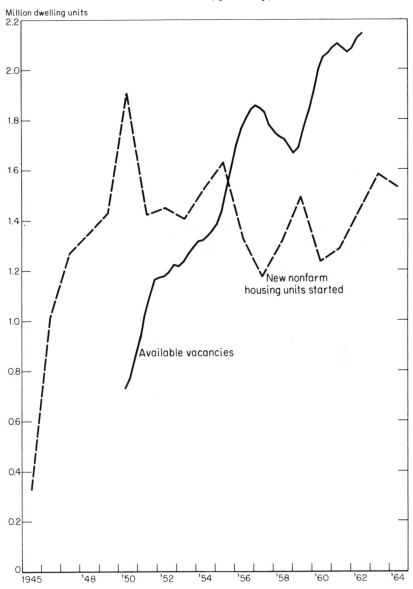

and the tendency to dilapidation. The lag in local cycles of new building behind vacancies at turning points ranges from three to five years; the lag is very consistent, with relatively small lead-lag deviations (mean 2.25 years) on thirty-six matched individual turns, a trend-adjusted mean correlation coefficient of -0.77, and a ratio of reference to specific total amplitude of 0.78. On a nationwide level the relationship of residential vacancies to new building appears more irregular and for an extended period in Germany vacancy rates and new building fluctuate concurrently.

NOTES

1. "The cause of the increase of building is from the natural increase of mankind, that there are more born than die" (N. Barbon, 1685). See also [46, p. 25]; [206, p. 33]; [134, p. 368]; [233, pp. 373–383]; [231, pp. 12 ff.]; [161, pp. 317–319]; [40, p. 67]; [245, Chap. 3, 7, 9]; [50, p. 41].

2. Marriage potential may be statistically approximated by the stock of unmarried women, from age 14 to 44, as in recent American vital statistics reports (see [24, p. 240]). "Marriage eligibles" have been counted as all single persons over 15, plus all divorced or widowed persons [145, p. 21]. For a weighted marriage rate see [59, pp. 205–210].

3. See [126, pp. 508–518].

4. [197, p. 47 (see also data on age of marriage and illegitimacy, pp. 35 ff., 41 ff.)]. John Hajnal, in his celebrated study, characterized Sweden as a country "where both the age at marriage and the proportion who remain permanently single are high" [119, p. 249].

5. See [248, App. B; and 97, Vol. II, p. 943].

6. [136, p. 10]. Spiethoff [239, p. 15] reported that the amplitude of cyclical movements for marriages is numerically much more limited than for migrations. He noted however that marriages moved in step with cycle movements.

7. The respective percentage ratios of standard deviations to means are: marriages, 7.8; building, 20.7; migration, 73.7.

8. D. S. Thomas in her valuable investigation of American and British marriage rates and business cycles found that a synchronous correlation of indexes of marriage and business activity yielded the highest correlation coefficient and that lagging a year reduced the coefficient by 29 per cent for the United States and by 33 per cent for Great Britain [248, pp. 64f., 81ff.]. Hexter found synchronous timing with monthly data for Boston between 1903 and 1916. The maximum correlation is found when marriages lag one month behind wholesale prices; Hexter noted how steadily "the coefficients diminish on both sides of concurrence." The relationship was tested for fifty-three different pairings [125, pp. 151 ff.].

9. See the authoritative and comprehensive collection [88, II, pp. 156f., 175f., 360ff., 304ff., 464ff.; 24, p. 365]. A recent illuminating study of migration

indicates that migration affected marital status differently for the manual worker, student, business, or professional person. See [138, pp. 115–143].

10. Sex disparities were prominent in both short and long migrations. Between 1868 and 1910 nearly two male immigrants into the United States were counted for every female immigrant. Since return migratory flows were predominantly male (and single), the net sex cumulative balance improved; but by 1910 female foreign born numbered only 77.6 per cent of their male counterpart. See [162, Table B-4]. Sex disparities were of course compounded by regional and urban size-class disparities, which together tended to reduce the proportions of males marrying [250, pp. 223ff.].

11. The monumental field survey of wage-earner families carried out by the Immigration Commission disclosed that between 10 and 11 per cent of native-born wage-earning families kept 1.5–1.6 lodgers per household; 30.1 per cent of foreign-born households kept 3.53 lodgers per household [272, pp. 423–425]. A similar survey of 25,440 wage-earner families in 1901 showed that 9 per cent of families took in lodgers [271, p. 22]. In Berlin the fraction of households with lodgers fluctuated cyclically around a trend which, between 1861 and 1905, fell from around 20 per cent to 10 per cent. Amplitude of fluctuation is indicated by the fall in the percentage share of lodging families in 1875 (a cycle peak) of 20.9 per cent and 1880 (a cycle trough) of 15.3 per cent. The absolute number of lodgers between the two dates fell 26 per cent [219, p. 133]. For European urban areas generally, subletting or sharing has involved as many as 15 to 30 per cent of dwelling units [141, pp. 25ff., 103, 123, 157, 266, 303].

12. The Census rate of 6.8 per cent in 1940 reflected depression levels, while the 6.6 per cent rate of 1950 reflected acute housing shortages; the 1960 rate of 2.2 per cent probably reflects a structural level which will tend to persist. On this whole issue, see the account in [114, pp. 79–85].

13. The vacancy rate averaged 3.28 for the first two decades (1801–21) and 6.57 for the closing two (1891–1911). See [223, p. 106].

14. [142, p. 30]; [140, pp. 110ff., 267ff.]; [141, p. 103]; [282, p. 22]; [239, p. 62]; [136, p. 17]. In America, many analysts have examined the "normality" of a 5 per cent vacancy rate. See [137, p. 354]; [257, p. 442]; [128, pp. 252ff.]; [230, p. 3]; [133, pp. 22ff.]; [124, p. 5].

15. This deals with only one turning point, the 1909 peak; but available data given in Cairncross suggest that the trough in vacancies came somewhere near the middle of the 1890's, as required for "lead" consistency.

CHAPTER 6

Price and Value in Long Local Cycles

A. INTRODUCTION

Our survey of long local cycles has so far recorded only the
movement of a network of physical activities—erecting buildings, subdividing lots, buying realty, extending mortgage credit,
foreclosing loans, migrating, marrying, and moving in and out of
homes. These activities involve a decision influenced by the
balance of returns over cost, which, at most points, will be
systematically affected by the level of price or value—the price
of used realty, the value of vacant urban land, the cost of new
building, the rate of interest on mortgage loans, the level of
money rents, and profits of realty undertakings.

This system of prices and values may play a purely neutral
role in building cycles by adapting itself to the movement of
physical activities and giving this movement a suitable pecuniary
expression. Such would be the case if the response of supply to
changes in effective demand was perfectly elastic at a constant
level of value. We know this is not the case, nor are prices and
values in the building and realty market constant over time. We
likewise know, or suspect, that different segments in the price
and value system will be unevenly affected by building cycles.
The markets concerned—for building materials and labor, for
mortgage finance, for urban land and used realty, for shelter
— differ considerably in procedures for price setting and in
degree of responsiveness to changes in demand and supply. The
ultimate sources of new supply are mobilized at different time
rates and respond in different rhythms to market signals.

Uneven change in relevant prices and values will alter the
crucial margins which motivate action by builders, buyers,
renters, developers, and mortgagors. This change in margins will
itself play an important role in the course of events which forms
long swings; the margins may restrain the impulse to fluctuation,
or they may augment it.

137

The purpose of this chapter is to describe this role, to the extent made possible by the available information. First we spell out the principal equilibrium relationships between realty prices, rentals, and the cost of new building. The characteristic features of the urban land market and the role played in this market by speculation are reviewed in some detail. Realty values are grounded in part on urban land values, and at the margin, where new land development occurs, the amplitude of fluctuation in turnover is, as we have seen, extreme. Likewise, realty values are grounded in the cost of new building, which resolves into costs of building materials, building labor, and mortgage finance. Following this preliminary inquiry into equilibrium price relationships and market behavior, the sources and weaknesses of time series available for analysis are described. Our information about price and value is woefully incomplete; methods and bases of valuation are not fully consistent; and some of our samples are very skimpy in the light of variations manifested. The conclusions to be drawn must take into consideration these qualifications.

B. PRICE SYSTEM IN RENTAL AND REALTY MARKETS

The price levels in realty markets are closely related to each other. The monthly rental price will be geared to the sale price of used rental property by capitalization of expected net rental income. An increase of rental prices will thus induce a corresponding improvement in sale prices for the properties involved. For single dwellings the capitalization factor over long time periods has ranged from 100 to 120 times the going monthly rental.[1]

If rent rates correlate with purchase prices of used rental properties, these purchase prices—along with those of owner-occupied dwellings—must, over extended periods, be closely geared to the cost of constructing similar structures, including the builder's profit. Of course, where there are poor facilities for rapid urban transportation, new construction will be handicapped by a rising price premium for access. New properties may avoid stigmas attached to old neighborhoods and may embody novel styles. The greater the attraction of new housing and the more efficient the facilities for transportation, the greater the depreciation of used realty. Since people have varied preferences for new and old housing, the markets for each will usually exhibit continuous interlinkage. As used realty prices get higher relative to new construction, some owners or occupants of old housing will be tempted to shift to new.[2]

The intensity of building is likewise related to the value of land. "In places where the value of land is high, each square foot is made to yield perhaps twice the accommodation, at more than twice the cost, that it would be made to give, if used for similar purposes where the value of land is low" [184, p. 447]. Since building arts are flexible and, by alteration of design, materials, layout, allow for nearly continuous substitution of broad classes of input factors for each other, the resulting input-output functions are readily differentiable and yield smooth continuous schedules of marginal value. The whole development of land and building in the metropolitan region of New York provides continuous illustration of the reciprocal influence between site value, style of building, and patterns of location [132, Chaps. 2, 6].

The complex of equilibrium price relationships serves a set of broad allocative functions. Dwellings are allocated to competing users, capital resources are used for alterations or for new building, the choice is made to buy or rent, and new building is put in housing or in other investment forms.[3] As usual, these price relationships will be more effective in promoting equilibrium, the greater the role of new investment in maintaining or augmenting supply.[4] Two basic prices are involved: the price of urban land and the cost of new construction.

C. PRICE OF URBAN LAND

The price of development land enters into the urban real estate market as an input factor, with indefinite physical, but limited economic, life expectancy. The price of development land will at the minimum be fixed by use of land for agricultural purposes [239, p. 151; 58, pp. 444 f.].

Above this minimum price, its equilibrium value for residential use depends upon two different types of influences. First, there is the influence of cost of adapting raw land to a form suitable for urban use. These costs include land assembly planning, land clearance, drainage, and public improvements for streets, sidewalks, sewage, and other public facilities. A second influence is that of relative preference: for larger lot size, for land further away from city centers, and for newer surroundings. These preferences will be affected by the efficiency of urban transportation and by techniques for dense construction. Improvement of techniques for dense construction—as were yielded by the automatic elevator or by steel frame construction—tends to cheapen the cost of producing urban buildings and thus reduces demand schedules for urban land. Improved methods of getting to and from work widen the radius of effective access and reduce the schedule of premiums paid for closeness. If the streetcar in its day had a revolutionary effect on land values, so much the greater has been the effect of the automobile and the expressway [282, pp. 92 ff.].

But if the value of urban land is thus basically an emergent from a competitive price process involving an interplay of utility and cost forces reaching equilibrium through adjustment of marginal values, it is also affected by a special force which involves the withholding of urban land from the market for the sake of capital gains or, as Henry George put it, "the holding of land for a higher price than it would then otherwise bring" [101, p. 255]. The value of undeveloped or vacant land will be gauged not only by capitalization of present and future incomes but also by the expected level of future land values. Thus, like the long-term investment value of money, the actual value of urban land "is largely governed by the prevailing view as to what its value is expected to be." In this sense its value is a "highly psychological phenomenon" in which, of course, present level, past trend, and future projections fold into each other [153, pp. 203 f.]. It was Henry George, in his classic *Progress and Poverty*, who first developed this truth and focused it on urban land value.[5] But it was Leon Walras who propounded a formal theory of land value which recognized the role of expectation concerning its rate of growth.[6] Only later did J. M. Keynes show how expectation variables played a role in the macroeconomic process [153].

It is not easy to measure the approximate importance to be assigned this speculative component in the value of urban land sites. In terms of market behavior, the volume of resources invested during most of the nineteenth century in vacant land held for purposes of speculative gain probably exceeded idle cash balances withheld by fear of capital loss. The practice of custom building on privately procured lots in the United States turned every potential homeowner into a potential land specu-lator. The phenomenal rise of land values in core areas of central cities or in business districts dazzled the imagination [60, pp. 415– 423]. Land was commonly sold on long terms of payment, and mortgage financing could readily be obtained. In Europe, speculative investment in urban land was not so widely diffused among wage-earners but was founded on even longer experience in urban land appreciation [233, II, pp. 109f., 239ff.; 180, pp. 59–85]. In England the practice of leasing rather than selling land, both agricultural and urban, for building purposes brought into existence a special class of investor who took long specula-tive positions in realty. In Germany the spectacular rise of land values generated by the relatively high rates of urban growth during the nineteenth century was accompanied by widespread speculative investment in urban environs by specially formed land-development corporations [283, p. 358f.].

Trade in urban land was facilitated by a market organization with professional agents, record-keeping facilities, insurance and advisory services. Ease of sale did not compete with high-grade bonds or government securities but probably com-pared favorably with many equity interests or participations. Thus, while the liquidity premium of undeveloped land was of a low order, liquidity considerations would rarely impede invest-ment attracted by hope for capital gains. And speculative investment was facilitated by the low costs of holding land idle. Undeveloped or unplatted land with high speculative value was commonly assessed in America at its farming or agricultural value, due to the unwillingness of the courts to venture far from established guides to value.[7] And assessment of both lots and farmland has been conclusively shown to run substantially under levels of assessment of improved urban land [261 (1959), Tables 7–10; and (1963), Tables 7–11]. In England vacant lots were not generally subject to property tax during our survey period; and undeveloped land on city outskirts used for farming purposes was generally assessed at its farming values [256, Chap. 7]. In Europe, property taxation of vacant land was not regarded as a serious deterrent to speculative investment [221, p. 272 ff.; 180, pp. 271 f., 276 f.; 80, pp. 14, 55; 239, p. 150 f.].

Given a fairly serviceable market organization, a tradition of a "bull market" in land values, and arrangements for purchase of land as an investment sideline and on instalment terms of finance, it is thus understandable that most growing cities of the Western World became surrounded by a ring of speculative land held for purposes of capital gains through urban development. Undeveloped parcels of land and vacant lots would drift into the hands of those who had the highest estimate of the future worth of the land and were prepared to act on the basis of their estimate. Their schedule of estimates would determine the collective supply schedule for land for development use and building. Against this schedule would be thrust a standard demand schedule derived from current demand for building sites. An increase in the demand schedule for land would in the first instance increase lot turnover, reduce the inventory of usable vacant lots and thus tend to increase land prices; and this change in price would exert a reflex influence on the supply function, chiefly through its effect on expected future values. The behavior of the supply schedule would doubtless depend upon the steadiness in price behavior to date and the consistency of its trend. On the other hand, an overdevelopment of lots could, if many holders should be forced to try to realize their investment (as occurred at crisis points in the business cycle), induce a forward movement of the supply schedule. It would seem, then, that substantial variation in both the psychological conditions of supply and building demand for vacant land would give the price of land wide scope for variation.

This variation need not be the same over time or in different places. The greater partitioning of land ownership in America, the infrequent use of the long-term ground lease, the policy of overdevelopment or creation of pockets of vacant land in or around growing cities, and our system of property taxation of vacant sites perhaps induced a lower mean level of site values, or a lesser differential between agricultural and urban land values, than in Europe where the tradition of land appreciation had deeper historical roots, where land on city outskirts was often laid out in princely holdings, and where land dealing was more of a professional business pursuit.

D. COST OF NEW BUILDING

The cost of new building in a given locality undergoing long waves would vary moderately if these long waves were not diffused throughout the economy. A booming local economy could attract additional building labor, building materials, and building finance by offering moderate premiums to attract mobile factors from other centers. Factors could then be released as growth rates receded. Long cycles in building costs would then measure migration premiums required to attract and repel input factors to local centers.

We have seen, however, in our survey of reference chronologies that local long cycles of residential building are to a high degree synchronized (see Table 1-1). They are thus part of a nationwide movement that is systematically influenced and to a degree interlinked both positively and inversely with kindred movements running their course in the Atlantic economy. We have also seen in Chapter 3 that it is not only demand for residential building that fluctuates in long swings. New homes require new stores, new schools and public buildings, new factories, and shops. We found that different types of urban building rose and fell together, and that with appropriate lags particular types of new construction are complementary in character.

If this is so, then the characteristics of the supply function of building—the response of suppliers of building to changed demand by means of a change in price or quantity—will play an important role in the process of long swings. If this supply function is highly elastic, then the cost of building would tend to be maintained, and shifts in demand would induce an appropriate shift of quantities. But if it were prices that responded freely, the variations in demand would spend themselves in high amplitude variations in building wage rates, costs, and prices. Some inquiry into the characteristics of the supply function is hence required to round out an investigation of building cycles.[8]

The supply function of building is not itself a simple function but a family of functions for the crucial input factors of building labor, investable funds, and building materials. With the rise of the business contractor, the segregation of a specialized wage-labor class, and the unions that this class brought into existence, it is reasonable to suppose that the supply elasticity of building labor was reduced. Unionization in the building trades was most effective and achieved the greatest job control in the metropolitan centers where, in addition, the greatest thrust of the building cycle was felt. But the full elasticity of pricing for the contractor component of building supply—and this went a long way when carpenter and contractor often consolidated roles—was unhindered by unionism. How easy for a master workman, serving as contractor, to scale up his terms of bidding when work was abundant and the order book was full and, conversely, to bid close, or to price down, when the demand for his services flagged [118, pp. 219f., 519f.].

Even if building labor and contractor services were available, and if the supply of building materials was readily expansible, more resistance might be encountered with the supply of investable funds. Investable funds must be partly accumulated by the investor and advanced as equity capital; these funds may be raised as loan capital borrowed at long-term interest rates. In the course of the long building cycle, mortgage interest rates would be affected by the well-known "Kondratieff" movement, which has alternatively raised and lowered interest rates, as well as agricultural prices, in long waves of approximately fifty to sixty years in duration.[9] In periods of Kondratieff upward movement, such as between 1897 and 1920, rising interest rates would put residential building, as apparent in Germany and England, under financial restraint.[10] Sensitivity to interest rate and capital flows is enhanced when mortgage lending is organized around legally prescribed or historically evolved interest "ceilings," such as prevailed in pre-1914 Germany or in post-1945 America [114, p. 78ff.; 156, p. 74–94; 136, p. 25f.].

Fully as important as the absolute level of interest rates are relative rates or differentials between yields of mortgages and of high-grade long-term bonds. These differentials must be interpreted in the light of the imperfect loan markets for residential mortgage credit and the resultant tendency for shifts in terms of lending to concentrate upon loan terms other than the quoted interest rates. The rationed—or imperfectly competitive—character of mortgage loan markets, and of many over-the-counter credit markets, has been alluded to in many investigations. See [122, pp. 39–50; 156, pp. 77f.; 206, pp. 25ff.; 229, Vol. II, pp. 617ff.].

Yield differentials have repeatedly played an important role in housing market analysis. The short-run movement of industrial and residential building in Germany was nearly inverted with a small residential lead [136, p. 45]. There was almost perfect inversion in American post-1945 short-run cyclical behavior of capital funds mobilized in nonfarm mortgage debt and corporate securities [115, pp. 22f.]. German analysts reported that an upward wave of industrial activity, while stimulating use and demand for shelter facilities, would tend to diminish the flow of funds needed to finance new construction [283, pp. 365f.; 213, p. 499; 240, p. 86]. Kuznets has demonstrated that, between 1870 and 1920, American long waves in residential building and railway construction were matched by inverted movements in rates in growth of industrial and other investment, so that for capital formation as a whole only a mild wavelike impulse is detectable.[11] In England, a similar inversion of long movements in rates of growth of residential building and industrial (or foreign) investment has been found to prevail in the whole pre-1914 period [45; 46; 245].

E. SERIES UTILIZED

For our tabulations we have utilized thirty-three time series. Five relate to rent and fourteen to sale prices of real estate. Six series relate to building costs, one to wage rates, three to building materials, and four to mortgage yields. Few of our series relate to the same area. Allowance must often be made for divergent statistical techniques used in compiling series or in classifying data. Our sampled series in any one class are too few to yield reliable measures of statistical significance. However, with these and other limitations, we can extract clues on the shifting balance between demand and supply in the interrelated markets for building input factors, housing for hire, improved real estate for sale, and unimproved land in process of development.

Our series on local price of improved real estate come from many sources. Two of the patterns measure real estate selling price in Paris and Berlin. For Berlin, the movement of these prices was derived from the appraised insurance value of purchased parcels of improved properties. While some influence of composition of sales by type, size, or class of property may affect the ratio, price should exert preponderant influence on per parcel value. The Paris index is derived from manipulation of ratios of sale prices for the same residential rental structure at different points of time within a twenty-year period. No allowance was made for alterations in the internal fittings or structure. The mean ratios of the second and third quartiles were computed, linked, and adjusted by a three-to-five-year moving average from 1841 to 1939. Separate study of the square-foot price for homogeneous types of property sold in 1939, but classified by decade of origin, showed that an annual rate of depreciation of 1.2 per cent per year fitted the observed value shrinkage. Applying this calculated rate of depreciation to actual sale price indexes yielded a rectified index which for 1841 to 1913 was utilized in our analysis. See [75, pp. 169–192].

Our two Manhattan series show estimated aggregate value of all realty and an average value per warranty deed. The latter measure is also available from 1877 onward for the State of Ohio and its sample groups for all platted nonfarm property. The average value of a deed, like the average cost of constructing a room, will reflect variations in "mix" as well as price. It will, however, reflect major movements of value levels, and it may provide a clue to shifts in realty price levels. The reliability of "consideration" quoted in deeds is evaluated in Appendix E.

Our rent data—analogous to our price and cost data—are of two classes. Two of our rent series (for Berlin and Hamburg) are for rent charged for occupied dwellings. This is the measure of rent ordinarily used in studies on the cost of living. The rent most significant in realty markets or in investment decisions is advertised rent charged on vacant dwellings. Series for the latter should respond more sensitively to changes in shelter market conditions. For the city of Hamburg, rent measures on both bases are available; for two other cities, a rental series on vacant units was included in our summary table. For Chicago and Manhattan, measures of rent on vacant dwellings are available only for relatively short time periods. Hence the returns for these two cities are not included in the summary tables, though they are discussed in the text.

Our price information for urban site values relates to three different areas and to different components of urban site values. Our fullest information is from Ohio public records of warranty deeds or transfer instruments for unplatted land, subject to the jurisdiction of incorporated municipal governments. Before platting, land is not divided into private lots or laid out into public streets and walks. Transactions in such unplatted land were separately reported in Ohio conveyance statistics and were analyzed for four sample area groups. Only so-called bona fide deeds (excluding deeds reporting nominal consideration) were utilized in this tabulation.

Another major source of site value data is drawn from a century of experience in America's third largest metropolis, Chicago. The land-value records and real estate history of Chicago were the object of a celebrated investigation by Homer Hoyt [134]. Hoyt utilized all available data and records to establish a chronology of long-swing peaks and troughs of land values from 1830 to 1933. He scoured the records to establish the aggregate value of land in the various districts of the city. His estimates of value were based upon sales of property, assessments, and contemporary informed opinion. Though the property sold in most downtown and business areas was improved, the values were estimated for sites alone. Sales consideration expressed in deeds formed the main basis for estimation prior to 1891. For the next twenty years, Hoyt relied upon appraisals, sales, advertised prices, and opinions. Between 1910 and 1929, estimates were based on a local annual real-estate value map. But for noncommercial districts, only sales of vacant land or of sites with negligible improvements were utilized. Since sales were fewer in trough years, estimation methods were cruder, including use of a percentage shrinkage derived from opinion of "current observers." However, shifts in land value were of the same magnitude as shifts in recorded deed consideration.[12]

Hoyt's estimates are dominated by values for improved urban land in a large, rapidly growing industrial city. The Ohio information related to site values of unimproved acreage land located chiefly in urban environs. Our third source of site-value information relates to vacant lots within a large and slowly growing European city—Paris.

Our series on cost of building was most complete on prices of building materials marketed to a large extent on a nationwide basis. Building materials make up somewhat more than half of the cost of building; for the United States and Germany, national or regional price series were found or contrived that reached back to the first decade of the nineteenth century and covered five long swings. The German series was compiled some years ago and is limited, for the early years, to relatively few local reporting sources [144]. The American series was contrived during this research by linking and weighting different series covering different periods and applying to distinct regional centers. It was found necessary to use arbitrary weights; in view of the diversity of regional price movements before 1861, some effect on over-all index behavior may have been produced by the weighting scheme. A detailed description of the new price series and its sources will be found in Appendix D. An independent check on our results may be found in a nationwide quarterly price series, derived from three to five reporting centers, of unit prices for pine timber. Average reference cycle patterns of our average price index, of the pine timber price index, and of a general benchmark pre-1861 series are set forth in Chart 6-1.[13] As expected, the general building price index is more sluggish in movement than the one-product index; but it has a similar conformation. Both lag at peaks.

Some seven series on building costs were analyzed covering four different countries. Three of these series (United States, London, and Germany) use a weighted average of factor input price levels (for building materials and building labor). Three other series allow for the additional influences of changes in productivity and in the quality and/or size of house rooms. While size probably did not undergo long cyclical fluctuation, the assortment of qualities probably responded mildly to cyclical influences. A seventh series shows the effect of building cycles on labor markets by tracing average hourly earning differentials between building and manufacturing labor in the United States.

CHART 6-1

Average Long Cycles, Ohio Valley Economic Pattern, Specific, Building Materials Price Index, Price of Pine Timber U.S., Reference 2 Cycles, 1821–1861

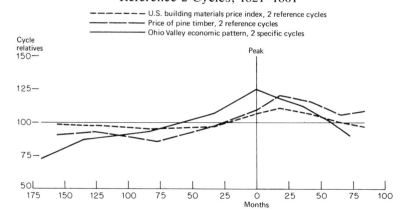

With regard to mortgage yield data, we were fortunate in finding long time series of mortgage yields in four countries: United States (1879–1932), Germany (1870–1913), Scotland (1816–49), and France (1879–1913). The American series represents average contract rates for mortgage loans recorded on Manhattan properties [114, pp. 492–503]. The German series represents average emission rates of German mortgage banks. These institutions, similar to our savings and loan associations, extended credit predominantly on urban mortgages. They raised capital not by accepting deposits, but by public sale of debenture instruments (*Pfandbriefe*) in capital markets. Net change in mortgage loan holdings closely corresponds in pattern of movement and level to *Pfandbriefe* issued. Our third series is of mortgage rates on landed securities for Scotland. This series arose out of the peculiar practice of fixing interest rates on mortgage loans by a conference of investors, accountants, and trustees who met semiannually and who were chartered for that purpose [102, pp. 134–136; 97, Vol. II, pp. 923ff.]. Our fourth mortgage yield series is the annual average rate charged on mortgage loans by the *Credit Foncier,* a nationwide mortgage-lending institution, established in France in the 1850's.[14]

F. SURVEY RESULTS

Vacant Land Price

Cyclical measures for vacant land value covering the Ohio and Paris experience are summarized in Table 6-1 and are graphically exhibited in Charts 6-2 and 6-3. The price of undeveloped Ohio acreage showed the widest range of movement, with highly irregular cyclical timing, of all our price series (see Table 6-1). Total specific amplitude of our four available local Ohio series was 336, or double the next most variable level of price and some 40 per cent above Ohio residential building amplitude. This wide range of amplitude in price per acre is obtained with annual series smoothed by a three-year moving average. However, we were unable to adjust for irregularities in the underlying data and for extreme variations in specific years. If we allow for the dampening effects of smoothing and of aggregation of county returns into county groups, the Ohio per-acre price amplitudes are comparable to the high amplitudes (mean value 681) yielded by the seven series in subdivision activity proper (see Chapter

TABLE 6-1
Summary Measures, Local Long Cycles, Price of Vacant Land

Measures	Paris[a] Mean	Ohio Price Per Acre,[b] Unimproved Land		
		Mean	*High*	*Low*
Full specific duration (years)	18.5	21.5	32.0	14.5
Specific cycle amplitude (cycle relatives)				
Full	132.2	336.1	390.6	216.3
Full per year	7.15	15.97	22.67	12.21
Fall per year	−7.99	−18.9	−24.18	−13.04
Full reference amplitude (cycle relatives)	104.8	187.7[c]	195.2	173.0
Secular weighted average growth per year (per cent)	2.933[d]	2.54	5.092	.401
Lead-lag turning points (years)	−1.33	−.94[e]	4.25	−8.25[e]
Average deviation (years)	4.00	2.77	5.25	0
Lead-lag reference pattern (years)	2.60	−.40[e]	3.50	−7.0[e]
Optimal serial correlation, trend adjusted				
Lead-lag (years)	n.a.	[f]	3	−2.0
Correlation coefficient (r)	n.a.	[f]	.601	−.314

n.a.—not available.

[a] Series 0273, which had four specific long cycles, in which six turning points were matched and two unmatched.

[b] Includes series 0252 through 0255, which had 6.5 specific long cycles, in which fifteen turning points were matched and two unmatched.

[c] Excludes 0252.

[d] For long specific cycles only, omitting high growth rate 1840–68 where level rose fifteenfold. Equivalent short-cycle rate would approach 4 per cent.

[e] Analyzing group IV on an inverted basis as other sample groups were inverted.

[f] Only series 0252, 0254 available.

CHART 6-2
Patterns of Average Specific and Reference Long Cycles, Ohio Statewide and Samples—Average Price per Acre Town Acres (Bona Fide Deeds)

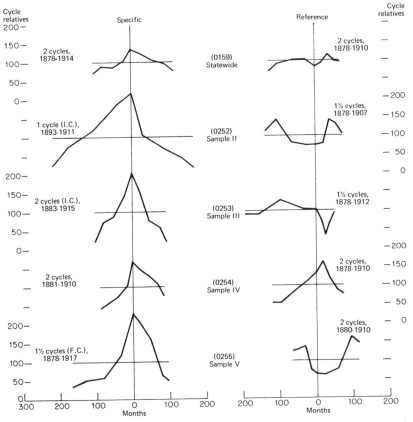

4). It is perhaps significant that mean amplitudes in the particular sample groups did not vary with secular annual rise of per acre price. Amplitude levels were nearly the same for the two sample groups with a low growth rate (for groups I and II, .456 per cent) or a high growth rate (groups IV and V, 4.624 per cent).

Whereas specific cycles in price per acre are clear-cut, there is relatively poor synchronization with long-wave movements in other phases of real estate and building markets. This is evidenced by the erratic form of the reference cycle patterns reproduced in Chart 6-2. Three out of four of those for the Ohio sample groups are governed by irregular forces; there is relatively poor correspondence of reference to specific amplitude.

CHART 6-3
Patterns of Successive Specific and Reference Long Cycles and Their
Averages, Paris, Price of Vacant Land

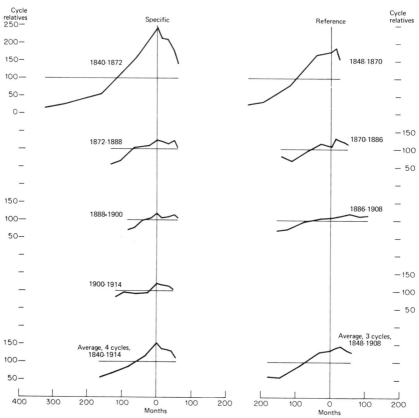

The statewide aggregate reference cycle pattern and correlogram
show little evidence of systematic integration with dominant
statewide movements. This irregularity of timing may be due to
the neutral timing pattern of the volume of development activity,
as indicated by measures for acres of land sold, dollar volume of
mortgages recorded, and value of consideration in bona fide
deeds. The development patterns reached turning points midway
in the residential building cycle. Irregularities in the price
behavior of development acreage sold would, under these circumstances, either induce a more complete inversion (as was the
case with groups II and V), shift back to positive timing (as with
group IV), or would leave intact the neutral position (group III).
The collection of all of these modes of response on the statewide

level perhaps caused the reference pattern simply to become irregular.

In almost all relevant respects, Paris price experience differs from that of Ohio (see Table 6-1). To what extent the difference reflects the pricing of developed lots in Paris and undeveloped acreage in Ohio is difficult to tell. The array of long cycle patterns shown in Charts 6-2 and 6-3 graphically indicates what our amplitude measure tells us numerically, namely, that Paris amplitudes of vacant land pricing are far below, some two-fifths, those of Ohio. Reference declines are very mild. Timing is positive but variable, with an appreciable lag of 2.6 on reference cycle timing but a lead of 1.33 years on six matched turning points. Vacant land pricing has nearly double the amplitude of fluctuation of used residential prices and tends to lead this series by about half a year. The only major specific cycle was the first wave, with its fifteen-fold rise of values between the 40's and 60's and its appreciable five-year period of decline. Thereafter the trend growth of vacant land values responded mildly, after appropriate delays, to very moderate residential cyclical rhythms.

It is worthwhile relating the land value experience of Chicago to that of Ohio and Paris. Tabular data for Chicago land value cycles are set forth in Table 6-2. The graph of site values over

TABLE 6-2
Land Value Cycles in Chicago, 1833–1933

Chronology of Cycles			Total Amplitude			
T	P	T	Rise	Fall	Full	Full per Year
1833	1836	1842	156	161	317	52.2
1842	1856	1861	143	84	227	11.9
1861	1873	1879	141	89	230	12.8
1879	1892	1897	122	49	171	9.4
1918[a]	1926	1933	58	87	145	9.7
Average 1842–1933			116	77.3	193.3	11.0

[a] Though Hoyt "dates" the rise for land values as commencing in 1920 (see 134, Table LXVI, p. 409), his "datings" are with reference to deviations from trend. Elsewhere he dates the "boom period" as 1918–26 and shows a 150 per cent increase for land values in 1926 over 1918 (p. 404). Hence we allowed \$3.333 billion for a 1918 land value, as opposed to \$2 billion in 1915 (p. 470). We have followed Hoyt in assuming that the cyclic long-wave process was smoothed out between 1897 and 1918.

time is reproduced in Chart 6-4. Excluding the near-apocryphal, first speculative boom-bust, with its extremely high annual rates of change, amplitude of total movement shows a marked receding tendency indicated by a skipped reference cycle (1897–1918), during which land values merely slowed up on the rise but did not fall in any general way.[15] The decline of amplitudes also showed up in the moderate behavior of amplitudes during the Great Depression. Mean amplitudes of rise are 116.0, of fall −77.3, and of both phases 193.3.

Oscillation of values was uneven among the different sections of the city and types of property. But though uneven, the shift of values was diffused. Timing was nearly concurrent with peaks and troughs of new building, with a slight lead in upturns.[16]

It is not easy to reconcile this scattered testimony about urban site movements in long swings, either with itself or with the

CHART 6-4
Chicago Land Values, 1830–1933

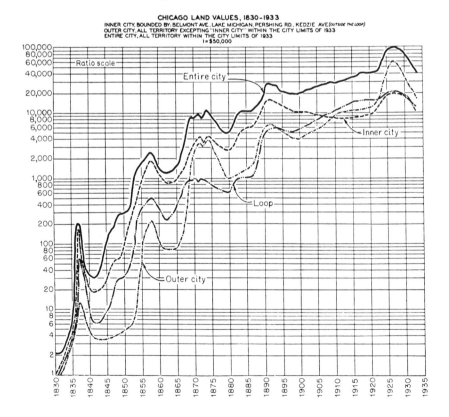

CHICAGO LAND VALUES, 1830-1933
INNER CITY, BOUNDED BY, BELMONT AVE, LAKE MICHIGAN, PERSHING RD, KEDZIE AVE (OUTSIDE THE LOOP)
OUTER CITY, ALL TERRITORY EXCEPTING "INNER CITY" WITHIN THE CITY LIMITS OF 1933
ENTIRE CITY, ALL TERRITORY WITHIN THE CITY LIMITS OF 1933
1 = $50,000

expectations raised by our analysis of the speculative characteristics of urban site values. Quite clearly this speculative
component was not uniformly active in all surveyed communities. It is noteworthy that, in the economically matured but
steadily growing metropolis of Paris, speculative activity in land
values could be very restrained. Our Ohio records indicate that
speculative exuberance was varied in its timing and was often
irregular in its reference behavior. Some of this irregularity may
have been due to incompleteness of submission for public
recording of true selling prices or, even if these prices were
properly reported, to variations in the "mix" of acreage land
being sold. The Chicago experience exhibited a powerful movement of site values in developed land.

Building Material Prices

Even in the nineteenth century, when urban land was at a
premium, the cost of building, including site improvements,
exceeded pure site costs. The most cyclically volatile surveyed
component of building cost was prices of building materials. In
this respect, the German and American series make an interesting parallel, since they both stretch across the five major waves
of the nineteenth century (see Charts 6-5 and 6-6 and Table 6-3).
The great war inflations took turns in severity. The inflation
generated by the Napoleonic wars reached higher peaks in
Europe than in America. The war inflation of 1860–70, which
came a few years earlier in America than in Germany, was more
severe in this country. The nonwar patterns are amazingly
similar, allowing for a more flattened version for Germany in the
1830's and for America in the 1880's. The average cycle patterns
of the first five successive cycles are graphed in Chart 6-7 (first
figure). The form and position are nearly the same, except for a
milder and shorter American decline. If the mean American
duration is longer (19.0 years against 16.8 for the German), the
total specific amplitudes are of the same order of magnitude
(90.4 and 97.4, respectively). The German pattern tends to lead
in timing of both peaks and troughs, and the American series
leads at peaks. However, the average peacetime pattern of the
American and comparable German and English cycles in the
middle and late nineteenth century shows that German price
experience was cyclically more vigorous than the American

CHART 6-5

Patterns of Successive Specific Long Cycles, U.S. and Germany,
Building Materials Price Index, 1802–1932

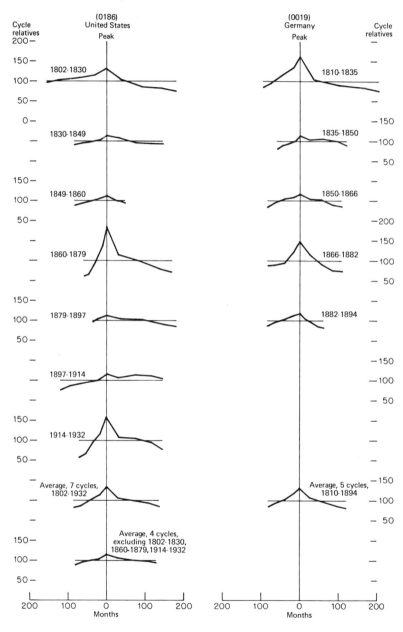

CHART 6-6
Long Reference Cycle Patterns, Successive and Average, U.S. and Germany, Building Materials Price Index

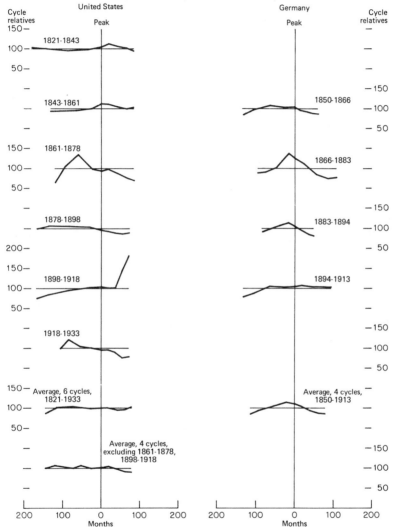

which, in turn, was more responsive to long swings than the English (see Chart 6-7, middle figure).

The very mild response behavior of the British price index, in comparison with the German and American, partly reflects a slower tempo of British long cyclical movement and partly the absence of war inflationary stimulus. The total English amplitude, between 1852 and 1911, is nearly as great as for the four

TABLE 6-3
Summary Measures, National Long Cycles, Building Costs and Building Materials Prices

Measures	Building Costs[a]				U.S. Differential, Building Trades, Manufacturing Hourly Earnings[b]
	Mean	Median	High	Low	
Full specific duration (years)	17.72 (2.56)	19.5	20.0	13.5	18.8
Specific cycle amplitude (cycle relatives)					
Full	50.6 (10.3)	42.6	85.1	30.6	47.9
Full per year	2.94 (1.15)	2.67	4.36	1.57	2.55
Fall per year	-2.60 (1.63)	-2.07	-4.61	-.39	-2.39
Full reference amplitude (cycle relatives)	34.1 (16.8)	31.0	64.6	12.9	19.8
Secular weighted average growth per year (per cent)[f]	-.025 (.875)	-.083	1.176	-1.110	.197[g]
Lead-lag turning points (years)	.67 (1.97)	1.00	3.20	-2.67	.66
Average deviation (years)	2.19 (.83)	2.64	3.14	1.00	2.30
Lead-lag reference pattern (years)	1.16 (1.12)	1.11	2.50	0	.75
Optimal serial correlation, trend adjusted[i]					
Lead-lag (years)	2.33 (1.26)	2.0	4.0	1.0	
Correlation coefficient (r)	.672 (.31)	.860	.912	.247	

Building Material Prices

Measures	U.S.[c]		England[a] (0275)	Germany[e] (0019)
	Peace Cycles (1830–1914)	All Cycles (1802–97)		
Full specific duration (years)	16.3	19.0	29.5	16.8
Specific cycle amplitude (cycle relatives)				
Full	42.7	90.4	42.8	97.4
Full per year	2.64	4.76	1.45	5.80
Fall per year	-1.93	-3.93	-1.69	-5.05
Full reference amplitude (cycle relatives)	15.2	37.5	7.4	58.0
Secular weighted average growth per year (per cent)[f]	n.a.	n.a.	n.a.	.171
Lead-lag turning points (years)	.33[h]	0.11[h]	-2.00	-.14
Average deviation (years)	4.67	4.06	3.00	1.24
Lead-lag reference pattern (years)	.75	-3.1	2.25	-.90
Optimal serial correlation, trend adjusted[i]				
Lead-lag (years)				0
Correlation coefficient (r)				.748

[a] Includes series 0275. 0020. 0014. 0076, 0167. Series 0078 is added in figures for full reference amplitude, secular weighted average growth, and lead-lag reference pattern. These series had twelve specific long cyles, of which thirty-three turning points were matched and two unmatched.
[b] Series 0313, which had four specific long cycles, in which nine turning points were matched.
[c] Series 0186. The peace cycles cover four specific long cycles from 1830 to 1860 and from 1880 to 1914, with eight matched turning points. The total cycle column includes one more long cycle with an additional matched turning point.
[d] Series 0275, which had two specific long cycles, in which five turning points were matched.
[e] Series 0019, which had five specific long cycles, in which nine turning points were matched.
[f] Excludes series 0275. 0020.
[g] Average of reference and specific secular movement, positive basis.
[h] Leads at peaks and lags at troughs.   [i] Excludes series 0076 and 0167 from building cost measures.

CHART 6-7

Long Cycle Patterns, Building Material Price Index, U.S. and Germany,
1802–1897, England, 1852–1912

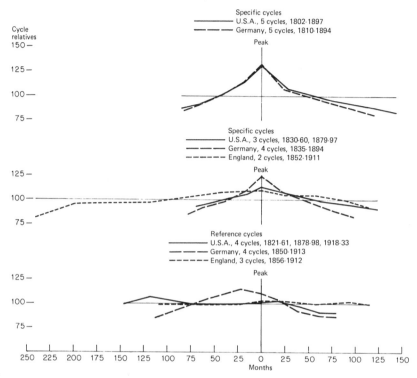

American nonwar cycles (between 1830 and 1860, 1880 and
1914), though annual rates of movement are much lower. Turning points are all matched and exhibit the same tendency to lead
found in Germany.

Amplitudes of long-wave movement for prices of building
materials—in America at least—are more vigorous in long
(building) than in short (business) cycles relative to corresponding fluctuations in building activity. Total specific short-cycle
amplitude of wholesale prices for building materials (monthly,
1892–1938) was one-fifth of the average short-cycle amplitude of
two monthly nationwide building-permit series which straddled
the period (Long, 1891–1916, and Babson–Bradstreet, 1908–38).
The corresponding long-swing fraction was over two-fifths. In
part, the difference in price behavior over short and long cycles
may be attributable to the different time periods studied. Our
long-cycle measures primarily reflect the experience of the

nineteenth century, when intensity of competition in product markets was relatively high. Prices of building materials in the first half of this century closely rivaled hides and leather with regard to frequency and magnitude of yearly price change.[17] During the short-cycle experience of the late nineteenth and early twentieth centuries, markets were sheltered and prices were increasingly administered.

Considering the intensity of competition which prevailed in building material markets of the nineteenth century, the confinement of long-cycle specific price amplitude to a third of residential activity amplitude is anomalous. This arises, in part, because our measures of building activity are confined to new building and omit coverage of repair and maintenance operations which account for from 30 to 40 per cent of all building activity in the United States and between 40 to 50 per cent for most European countries. See [136, p. 7f.; 107, p. 83]. Repair, maintenance, alterations and additions fluctuate moderately both in short and long cycles and their derived demand for building materials would likewise fluctuate moderately. For seven major cities Burns found that total specific amplitude of short cycles in additions and alterations was 20 per cent under amplitude measures for new building. His explanation is still cogent [39, p. 53]:

Although the repairs and alterations of actual life merge into new building, there is an important distinction between the two. As we have already stressed, little new building is likely to be undertaken, unless the business outlook and the state of the building and capital markets are deemed sufficiently favorable to justify investment in long-lived goods. On the other hand, if certain alterations are not made, production must come to a standstill, or premises cannot be rented, or considerable discomfort must be tolerated by owners occupying their own houses. Not infrequently, the full cost of alterations or repairs can be recovered within a year or less, even when the year is one of acute depression. It may also be more convenient to make needed repairs when business is dull than when business is booming. Hence alterations and repairs are distributed more uniformly over time than is new building.

Building Costs

Building costs should have a much dampened range of movement compared with prices of building materials. The more lively movement of prices for materials is joined to the more sluggish cost behavior of building labor. Hence, Table 6-3 records a total mean specific amplitude for cost of building which is nearly half the amplitude of prices of building materials. While materials' prices tend to lead at turning points, building costs tend to lag. However, this lag is variable and shows up only on reference cycle patterns for Victoria, Australia, and Glasgow, Scotland (see Chart 6-8). For the three national building-cost indexes—the United States, England (London), and Germany—sluggishness is dominant in reference cycles, with only the slightest suggestion of cyclical behavior.

The cyclical movement is perhaps more perceptible in the individual than in average cycle patterns, due in part to the offsetting character of the long-wave price movements which turned up reference-cycle patterns in the 1900's and turned them down in the 1870's and 1880's. But these price movements are not part of the building-wave process. Our average reference cycle pattern thus represents a kind of deflated version of building costs in which the element of the Kondratieff long-wave price movement is rubbed out. This same kind of deflation was at work in the German and in the American cost indexes as well.

The sluggish behavior of building wage rates cuts down the relative long-swing amplitude of over-all costs of building. Labor costs in absolute terms are important as an element in total building costs, and thus they affect the whole scale of values for property and rentals. Tension in the labor market would be reflected in building-trade earning differentials, or the percentage margin over hourly earnings in manufacturing. Any tendency for building booms to be retarded by shortage of labor or inelasticity of the labor supply function should be indicated by upward movements in pay differentials.

Recent work in American hourly earning statistics made it possible to compute percentage differentials back to 1860. The series expresses the value of hourly earnings of building trade workers as a per cent of hourly earnings of workers in manufacturing (see Chart 6-9 and Table 6-3).[18] The differential had little or no tendency for secular upward growth, despite the greater role of union power in the building trades, ending up in the mid-twentieth century not far from where it was located by Adam Smith in the mid-eighteenth century. The slight upward course of

CHART 6-8
Patterns of Average Specific and Reference Long Cycles, Building Costs, Five Areas

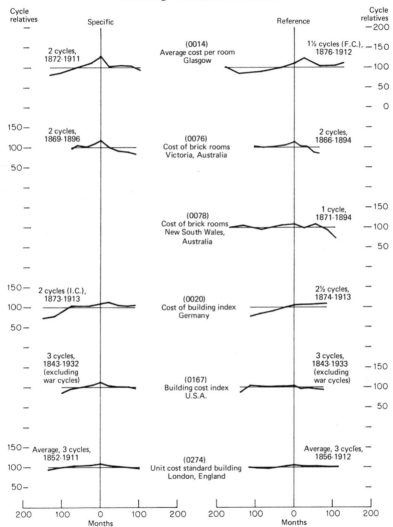

Cycle relatives — Specific — Reference — Cycle relatives −200

(0014) Average cost per room Glasgow — 2 cycles, 1872-1911 — 1½ cycles (F.C.), 1876-1912 −150

— 100

— 50

— 0

(0076) Cost of brick rooms Victoria, Australia — 2 cycles, 1869-1896 — 2 cycles, 1866-1894

150— 100— 50—

(0078) Cost of brick rooms New South Wales, Australia — 1 cycle, 1871-1894 −150 —100 — 50

(0020) Cost of building index Germany — 2 cycles (I.C.), 1873-1913 — 2½ cycles, 1874-1913

150— 100— 50—

(0167) Building cost index U.S.A. — 3 cycles, 1843-1932 (excluding war cycles) — 3 cycles, 1843-1933 (excluding war cycles) —150 —100 — 50

(0274) Unit cost standard building London, England — Average, 3 cycles, 1852-1911 — Average, 3 cycles, 1856-1912

150— 100— 50—

200   100   0   100   200   200   100   0   100   200
Months   Months

the differential (0.2 per cent per year) was chiefly due to our use of union-based records of building-trade hourly earnings, whereas hourly earnings for manufacturing were measured both for union and nonunion plants. Amplitude on the whole was slight. Total specific cycle amplitude was only 47.9 cycle relatives and total reference amplitude was only 19.2 cycle relatives.

CHART 6-9
Successive and Average Long Cycle Patterns, Average Hourly Earning Per Cent Differentials in Building Trades and Manufacturing, U.S., 1860–1937

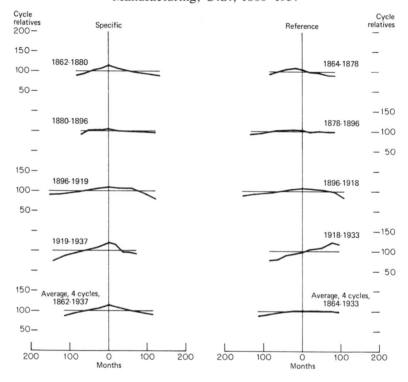

The timing history of the differential is significant. At the first four turning points, the differential led by a mean of 1.25 years; at the last three, it lagged by 3.67 years. This shift reflects the market influence of the building-trade unions, which could not, however, permanently widen the differential.

The mild amplitude of the building-trade wage differentials over reference cycle periods, together with the unresponsive movement of building-trade wage rates—except in very severe depressions—indicate that building cycles were not appreciably curbed by pressure in labor markets. Neither were these cycles curbed, as we have shown earlier, by pressure in markets for building materials. We turn to capital markets, and primarily to the record of differential interest rates, to see whether pressure there was more acutely registered than in material and labor markets.

Mortgage Yield Differentials

Three of our mortgage yield differential series are shown in Table 6-4. The French data were not included because the years covered were too few to establish more than one long-cycle chronology, though interesting cyclical characteristics are indicated (see Chart 7-1). Successive specific and reference cycle patterns are presented to permit close consideration of the behavior involved (Charts 6-10, 6-11, and 6-12).

There are eight clear-cut and systematic specific cycles in the three countries, with total specific amplitude for the German and American series at 134–135, nearly three times the amplitude of the American building-wage differential. (For the one clear-cut specific cycle in the French series, 1880–99, specific amplitude was about one-fourth less; considering the dampened character of the French long-wave process, that was considerable.) The much higher level of the Scotch amplitude and the much longer lag on both peak and trough, nearly approximating neutral timing, are probably due to the negotiated and crudely calibrated adjustment of mortgage rates by an investor-borrower state council. The rates were fixed at conventional levels and were adjusted in multiples of 25 basis points. Mortgage rates fixed in this way should lag on reference chronologies and should involve higher peaks and lower troughs, with a corresponding higher amplitude. If the series had been smoothed by a moving average, or by averaging peak and trough values, presumably Scotch amplitudes would have corresponded more closely to American and German amplitudes.

The characteristics of reference-cycle patterns are equally interesting. There were altogether seven and a half reference cycles surveyed for our three countries. In each case, the patterns are positive, rising in reference expansions and falling in reference contractions. There is variability in timing as witnessed by the individual reference patterns. On the available evidence, Manhattan indicates a tendency to lead, but this was not consistent and did not prevail at turning points; for that reason it possibly was not significant. The German tendency to lag was a little more prominent and shows up on both reference cycle phasing and turning-point counts. There were altogether five lags, three leads, and five synchronous timings for the two countries on matched turning points. The Scotch tendency to lag

TABLE 6-4

Summary Measures, Long Cycles, Mortgage Yield Differentials, U.S., Germany, Scotland

Measures	Mean	Manhattan," U.S.	Germany[b]	Scotland[c]
Full specific duration (years)	14.6	16.6	14.7	12.5
Specific cycle amplitude (cycle relatives)				
Full	166.4	134.2	134.2	230.8
Full per year	11.91	8.16	9.12	18.46
Fall per year	−15.92	−8.21	−8.39	−31.17
Full reference amplitude (cycle relatives)	88.2	66.6	59.2	139.1
Lead-lag turning points (years)	.88	.16	.67	1.80
Average deviation (years)	1.44	1.55	1.66	1.12
Lead-lag reference pattern (years)	.85	−.90	.75	2.70

[a] Series 0268. which had 3.5 specific long cycles. in which all seven turning points were matched.

[b] Series 0267. which had 2.5 specific long cycles. in which all six turning points were matched.

[c] Series 0300. which had two specific long cycles. in which all five turning points were matched.

CHART 6-10
Patterns of Successive Specific and Reference Long Cycles and Their Averages, Mortgage Yield Differentials, Manhattan

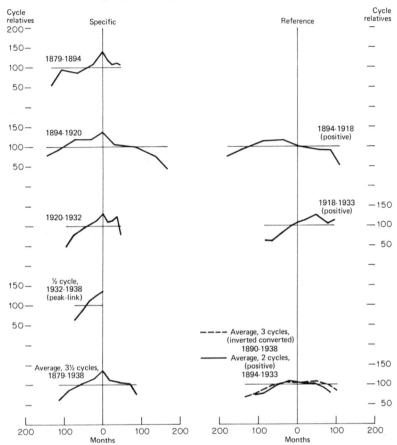

was certainly reinforced by the sluggish kind of pricing decisions made.

Because of timing variability and near absence of upward trend, less than half of the total specific amplitude is retained in reference cycles. Nevertheless, the reference falls are unambiguous. The patterns clearly reflect a consistent response of capital markets to long building expansions and contractions; they indicate that during long expansions capital funds were procured by paying widening interest differentials. Long building contractions are in turn accompanied by improving terms of finance and more favorable access to loan markets. This in

CHART 6-11
Patterns of Successive Specific and Reference Long Cycles and
Their Averages, Mortgage Yield Differentials, Germany

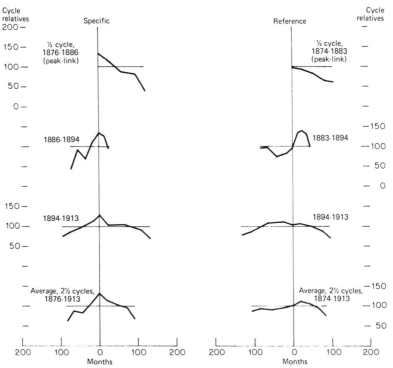

general confirms the hypothesis of Guttentag that short cycles would appear to be related "mainly to changes originating in the mortgage market" as opposed to long cycles which appear to be actuated by changes in demand [115, p. 281]. Our results also reinforce the suggestion of positive association disclosed in earlier investigations between long expansion periods and either "large or increasing spreads."[19] Finally, the tendency to positive covariation of yield differentials and fund flows has in general been confirmed in the American postwar experience. Particularly since mid-1953, the "influence of yield spreads on gross flows," moving at a lag, "has been particularly evident" [156, p. 13].

Rentals

Shifts in cost of land and of new building must now be related to shifts in prospective building rental revenues. If rates of rental

CHART 6-12
Patterns of Successive Specific and Reference Long Cycles and Their Averages, Mortgage Yield Differentials, Scotland

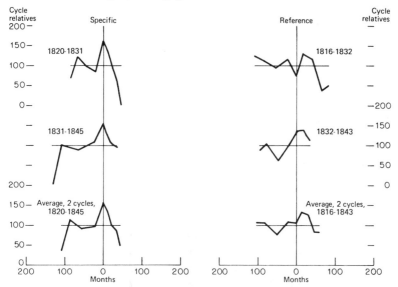

fluctuate in harmony with building costs, including site values, then the deterrent effect of higher building costs on new construction would be offset. Our information on rents indicates that this offset at least partially occurs (see Table 6-5 and Charts 6-13 and 6-14). Rentals exhibit a long swing, rising in building expansions and falling in building declines; moreover, varying somewhat more than building costs, if rentals for vacant units are the working guide to rental incomes of newly built properties. Total reference amplitude for vacant units was some 52 cycle relatives (61 for specific) against a mean total reference amplitude for building costs, covering materials and labor costs, of 34 cycle relatives (51 for specific). Shifts in rental returns for new construction would thus have exceeded the range in fluctuation of building costs alone. The excess would go at least part way in redressing the balance of additional cost growing out of higher land charges and higher interest costs for mortgage finance.

If rental incomes of newly built properties more closely approximates rental incomes of occupied, rather than vacant, dwelling units, then a much lesser amplitude of rent fluctuation and a smaller offset against shiftings in site values, building

TABLE 6-5
Summary Measures, Local Long Cycles, Rent

Item	Units	Occupied Dwellings[a] Mean or Total	Vacant Dwellings[b]			
			Mean or Total	Hamburg[b]	St. Louis[c]	Glasgow[d]
A. Totals						
1. Number of series		2	3			
2. Number of specific long cycles		5	6	2	1.5	2.5
3. Number of turning points (TP):						
a. Matched		10	12	4	4	4
b. Unmatched		3	2	0	0	2
B. Mean values						
4. Full specific duration	Years	15.15	12.4	12.5	11.3	13.5
5. Specific cycle amplitude						
a. Full	Cycle relatives	37.2	60.7	74.0	43.5	64.6

	Units					
b. Full per year	"	2.27	4.89	5.92	3.95	4.79
c. Fall per year	"	−2.13	−4.14	−6.57	−3.17	−2.67
6. Full reference amplitude	"	22.6	51.8	68.1	39.1	48.1
7. Secular weighted average growth per year	%	.814	n.a.	n.a.	n.a.	n.a.
8. Lead-lag (LL) TP:						
a. LL	Years	.30	−2.28	−4.25	−2.1	.5
b. Average deviation	"	1.72	2.46	1.88	3.00	2.5
9. LL reference pattern	"	.38	−2.3	−4.0	−2.9	0
10. Optimal serial correlation trend adjusted:						
a. LL	Years	−.5	−2	−4	0	n.a.
b. Correlation coefficient	r	.75	.637[e]	.750	.523[f]	n.a.

n.a.—not available.

[a] Includes series 0025 and 0031, which had five specific long cycles in which ten turning points were matched and three were unmatched.

[b] For series 0032, 0083 and a Glasgow series.

[c] For items 1–9 series 0134 of St. Louis rentals 1890–1914 by Albert Rees [218, p. 97f.]; for item 10 series 0083, running to 1933, was used.

[d] Results only approximate since between 1870 and 1912, 10 years omitted (1891–95 and 1896–1900) [46, pp. 16 ff.].

[e] Excludes Glasgow.

[f] Includes war period.

CHART 6-13
Patterns of Average and Specific and Reference Long Cycles,
Rent, Six Cities

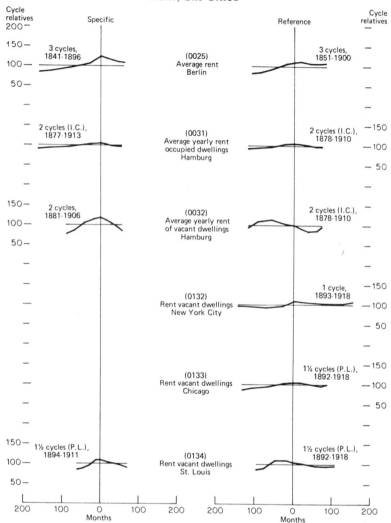

costs, and interest charges, are observable. The amplitude of reference fluctuation of occupied rentals was only some 23 cycle relatives (37.2 for specific), giving evidence either of the strength of contract frictions for occupied rentals or of a tendency for fluctuating demand to seek vacant facilities.

If newly built properties embody innovations which result in the formation of distinct housing submarkets, then neither the

CHART 6-14
Correlogram, Rent Series (Trend Adjusted) Five-Year Moving Averages

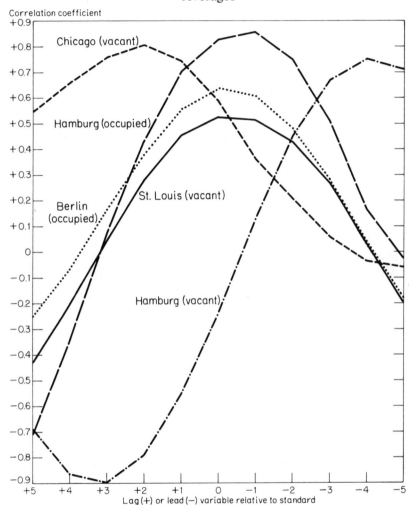

Correlation coefficient

Lag (+) or lead (−) variable relative to standard

rentals of vacant nor of occupied housing units belonging to other submarkets would govern rent levels for new building. The evidence on timing interplay between occupied and vacant rentals is suggestive but not fully consistent nor does it clearly point to the emergence of distinct submarkets. On the mean values, vacant rentals lead occupied rentals by a margin of 2.25 years on twelve matched turning points, 2.3 years by reference cycle stages, and 2 years on correlogram values. The Hamburg rent correlograms clearly exhibit this relationship and over the full range of two pre-1914 cycles (see Chart 6-14). St. Louis reference cycle patterns exhibit the same clear lead. However, the lead over residential cycles is greatest for Hamburg, falls to less than one year for St. Louis, and—according to the correlogram and reference cycle patterns—turns into a lag for Chicago and approximately simultaneous timing for Manhattan and Glasgow. Since nonrental residential construction would affect the correlation in the Chicago and St. Louis series, variation in timing is understandable. But variation in such cities as Hamburg, Manhattan, and Glasgow—where rental construction dominates—is more difficult to explain.

That variation in timing is in some sense structural and not random is indicated by the correlograms of our three vacant rental series (Chicago, Hamburg, St. Louis). The Hamburg correlogram exhibits classical neutral timing inverted to that of vacancies. High positive coefficients for high lead values in vacant rentals are matched, as we have seen, by high negative coefficients for vacant units of the same serial order (see Chapter 5). This is as expected and is confirmed by multiple regression analysis, as will be seen later in this chapter. Rent prices for vacant units in Hamburg respond perfectly with little lag to cyclical shifts in the relative number of vacant units. But with the same vacancy pattern in St. Louis (see Chart 6-14), the rental correlogram of cycle pattern does not exhibit this inversion, nor is it indicated in Manhattan or in Chicago.

The classical form of the Hamburg rental market and its long cyclical swings stands out clearly in contrast to Glasgow. For both cities, between 1870 and 1911, rentals for occupied and vacant dwellings were separately tabulated. The Glasgow data is imperfect, since for ten years it was necessary to interpolate estimates.[20] For both cities the resultant average reference-cycle patterns are shown in Chart 6-15. The Hamburg pattern is a classical instance of neutral timing perfectly inverted to its vacancy pattern. The Glasgow vacant rental is less well outlined, and can be analyzed at best either as irregular or with an expansion phase of II–IV and a contraction phase of IV to II.

The more sensitive differential between occupied and vacant rentals should correspond inversely with building if the same housing submarkets are involved. When occupied rentals exceed vacant rentals, residential building should be discouraged. When

CHART 6-15
Patterns of Average Reference Long Cycles, Average Rent of Vacant
Dwellings, Glasgow and Hamburg

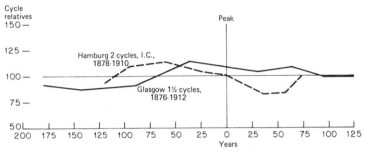

vacant rentals rise relative to occupied rentals, residential building should be encouraged. Hamburg experience conforms to
expectations with its perfect neutral timing. The corresponding
chart for Glasgow shows less rationale. Even allowing for the
indicated upward trend in the differential, corresponding to a
secular accumulation of deteriorated property, observed oscillations are poorly related to oscillations in vacancies or in building.

The structure of the rental markets in Hamburg, Glasgow,
Manhattan, and Chicago diverged significantly with regard to the
position and function of vacant units. Vacant units in Hamburg
appear to be more like occupied units; in Glasgow vacant units
may have corresponded more to substandard units, toward
which demand would gravitate in depressed times. If these units
were characterized by negative income elasticity to some significant degree, then some of the differences in our rental
patterns for vacant units is explicable. Boom building periods
would then be associated with positive occupied-vacant rent
differentials. Regression analysis of Hamburg observations
showed that changes in long cycle relatives of occupied rentals
for corresponding long specific cycle phases were 35 per cent of
the changes for vacant rentals.

For Chicago and Manhattan, however, variability of vacant
rentals seemed more restrained. For the one specific cycle that
could be identified in the two series, amplitude both total and per
year was of the same order of magnitude as our measures for rent of
occupied dwellings. Mean total specific amplitude for Manhattan
and Chicago was 41.2, or only 107.5 per cent of mean occupied
rental and two-thirds of other vacant rentals. Rate of amplitude

per year was 2.31, or only slightly above that for occupied rentals. Inspection of the chart will show highly dampened reference cycles. Yet Manhattan and Chicago should have experienced lively rental markets.

Perhaps restrained amplitude and timing in these cities are due to the fact that the survey of vacant dwellings was restricted to advertised rentals for dwellings characteristic of mean family incomes of workmen. Since advertisements specified little information regarding quality of accommodations, the mean quotations may reflect changes in "mix" offsetting shifts in level [218, pp. 97ff.]. It is known that less desirable units in every price class have a higher vacancy incidence and correspondingly will tend, in good times, to predominate in want ads. In bad times, the incidence of vacancies among higher quality units will rise. The systematic shift in composition of vacant units will dampen the amplitude of the mean value of the observations, since the peak rentals will predominantly measure less desirable units and trough rentals will reflect the availability of better units.

The varied behavior of rentals for vacant and for occupied units explains why highly diversified views regarding rental behavior could all derive some semblance of empirical justification. At the one extreme was the view that "rents are more sensitive than other real estate prices. . ." [217, p. 101]. Other analysts have stressed the "notoriously sticky" behavior of rents.[21] Both views are consistent if a distinction is made between vacant and occupied rentals.

Real Estate Prices

Variations in the value of vacant land and in the level of rentals, both for vacant and occupied dwellings, will tend to affect selling prices of improved nonfarm property. We have nine series whose tabular results are brought together in Table 6-6 with graphic results shown in Chart 6-16. For both the Ohio and non-Ohio series the mean specific total amplitude was near 100 and the per year rates of specific declines were relatively high (−7.45). These amplitudes are less than one-third of those reached by prices for acreage land, but are nearly twice the amplitude of cost of building and of vacant rentals. This relatively active response of real estate selling prices to swings in

TABLE 6-6

Summary Measures, Local Long Cycles, Real Estate Price

Measures	Ohio[a]				Non-Ohio[b]		Totals			
	Mean	Median	High	Low	Mean	Median	Mean	Median	High	Low
Full specific duration (years)	13.96	14.0	14.5	13.4	18.95	20.75	16.17	14.50	21.0	13.3
Specific cycle amplitude (cycle relatives)										
Full	97.92	101.8	121.6	70.6	108.42	104.4	102.6	101.8	148.7	70.6
Full per year	7.06	7.63	9.12	5.04	6.04	5.94	6.44	6.33	9.12	3.73
Fall per year	−7.18	−8.35	−10.84	−3.53	−7.78	−6.24	−7.45	−6.72	−15.20	−3.46
Full reference amplitude (cycle relatives)[c]	67.5	64.5	88.4	52.6	57.2	53.3	62.4	64.5	88.4	34.1
Secular weighted average growth per year (per cent)[d]	1.075	1.188	1.860	.337	.621	.723	.905	.956	1.860	−.325
Lead-lag turning points (years)	−.53	−.25	−1.33	−3.33	1.02	1.28	.16	0	3.67	−3.33
Average deviation (years)	2.85	2.89	4.52	1.55	2.23	2.11	2.57	2.40	4.52	1.55
Lead-lag reference pattern (years)[c]	−1.20	−.83	1.00	−4.15	.813	1.00	−.194	−.37	3.05	−4.15
Optimal serial correlation, trend adjusted[e]										
Lead-lag (years)	.75	1.0	4.5	−3.5	−.17	.5	.36	.5	4.5	−3.5
Correlation coefficient (r)	.805	.780	.970	.690	.318	.674	.596	.690	.970	−.402

[a] Includes series 0247 through 0251, which had eleven specific long cycles, in which twenty turning points were matched and five unmatched.
[b] Includes series 0036, 0026, 0095, and 0096, which had 11.5 specific long cycles, in which twenty-one turning points were matched and six were unmatched.
[c] Excludes series 0096.   [d] Excludes series 0250.
[c] Excludes series 0250.   [e] Excludes series 0248 and 0095.

CHART 6-16
Patterns of Average Specific and Reference Long Cycles, Real Estate
Sales Price, Nine Areas

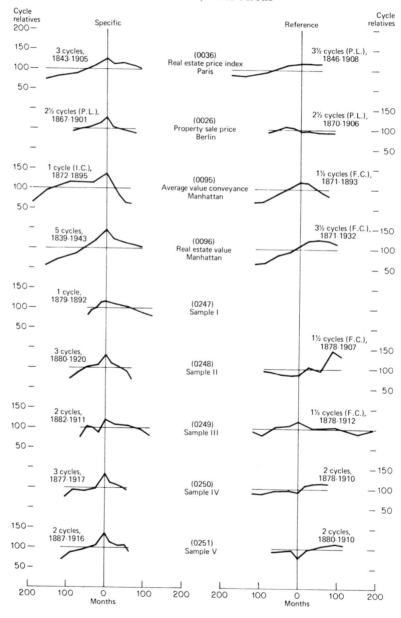

demand reflects the fluidity of market pricing characteristic of real estate markets, which may try to take off on speculative flights characteristic of urban land values. But in flight, prices for existing improved property are related to the movement of building costs, which govern the terms on which new construction is made available. Real estate selling prices will also reflect anticipated rental revenues. The behavior of the selling price of improved nonfarm property thus embodies a kind of weighted average of the price patterns for cost of building and land values, on the one hand, and of property returns on the other hand, as indicated by rental movements.

If our mean values reflect the typical order of magnitude then the amplitude of selling price of improved property (including land) is approximately double that of the cost of building new structures (excluding land and builder's profit). The approximate long-cycle component amplitude indicated for unimproved site value alone is somewhere near 200 cycle relatives, if our Ohio acreage value sets proper outer limits. But site values play a smaller role in realty value than cost of building. The proportions of site value to building cost for residential property of the kind principally reflected in our analyzed series changed over the years. Excluding all improvements (roads, sidewalks, grading, utilities, parks, curbs, and so on) which build up site values, it is doubtful that a four-to-one ratio of building cost to bare site value would be far out of line. In that case, a 34 per cent amplitude for building costs and a 200 per cent amplitude for site value would yield a total amplitude of realty improved values of 67 cycle relatives, or about what was observed for improved realty price swings.

It is worthwhile checking these estimates of real estate value and building cost movements, drawn from fragmentary data, with records of other experience and with judgments of other investigators. Our findings are reaffirmed by the report of David Blank that in most periods the market price of homes fluctuates more widely over the short run than do construction costs, the difference in rise or fall perhaps amounting to as much as 10 per cent in a period of several years. The long-run movement of prices and home-building costs "is remarkably similar" [21, p. 78]. This finding in its own way confirms the substantial emphasis which courts have placed on cost of reproduction in determining value. "The most strikingly distinctive feature of *judicial* valuation . . . is to be found in the proneness of the courts to single out the estimated replacement cost of replaceable property, minus certain allowances for depreciation, as the most reliable index or measure of value [25, p. 150]. The courts would find refuge in a rule which constitutes a safe upper limit of value. For the same reason, professional appraisers have come to feel it an unsafe guide in particular cases. This is partly due to inapplicability of general depreciation rates to the individual property and partly to circumstances which have impaired or built up going concern values or have made the property not worth reproducing [25, pp. 150–176]. Both courts and appraisers in their own way recognize the truth set forth in our empirical findings: that average prices of improved realty fluctuate with greater amplitude but in close correspondence to building costs.

Vacancy and Value Shiftings

By its nature, any movement in vacancies is a public event. The empty dwelling is talked about by neighbors and street observers and will often be listed with dealers or formally advertised to the public. Vacancies are thus highly visible and serve to signal the shifting currents of demand and supply for shelter. The signal is communicated quickly and evaluated by participants in the real estate market with the interpretive skill developed by artisans in a craft. Signals require evaluation since only in recent years have up-to-date comprehensive vacancy statistics for our large cities been collected and made public. The vacancy rate as a single magnitude has only acquired common notoriety since our experience with rent control. Even now, however, a given value of a vacancy rate will need to be interpreted in the light of its derivation by way of type of building or location, any cumulative drift, and other abnormal factors.

The change in vacancies has potent effects on the financial operations of rental property. The variable or "user" costs of using shelter facilities are slight and irregular and may be wholly offset by handling charges of tenant management.[22] The larger part of additional revenue obtained by filling a vacancy will go to swell profits or to reduce losses. Since the profit margin of the landlord is not a large one, a slight movement of the vacancy rate will have multiple effects on profits of operation. As we have seen, rent levels on vacant properties "lead" peaks and troughs of building activity proper, but in their turn they lag behind peaks and troughs of vacancies proper. For the same reason that rents begin to move, sale prices of rented property, in their own dampened way, will respond to cheerful news. Still more indirectly, there will be a tendency for values of vacant lots to rise.

The predominant role of vacancies in generating changes in rent has been indicated by multiple regression analysis.[23] The linkage of rents to vacancy rates has been graphically exhibited for a number of leading cities in terms of an "occupancy-rental pattern" which has definite form under given market conditions [22, pp. 181–208; 91, pp. 241–247, 263ff.]. The influence of vacancies on rent is paralleled by similar "market-clearing" functions, which seek to explain short-term interest rates by "excess bank reserves" and wage-rate changes by unemployment.[24]

Only in the United States, and perhaps in a few of the smaller communities in Europe, was there an extensive market for single-family residences and a stock of vacant single-family dwellings awaiting sale. A much smaller proportion of the owner-occupied stock will be vacant for this purpose, since it will be advantageous for an owner to continue to reside in a property until it is sold. The mean rental vacancy rate for the period 1960–64 was between four to five times the corresponding rate for owner-occupied dwellings [269, p. 699]. A given change in demand for sale property tends to affect prices of the vacant sale units much more dramatically than the rental market. The different buyers and sellers who succeed each other for purposes of completing one or two transactions on the owner-occupancy market develop comparatively little rational awareness of market trend or market behavior. The realized level of selling prices in such a market should tend to be abnormally sensitive to changes in stocks of vacant properties on the market for sale.

In a perfect market the shift in demand which is recorded in the movement of vacancies, allowance being made for any new construction or retirement of old structures, would directly affect both selling prices and rental rates; and any influence of vacancies on building would be transmitted through the price effects. As Cairncross and Tinbergen noted "the stickiness of rents, closely connected with the long duration of letting contracts and further imperfections in this market, prevents such a rapid adaptation." Tinbergen accordingly concluded, as did

Cairncross, that "the number of unoccupied houses influences building activity independently of its indirect and lagged influence through derived price changes [252, I, p. 93; 46, pp. 15f.]. For the cities of Stockholm and Hamburg it was possible to conduct multiple regression analysis on residential building and to evaluate the direct influence on vacancy rates against the influence of rent which, as we have just seen, is itself influenced by vacancies lagged for an earlier period. Owing to the choice of units, the regression coefficients can be interpreted as specifying the multiplied response in building (in terms of per cent deviation from trend) induced by a 1 per cent change in the explanatory factor. For both Stockholm and Hamburg the regression results, summarized in Table 6-7, indicate that a 1 per cent change in vacancy rates is from three to four times more potent in affecting building, though with a longer lag, than a 1 per cent change in rent or in income variables. However, some of the variables are statistically suspect; there were a number of inconsistent regression runs from Stockholm. Hence the elasticity coefficients are only broadly significant. These results, it must be added, were obtained from analysis of short-run movements, derived by computing deviations from a nine-year moving average; analysis of longer waves with longer time lags might alter results appreciably.[25]

Since vacancy rates constitute, both directly and through a derived influence on price, the main working mechanism of the housing market, it is not surprising that vacancy rates have from the outset been singled out for special attention by students of building cycles. A German commentator, writing in 1905 about a long building cycle in Munich between 1805 and 1911, noted that only "when the number of vacant dwellings is under 3 per cent can one speak of a rising housing need" which "gives the impulse to a higher level of building activity" [220, p. 80f.]. Emmy Reich in her extended study of Berlin, so often cited in these pages, described the mechanism of the housing market and signals for advance and retreat in terms of movement of vacancy rates. The British report which first brought to light the long-swing movement in London housing production did not fail to note that the variation in the number of empty houses was closely associated with it [238, p. 169]. Hoyt pivots his version of the upswing phase of the Chicago building cycle around the tendency for vacancies to disappear as "people crowd into all

TABLE 6-7

Regression Coefficients, Rent, Vacancy, Incomes on Residential Building
(in Terms of Deviations from Trend); Hamburg 1878–1913, Stockholm 1884–1913

| | Vacancy | | Rent | | Total Income, | Corporate Profit |
Item	Hamburg	Stockholm	Hamburg	Stockholm	Stockholm	Rate, Hamburg
Regression, simple	−15.5					
Regression, multiple, excluding rent	−20.1	−4.4			4.29	1.72
Regression, multiple including rent and other factors	−16.5	−3.7	5.20	1.14	3.75	1.71

SOURCE: Tinbergen [252, I, pp. 103–111]. Vacancies were lagged 3 years for Hamburg and 1.5 years for Stockholm. Other terms were lagged one year, except corporate profit rate in second line, where a zero lag was used.

the available space" so that "rents of old buildings rise" [134, p. 375]. Summing up these studies in his comprehensive analysis of the German housing and building market before 1914, Hunscha estimated that between 20 and 40 per cent of new housing demand was concurrently either underprovided or over-provided, while the time gap between new demand and new supply runs to one to two years [136, p. 16]. Cairncross reduced the "logistics of the building cycle" to the "magnitude of the swing in empty houses that builders are prepared to treat as normal" [46, p. 31f.]. It was not long before formal sequence models were designed and statistically evaluated showing a building cycle revolving around a decision lag and the cumulation of a building "deficit."[26] And the practical experience of a prolonged siege of rent controls showed that vacancy rates were at once the supreme test of the "normality" of a market, the criteria for release from rent control, and the best means of predicting the expansive power of rent movements.

G. SUMMARY

Prices at four different levels—urban site values, building input factor markets, rental values, and values for improved residential properties—correspond to basic markets in which the new and the old are continually adjusted on a plane which aligns techniques, returns, and benefits in shifting equilibria. The market for vacant land includes raw farmland or wasteland as well as developed lots which are graded, landscaped, and equipped to serve as building sites. Vacant sites traditionally have zero wastage and low costs of upkeep; they tend to appreciate rather than depreciate over time; investment in them can be financed with long-term loans at moderate interest rates; they are either tax exempt or usually subject only to a diluted property tax; and they have access to organized realty markets which provide a fair measure of liquidity. As an investment asset, vacant urban land is tangible, can be evaluated best with local knowledge informally absorbed, and is not especially subject to economies of scale. Hence investment in land for capital gains has been a basic feature of urban land markets. The gains involved have generally been of a long-term nature, since trading costs would preclude the in-and-out movement common to speculative markets for primary staples or standard investment securities. Prospects for capital gains depend on values expected to be maintained or value growth rates to be sustained over a long forward period. Thus urban land values have acquired an elasticity of response and a potential for cumulative movement unique to any major productive input factor. It would be expected that land value movements would be slow to start, would develop considerable momentum, and would persist long after reversal was signaled.

Something like this is indicated by our survey returns for sale values of undeveloped urban land in Ohio. The 5½ long specific cycles in acreage values experienced a total mean amplitude of 336 and a reference amplitude of 188 cycle relatives. These cycles moved irregularly but with a strong tendency to invert, with a lead of a year or two relative to residential building (or a lag of six to seven years behind building cycles). Value levels for subdivided vacant lots and building sites exhibited a lesser degree of instability, with nearly concurrent timing. Paris means amplitude for subdivided vacant lots was 132.2 and Chicago's record, over a comparable stretch of years, was 193.3 cycle relatives. In both areas amplitudes receded as urban growth rates slowed down.

The cyclical shifting of urban site values was accompanied by a lesser movement of building costs, dampened by the greater supply elasticity. The price response of building materials to long-swing shifts in building for the five long cycles which spanned the nineteenth century were studied in Germany and in the United States. A striking parallelism of form and regularity of timing characterized the two sets of long cycles. For both countries the century included two wartime inflations—around the Napoleonic wars and around the 1860's-1870's. The American mean duration was somewhat longer (19.0 years compared with 16.8 years); the American mean total specific amplitude was a little less (90.4 compared with 97.4); and the yearly rate of fall was of lesser magnitude than that of Germany. American timing around reference turning points was more variable, so that mean American reference amplitudes (37.5) were a full third under the German (58.0).

In settled peacetime periods, mean reference amplitude was minimal for the United States and England. For England (1870–1913) it was only 7.4 cycle relatives, for the United States (1830–60, 1880–1914) only 15.2 cycle relatives.

Our measures for total unit building costs—reflecting changes in building material purchase prices, productivity shiftings, and unit labor costs—exhibited a corresponding degree of responsiveness to cyclical shifts in demand. Total specific amplitudes for twelve long cycles in unit building were only 34.1 ± 16.8 cycle relatives, reflecting the very sluggish behavior of building-trade unit labor costs. This probably accounts for the clear-cut tendency of building costs to lag two or more years at turning points, in reference cycle measures and on correlograms.

An insight into the impact of building cycles on conditions in the labor market is afforded for America by building-trade earning differentials over manufacturing hourly wage levels. A definite cyclical pattern was exhibited, tending to lead at the earlier turning points and to lag at the later ones. Mean total specific amplitude was 47.9 cycle relatives, of which only 19.8 survived timing variabilities for inclusion in reference amplitude. The effect of a relative wage change of around 1 per cent per year on a demand for building, which fluctuates nearly ten to fifteen times that much, is inappreciable.

Of larger magnitude is the price premium paid in the capital market to mobilize the funds needed to finance building booms. Interest rates themselves moved sluggishly in long fifty to sixty year movements and showed little direct responsiveness to building cycle rhythms. But relative differentials of mortgage yields over bond yields for three countries exhibited distinct long specific cycles, with a mean duration approximating that of the relevant reference cycles. A positive cycle of mortgage rate differentials means that building expansions mobilize capital by paying a rising interest premium; conversely, building contractions would be impeded by relatively easier terms of finance. Of eighteen potential turning points, none were unmatched and mean deviation in timing from the mean lead-lag was only 1.44 years. Mean characteristic total specific amplitude, allowing for special characteristics of our Scottish series, was some 134 cycle relatives; and between 60 to 70 of these relatives carry through to the reference level. The tendency for the mortgage yield differential to lag was greatest in Scotland where mortgage rates were negotiated by a quasi-public cartel. In Germany, France, and the United States the differential led or lagged according to circumstances.

These cost shifts for land, labor, building materials, and

finance were in part offset by a parallel movement in rentals. This movement was considerable for vacant dwellings (specific amplitude of 60.7 and a reference amplitude of 51.8). With a two-year lag, these swings in value, somewhat dampened, became reflected in occupied rentals, which, in turn, enter into the income stream. Vacant rentals affect incentives to build additional rental facilities. The positive and substantial covariation of building costs and rentals means that landlords have passed on to ultimate users the higher costs of building and at least some of the burdens of appreciated urban site values and higher interest charges on mortgage credit.

Though rental returns did not seem to rise (or fall) on the scale matching the cost of land, building, or finance, selling prices of old realty (chiefly dwellings) more nearly achieved this result. They showed a mean specific total amplitude range of 98–108 and a reference amplitude of 57–68, as compared with 51 and 34 for building costs alone.

NOTES

1. See [114, pp. 406–425; 195, pp. 14–41; 13, pp. 101–136].

2. For data and survey see [114, pp. 407–425]; for French capitalization rates over five centuries see [228, pp. 446f.]. British capitalization data is presented in [46, pp. 212–215].

3. For two interesting statements of these allocative functions, see [256, pp. 43–46; 217, Chap. 12].

4. See my paper [111, pp. 37f.].

5. The rise in the value of land because of its greater scarcity as population grows is augmented by "the confident expectation of the future enhancement of land values" and this leads to "speculation, or the holding of land for a higher price than it would then otherwise bring." In every growing city "much vacant or poorly used land is withheld from use" and at the limits of the growing city "we shall not find the land purchasable at its value for agricultural purposes, as it would be were rent determined simply by present requirements; but we shall find that for a long distance beyond the city, land bears a speculative value, based upon the belief that it will be required in the future for urban purposes. . . [101, pp. 255–257].

6. See especially [276, pp. 270, 386–392, 425ff.; 277, pp. 257–360].

7. How far assessors could go in assessing land for its probable future, rather than its actual present market value was—as Bonbright reported in 1938—a "much litigated question," with courts generally reluctant to go beyond "value based upon the present use in the absence of clear proof that there is or will be another use" [25, I, p. 489].

8. In this inquiry, I have drawn upon my earlier discussion of this subject in [107, pp. 78–86].

9. The systematic movement of interest rates in the Kondratieff periods is well-established fact. See, among other works: [76, II, pp. 53 ff.; 183, pp. 206–215; 177; 154, II; and 229, II].

10. The structural change in the influence of financial conditions on German residential building, reported by Hunscha between 1895 and 1900, may reflect this basic shift [136, p. 31].

11. "... when population-sensitive capital formation was increasing more rapidly, other capital formation was increasing less rapidly." This inversion in timing "resulted in so much cancellation that the comprehensive capital formation totals fail to reveal distinct long swings" [161, pp. 333, 351].

12. Thus percentage decreases from peak are listed for Hoyt's land value and for consideration in deeds [134, p. 405]:

	Land Value	Deed Consideration
1873–78	56	51.4
1892–98	33	65.0
1926–32	60	51.5

13. The benchmark series was compiled by T. S. Berry; see [16]. He used methods devised by Edwin Frickey [94, 95]. Arithmetic deviations were taken from link relatives of nine annual series; deviations were standardized for amplitude by expression in quartile deviations. Averages of middle quartile units were taken for each year, converted back to percentages, and cumulated into a time series. See Appendix A in Berry. The nine types of series from which the "pattern" is extracted include: Cincinnati prices, steamboat launchings and tonnage, toll receipts (Ohio canals), public land sales, imports and exports, immigration, and bank and finance series.

14. The rates were obtained from the *Credit Foncier* by Lucien Flaus, Paris, and kindly made available by letter, 30/11/62, to this author. See [93, p. 36]. On operations of the *Credit Foncier* see [170, pp. 241–254]. The mortgage loans are "principally on city buildings and town lots" (p. 248).

15. See Hoyt's detailed canvass of the period [134, pp. 200–232]. Hoyt concluded that "there was no general land boom in which values took a sudden spurt" and no "wild excitement" but a "steady advance" of land values "in the Loop, the North and Northwest sides along the newly extended elevated lines and in the outlying centers. . . . [The] painful remembrance of the aftermath of 1890 checked any tendency toward reckless speculation" (p. 207). Nevertheless in 1909 market opinion was described as "firmly convinced" that prices would "never stop going down" (p. 223).

16. In Hoyt's datings, land values and new construction begin at the same time, land values reach a maximum position above "normal" four months before construction; the decline begins concurrently; but construction reaches a trough 1.7 years ahead of land value (p. 409). Using our datings, out of eight turning points, three represent leads, one a lag, and four concur. At peaks the lead is zero; at troughs, −1.

17. Annual per cent change in prices over the whole period 1784–1861 was for the several commodity classes: building materials, wood—5.49; building materials, other—6.38; ferrous metals—3.96; nonferrous metals—6.36; fuel

and lighting—7.42; grain products—13.0; hides and leathers—6.61. See [18, pp. 424–425].

18. The stimulus for the preparation of this series was a paper by Earl A. Thompson, "Induced Innovation and the Building Cycle," read at the 1962 session of the Econometric Society (brought to my attention through the courtesy of Victor Fuchs). Thompson prepared an index purporting to represent skilled and unskilled pay differentials within the building trades. This probably has a wider margin of error than the building-trade–manufacturing differential; in any case, it exerts little or no influence on the sluggish process of technological improvement in building. Thompson reports a skill differential lead by some three years, or by more than our occupational differential. Using our over-all building chronology, we derive a net lead (inverted basis) of −.8 years (on 9 turns, average deviation 2.27 years). See also [64, p. 379].

19. Grebler et al. [114, p. 226] found in a comparable series that "none of the three contraction phases was accompanied by a high spread"; our cycle patterns show that contraction phases at a lag were accompanied by falling spreads. Of course, at particular points of time other influences operative in the capital market and in building will affect either the yield or building magnitudes. Hence, irregularities and consequent dispersion around our mean cyclical standings is to be expected. The striking fact is that dispersion is comparatively so restrained. Our conclusions are derived from comparison of Manhattan mortgage yields with Manhattan building, not with nationwide building series. Grebler et al. compared building and yield differentials by grading whole long expansion or contraction phases with mortgage yield spreads as "large," "small," or "changing." Hence our more detailed analysis refines their conclusions.

20. Figures for 1891–94, 1896–1900, and 1909 were linearly interpolated. See [46, p. 16]. The listed values in the source of rentals of "all houses" were converted to "occupied houses" by the formula $V \cdot r^c + (1,0 - V)r^0 = r^t$, in which V = vacancy rate, r^c = mean rental for vacant houses, r^0 = mean rental for occupied houses, and r^t = mean rental for all houses.

21. [46, p. 15]; [252, II, p. 93; 206, p. 41]. The virtual doubling of personal income between 1914 and 1919 in the United States generated an increase of the BLS rent index of only 8 per cent and in net rental income of only 35 per cent [67, p. 117]. Even more striking is the limited fall of only 18 per cent in the BLS rent index between 1925 and 1933–34 though house purchase values fell by 31 per cent [91, p. 55].

22. Perhaps "user" charges, as the term was developed by J. M. Keynes [153, pp. 66ff.] is more rightfully applied to housing rentals than to use of other structures or facilities.

23. Our most acceptable econometric test has related rent indexes to vacancies and family income (with some other factors included). The regression coefficients measure elasticities because of the unit values used. Vacancies emerged as the most important explanatory influence.

1914–37	*Family Income*	*Occupancy Ratio*	*Source*
Chawner Regression	.778	2.5	[52, p. 56]
Derksen Regression	.52	4.9	[72, p. 97]
Klein Regression	X	2.0	[157, p. 109]

24. "We shall regard the excess reserves as inventories of money available to the borrowing public at the going interest rate. When the banks accumulate large excess reserves they find that there is a glut of the money market and that the price of money, interest rates, must fall." L. Klein [157, pp. 101, 21f.]. See also, [22, pp. 283–299; 82, pp. 383ff.].

25. Thus the "income" variable for Stockholm was national income, while Hamburg building would be only dubiously influenced by nationwide corporate profitabilities. The rent index, too, was very hypothetical before 1915. Actual average rents per room in Stockholm are only available from housing censuses taken in 1894, 1900, 1905, 1910, and annually after 1915. The rent index before 1894 was estimated from a cost of building index. See [172].

26. The sequence model was designed by Jan Tinbergen and J. Polak [253, pp. 241ff.]. In this model, $B_t = aD_{t-b}$, in which a is a parameter indicating degree of response to demand, b represents a lag of response, D_t represents accumulated deficiency or surplus. Period and amplitude of fluctuations and character (damped, explosive, etc.) will depend upon the relative magnitudes of the two parameters.

CHAPTER 7

Long National Residential Building Cycles

A. LONG CYCLES, TEN COUNTRIES, AND AVERAGE CYCLE PATTERNS

Our inquiry until now has concentrated primarily upon the local cycles. The theater of action was an urban community or region inclusive of rural environs and representing an area over which building resources could move with some facility. In this theater we encountered the influences and mechanisms making for long waves in urban residential building, real estate market activities, and demographic movements. These influences and mechanisms are, in the first instance, local and depend upon the structural lags and leads built into the real estate market and its characteristic responses to demand stimuli, its supply elasticity, and the prevailing state of expectations. But at many points these influences and mechanisms join with their counterparts elsewhere, resulting in a broader nationwide movement, which has affected markets for capital, building labor, building materials, and manufactured goods.

We shall now see that this broader nationwide movement has involved long waves in urban building. Chart 7-1 shows time series of residential or related categories of building for ten countries, spanning the larger part of the nineteenth century and reaching well into the twentieth. In Chart 7-2 is a pair of series tracing the use of strategic building materials in England back to the early 1700's.

Inspection of Charts 7-1 and 7-2 discloses a widespread tendency for building to fluctuate in the longer rhythm which we found characteristic of local building and related real estate activities. Only the Danish series is free from perceptible long swings, which however emerge in rates of growth for the same series. The French and Swedish series were too short to permit a

CHART 7-1
Residential or Building Construction, Ten Countries, 1840–1955

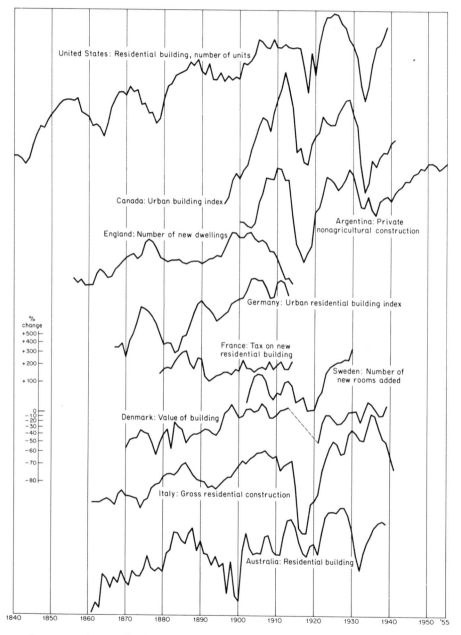

SOURCE: Appendix B, 0057, 0062, 0049, 0055-0056, 0037, 0140, 0155.
Appendix H, 0018.

CHART 7-2
Building, England and Wales, 1700–1849

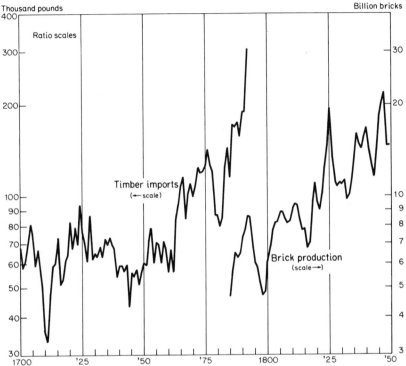

satisfactory rendering of cycle patterns out of the crude data of experience.[1]

The Canadian graph is an attempted measure of central city residential building experience, as indicated by building permits.[2]

The time series spread out over Charts 7-1 and 7-2 depict the patterns of fluctuation as they occurred on a year-to-year basis. In Charts 7-3 and 7-4 these patterns are distilled from historic experience using the technique of the nine-stage cycle pattern which has become so familiar in this work. The graphic patterns are supplemented by tabular summary measures presented in Table 7-1. To clearly indicate the degree of conformity that was embodied in these average patterns they are drawn as a zone bounded by the mean deviations of the individual cycle standings from the average standings, those "bleak symbols"—as Mitchell once called them—of intracyclical variability.

This variability arises in part out of the basic fact that the

CHART 7-3
Average Long Specific Cycle Patterns, Three Countries, 1711–1941
(Cycle Relatives Charted Plus and Minus Mean Deviations)

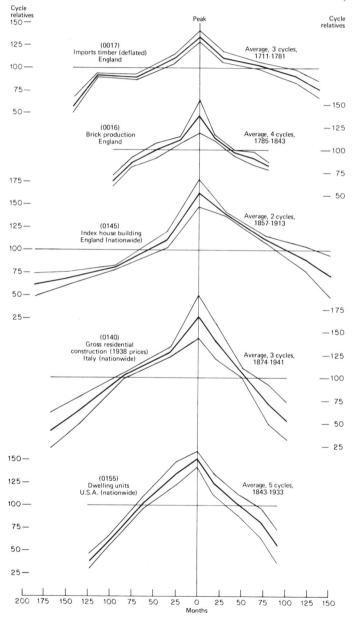

CHART 7-4
Average Long Specific Cycle Patterns, Five Areas, 1867–1933 (Cycle Relatives Charted Plus and Minus Mean Deviations)

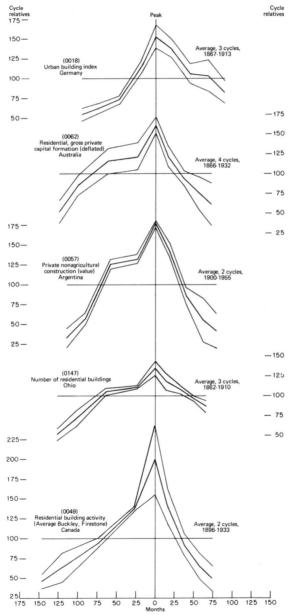

TABLE 7-1

Summary Measures, 31.5 Specific National Long Cycles, Building Activity, Seven Countries

A. Identification and Duration

Country	Series No.	Item	Years	Number of Specific Cycles	Mean Duration (Years)
Great Britain	0016	Brick production	1785–1849	4	14.5
	0017	Timber imports	1711–1781	3	23.3
	0145	House building	1853–1914	2	28.0
Germany	0018	Urban residential building	1867–1913	3	15.3
Canada	0049	Residential building, urban (Buckley)	1896–1941	2.5	16.7
	0050	Building activity (Firestone)	1896–1941	2.5	17.5
Argentina	0057	Nonfarm building	1900–1955	2	16.5
Australia	0062	Nonfarm gross residential capital formation (deflated)	1861–1939	4	16.5
Italy	0140	Gross residential capital formation (deflated)	1861–1941	3	22.3
Ohio	0147	Number of residential dwellings	1857–1914	3	16.0
U.S.	0155	Number of residential dwellings	1840–1939	5	18.0
U.S.	0271	Value of residential building	1843–1939	5	18.0

B. Amplitude, Secular Measures

| Country | Series No. | Amplitude Specific | | | Secular Weighted Average Growth Rate Per Year Short Cycles | Average Per Year Per Cent Change Overlapping Short Specific Cycles |
| | | Total | | Per Year Fall | | |
		All Years	Per Year			
Great Britain	0016	123.5	8.52	−8.53	1.846	1.91
	0017	133.9	5.74	−5.05	n.a.	n.a.
	0145	191.6	6.84	−7.26	1.680	.90
Germany	0018	169.4	11.07	−9.67	2.338	2.64
Canada	0049	424.8	23.85	−43.77	1.188	5.05
	0050	164.7	9.41	−10.61	n.a.	n.a.
Argentina	0057	280.0	16.97	−19.39	−.097	1.91
Australia	0062	208.8	12.66	−16.67	2.08	2.79
Italy	0140	239.3	10.71	−13.69	2.216	2.23
Ohio	0147	131.3	8.21	−9.06	2.547	3.08
U.S.	0155	207.3	11.50	−12.50	2.977	n.a.
U.S.	0271	220.1	12.23	−14.17	4.00[a]	2.35[a]

n.a.—not available.
[a] Average, 2 segments.

historic environment, within which building waves ran their course, was changing in character. Even two successive waves would touch different historic epochs; the terminal troughs in three successive waves would span over half a century. A changing environment and the shifting course of historic development would affect the form and character of long-swing movements. It is important thus at the outset to establish in some valid sense the *representative character* of the nationwide average cycle pattern and the consequent meaning of the zone of mean deviations. In our analysis of local long swings we encountered instances where the average pattern does not embody a recurring pattern of experience marred by irregularities. The average pattern in these instances offsets and helps to erase divergent types of experience embodied in successive patterns. In such instances the "average" represents the cumulative aggregate, not a typical pattern running through it. In our investigation of local cycles it would have been tedious formally to have examined the credentials of every average pattern before its use. But at the threshold of our study of nationwide average patterns presentation of such credentials is called for.

If the successive individual wave movements conform closely to a typical pattern they should be uniform at least in certain crucial respects: underlying secular change, sign of stage movements, predominance of phase (expansion or contraction), degree of duration, dispersion, and presence of clear-cut secular trend in amplitude or duration. There are other measurable characteristics but these should suffice to indicate the representative character of the average patterns and the meaning of the zone area of deviations bounding these patterns.

The first suggested measure, that of secular change, may be probed by a comparison between two measures of secular change measured by (a) per cent change per year and (b) average short-cycle standings (see Table 7-1). The magnitude of secular change corresponds to the upward tilt of our specific patterns themselves (Charts 7-3 and 7-4). In this very elementary respect, all successive long cycles conformed to the secular drift, i.e., the mean annual values of each successive long cycle were greater than its predecessor.

Stage movements are more variable, and some divergence in sign of stage movements in particular cases is to be expected. It is striking, however, that, out of 252 surveyed stage movements, in only 5.7 per cent of the cases was there a direction of change different from that of the series average. This means that individual cycle patterns with regard to this feature of general shape conformed to a structural type.

Another basic feature of general shape is balance of cycle pattern or relative predominance of expansion over contraction months. Expansions predominate in all of our average patterns. Out of thirty-five individual cycle patterns, 80 per cent conformed to type in this regard. In only 12 per cent of the cases were contractions longer; in another 8 per cent the two phases were of equal duration.

With regard to durations, the deviation bars attached to the charts and figures cited in the tables show that dispersion generally was as wide between, as within, series. For the nine countries involved, our mean duration was 19.09 years, with a mean deviation of 3.64 years. The mean deviation for the corresponding country series is 3.4 years, nearly the same magnitude. A relatively low mean variation was characteristic of country series generally and even prevailed for the one case, Great Britain, where three different series covering different segments of over 200 years of building experience yielded radically different duration levels. For the earlier eighteenth century and later nineteenth century, waves of extraordinarily long duration were involved, averaging 23.3 years in the earlier period and 28 years in the later period. But between the two periods there was a succession of four clear-cut long waves, with a duration range between 11 and 17 years and a mean duration of 14.5 years. Total amplitude experienced was comparable to the earlier eighteenth century movement as shortness of duration was offset by greater intensity of action. Yet, though the three series had a wide range of durations—from 14.5 to 28.0 years —the diversity of duration experience within a series and the historic experience involved was relatively narrow.

The final feature selected to test for the presence of structural conformity between average individual patterns of our surveyed series has regard to trend of duration or amplitude. If long waves were systematically growing longer or shorter or greater or lesser in amplitude, then the average pattern of a series would not incorporate all the systematic elements present in its component individual patterns. Both mean duration and amplitude could then more accurately be described and graphed in trend-adjusted terms and supplemented by trend factors for amplitude and duration. If there is no systematic trend indicated for amplitude and duration, then the variations both within and between series probably correspond to the circumstances in the historic environment which hinder or accelerate the swing process.

Tabulation of the direction of change of successive long cycle standings indicates some slight tendency for both amplitudes and durations to decline. For nineteen instances of successive cycles in seven countries, some eleven were downward both with regard to duration and amplitude. If we compare not successive but terminal cycles, the picture changes. From initial to terminal cycle, durations were shorter for both nineteenth and twentieth century United States and Great Britain but longer in eighteenth century Great Britain, Germany, and Italy. American, British, Australian, and Italian amplitudes terminated at a higher level than they originated. With this mixed picture no clear trend of amplitude or duration is indicated and the average represents a persistent central tendency. There are probably systematic elements in our residuals which could be isolated and separated from the mean values and their residuals. I believe, however, we can be satisfied that our mean values approximate a form of movement running through the individual cycle patterns.

The dispersion from these mean values in absolute terms will only be crudely measured by the mean deviations. The number of observations was too few to assume a normal distribution of these. We insert the deviations in the charts only as a rough index of the scale of dispersion. In terms of acceptable statistical measures, our bounded zone of mean values and deviations probably overlaps substantially with the interquartile range, which, for these purposes, would have been equally suitable as an index of the scale of dispersion. While this index probably serves satisfactorily between series and phases of a given series, it is biased in its distribution of dispersion between stages of a phase. Allowance will need to be made for the tendency of this measurement technique to minimize deviations at mid-stages (II, III, IV, VI, VII, VIII) and to maximize them at troughs and peaks (I, V, IX). The bias is not serious but it will systematically warp the distribution among the cycle stages of the scale of dispersion indicated in our charts.[3]

B. RATES OF PER YEAR CHANGE, LONG CYCLES

The average cycle patterns which we have just reviewed graphically spell out the form and character of the long-swing movement characteristic of urban building in the open markets of classical capitalism. In outward form these patterns are similar to the patterns of movement of industrial output etched out by business cycles. There is the same smoothed rise and fall, the same predominance of expansion over contraction phases, the same upward tilt signifying growth. Does the similarity extend to the annual *rates of change* implicit in these cycle patterns? To answer this question we took the "first differences" of successive cycle relatives and divided the differences by the average interval (called a "segment") between the middle of the earlier and the middle of the later stages. The results represent percentage rates of movement of cycle relatives per year between segments of a cycle.[4] These yearly rates can readily be converted into the more common monthly rates used elsewhere.

For virtually all expansion and for most contraction phases our methods smooth out irregularities in intervals between peak and trough years, since the successive cycle stages will embrace two or more adjoining years. But short contraction phases which last for four years or less receive very little or no smoothing, and contractions which endure for six years receive only bivariate smoothing between paired sets of adjoining values. Of our surveyed national experience, series 0147 for Ohio and series 0016 for England (1785–1849) have relatively short mean contraction phases of 5.4 and 6.6 years, respectively, and hence allowance in these instances will need to be made for an increase in variability of rates of change due to reduced smoothing. And of course, for all our series—except in the highly volatile ones where a moving average was substituted for the original series—peak and trough values are unsmoothed. The tendency to "peakedness" would be random in reference cycle patterns, except where turning points coincided, but would be biased to extreme values where specific cycle patterns are concerned. Our basic statistical procedures would tend to depress terminal values and to elevate peak values and thus tend to generate some rise in rates of change between stages I–II and IV–V and some fall between V–VI and VIII–IX.

The graphs of the average rates of change between cycle segments for nine of our nationwide series are presented in Chart 7-5. The vertical axis is scaled in terms of percentages, the horizontal scale is in terms of years to or from stage IV–V. The percentage changes to the right of stage IV–V occur during the contraction phase; the percentage changes to the left of the zero point correspond to the expansion phase. The intervals between stages are all scaled on the horizontal axis except interval IV–V, which is assigned a zero time value in order to align uniformly all IV–V stages of the different series.

As with the average cycle patterns, these average rate-of-change patterns are extended into a zone bounded by the mean deviations from the changes. The minor bias previously noted, which tends to reduce deviations at mid-stages and to enlarge them at turning points, will operate here to the extent rates of change will be involved.

Unlike our cycle pattern charts, the time scale no longer is standardized at one cycle relative for one month. A 1 per cent change in our vertical scale now corresponds to six months of cycle time; hence a 45° slope to the rate-of-change pattern means that the rate is changing by .166 per cent per month or 2 per cent per year.

The rate-of-change patterns graphed in Chart 7-5 exhibit a comparable movement in the mean values and zone of deviations. The movement of the deviations corresponded, with only nine exceptions, to the movement of the mean values. Divergences were concentrated in intervals IV–V, VI–VII, and VII–VIII.[5]

If rates of change were constant in expansion and contraction with merely a reversal of sign, our graph would be made up of two parallel discontinuous straight lines, one in the positive scale (for expansions) and the other in the negative scale, and at equal distance from the origin. If rates of change steadily changed, as in a sine function, then the change pattern would reproduce the function, but shifted to neutral timing, showing the rate peak and rate trough midway in the reference phases. If the rate of change steadily fell during expansions and became negative at the peak, then the change function would decline during the expansion and cross into the negative scale between IV–V and V–VI. This would represent an expansion steadily being sapped of its driving force. Since rates of change of building, as well as

CHART 7-5
Average Patterns of Yearly Rates of Change from Stage to Stage of Building Cycles, National Building Activity, 1711–1955

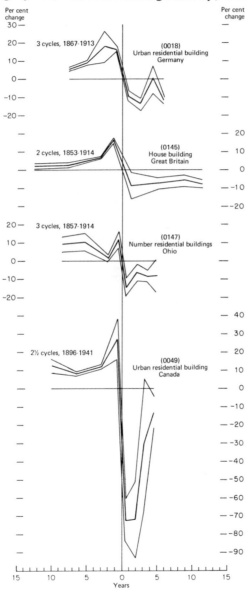

CHART 7-5
(Concluded)

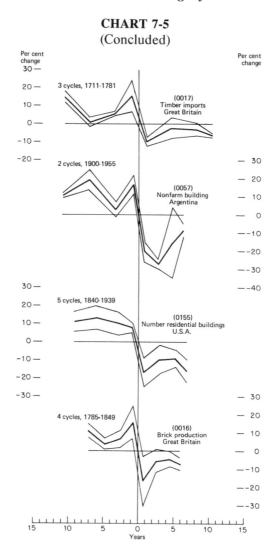

building itself, elicit response and exert influence, careful consideration of rates of change seems indicated.

It will be interesting to compare our change patterns with the characteristics of similar change patterns for short cycles. Since for short cycles our time series would need to be on a monthly or quarterly basis to yield eight rate-of-change estimates, we have supplemented measures of aggregate output with proxy measures on imports and wholesale prices that conform well to movements of productive activity in four countries: United States, United Kingdom, Germany, and France.[6]

These average business cycles change patterns for four countries show certain interesting structural characteristics. Rate-of-change peaks in average patterns generally occur early in expansions. In our eleven national series, peaks were reached three times each in the II–III and IV–V segment but five times in the III–IV segment. Characteristically the high point of expansion is reached earlier in output expansions and somewhat later in import expansions. Countrywise, the United States tends to later peaks and Germany and France to earlier peaks, with the United Kingdom tending to a middle position. This ranking is based on average patterns and may conceal disparate movements in individual cycle experience.

Contractions exhibit a greater tendency to dispersion. Output troughs concentrate in the intermediate segments, as do prices. Import behavior is oddly dichotomized. Two of the countrywide series reach troughs at the beginning and two at the end of the contraction. The tendency to secondary relapses and pickups, characteristic of American comprehensive reference series, is reproduced in American specific cycles behavior but is found for three other countries only in the more volatile import series.[7] There is likewise little evidence, apart from U. S. experience, for the "striking and significant fact," noted by Abramovitz, that with respect to the rate of change in output "contractions and expansions are not symmetrical." Patterns of industrial output during expansion periods he found to be highly "variable." They sometimes reached their maximum points at the outset, more usually in the middle but rarely at the close of the expansion periods [2, pp. 359, 377f.]. During contractions, Abramovitz found that the most rapid rate of decline was reached "well before" the cyclical trough, in most cases at segments VI–VII but at adjoining segments also. The non-American experience was more inclined to exhibit symmetry of form between expansion and contraction behavior, with peaks and troughs in rates of change characteristically being reached within expansion and contraction phases and with some approach to a sinelike form. The dichotomy between expansions and contractions and the tendency for greater variability during expansions than in contractions is to be found, curiously enough, in the pre-1848 English behavior.

Rates-of-change patterns in our building cycles exhibit the same range of diversity and some of the characteristic tendencies of business cycles. Building expansions, like business cycle expansions, are often sinelike. Only one building expansion (0155) shows the declining tendency exhibited by only a few short industrial cycles. Building expansions seem, however, to be characterized by greater buoyancy of spirit, with a crescendo reached late in the expansion or at the peak. This variation from the sine form, in my judgment, is partly but not wholly, the product of statistical bias in our smoothing procedure.

The same field of variation in change patterns is found in the contraction experience with building cycles. Three of our series exhibit a sine formation. For five of our series, however, a secondary decline occurs in the rate of fall, which pulls down the rate at the terminal trough. This corresponds to the tendency, uncommon in short cycle output behavior, for low levels of the rate of change to persist in the contraction (series 0017, 0140, 0155, 0145, 0147).

C. RELATIONSHIP OF LOCAL AND NATIONAL LONG CYCLES

If we now compare nationwide long cycles in residential or related building with counterpart local long cycles, we observe a curious and striking family likeness. Let us commence with the simple property of duration, the data for which is set forth in Table 7-2. We take our national and local series as they come and tentatively allow each an equal weight.

The results are striking. As expected, the absolute range of local variation is wider, as is indicated by the standard devia-

TABLE 7-2
Summary Tabulation Nationwide and Local Cycles—Duration

	Local	*National*
Number of series	30	10
Number of cycles	81	30.5
Mean duration	19.67±5.00	18.96 ± 4.36
Median duration	18.45	17.3
Ratio high to mean	1.68	1.48
Ratio low to mean	.54	.77

SOURCE: Chapter 2, Table 2-2; Chapter 5, Table 5-1.

tions and by corresponding ratios of the extremes to mean values at the upper and lower ends. But the mean and median values are nearly the same and the standard deviations are close together. Though the national sample of series is relatively small, the range of historic experience surveyed is wide, and the pattern of results reached would probably persist with much larger samples of nationwide or local cycles. The import of our table is, that with regard to duration, nationwide cycles center at the same value level as local cycles, have comparable cluster characteristics, and experience a relatively wide absolute range of dispersion. This indicates or implies a high degree of coalescence of local cycles, for otherwise mean local cycles would systematically be shorter and nationwide cycles appreciably longer.

A different kind of coalescence is exhibited by amplitude characteristics, which are detailed in Table 7-3. The range of nationwide amplitude is cut off by aggregation, as was the case with duration, but the center of the national distribution is around two-thirds that of the local. In aggregation some 30 per cent of local amplitude was eroded away. If we strike an average of the national experience for the mid-nineteenth century and later of the three countries most fully represented in the local returns—the United States, Great Britain, and Germany—we derive an implicit erosion rate of 34.6 per cent. These erosion rates of mean local amplitudes among nations correspond to erosion rates for five Ohio local groups when compared with statewide aggregation (32.7 per cent), five major U.S. areas, including the state of Ohio (36.6 per cent), and three major

TABLE 7-3

Summary Tabulation Nationwide and Local Cycles—Total Specific Amplitude

	Local	*National*
Number of series	30	10
Number of cycles	81	30.5
Mean total amplitude	306±92.37	214.3±83.16
Median total amplitude	288	200.2
High (ratio to mean)	1.58	1.98
Low (ratio to mean)	.59	.58

SOURCE: Chapter 2, Table 2-2; Chapter 5, Table 5-1.

German cities (45.1 per cent). These erosion rates represent the shrinkage in mean local specific total amplitudes emerging in the amplitude measure of the corresponding territorial aggregate.[8]

The erosion of amplitude in aggregation results from differential coverage and from variations in timing, which put some cities and areas in the lead and cause others to lag. Out of thirty-two matched turning points for the five local and regional American series, there was considerable variation from period to period, the mean deviation of the five local series being 1.39 years. A similar range of variation between timing of local and national cycles was found in Germany and in Great Britain. For the seventeen non-Ohio cities for which specific turns could be matched with national turns, fourteen had mean lead-lags of less than two years and none exceeded four years. The mean lead-lag, signs disregarded, was only 1.34 years. The over-all mean deviation at these measured lead-lags for twenty-eight local series was 2.61 years.

This expected conformity of regional to national movements shows up in the one instance when our survey included regional series. Australian brick production is fortunately available for a long time period for three major regions. The resulting set of specific and reference patterns graphically exhibit the expected high degree of conformity of regional to nationwide patterns of movement. The reference frame here is the national chronology of total, gross, nonagricultural capital formation, since brick production would be associated with all varieties of construction activity, not merely building. Since brick production itself experienced an erosion of specific amplitude of 13.6 per cent when measured on a national reference construction frame, it can be seen that the mean erosion of the three provincial areas, 22 per cent, indicates a high degree of convergence of provincial and national movements in brick production. It appears that the larger the level of aggregation the greater is the conformity to the national aggregate.

D. CONVERGENCE OF NATIONWIDE AND LOCAL CYCLES

Nationwide and local cycles, then, do not run independent courses but to a high degree conform to each other. However, local and national cycles can run a wide range in terms of amplitude and duration; and the response mechanisms and speculation potential of urban communities will be quite different both over space and in time. It would seem almost unavoidable that local cycles would offset each other or neutralize each other in conformity to the rule, suggested by Arthur Burns in his unpublished manuscript study, "that cyclical amplitudes become narrower as the geographic scope of a building series becomes wider" [39, pp. 59ff.]. This tendency to dispersal would be promoted from the supply side. It would be easy for any given impulse of long cyclical expansion in one area to work its way if the converse state prevailed elsewhere. Mortgage funds, building labor, and building materials could more easily be obtained; and an increase in demand for building would be satisfied with a lesser degree of price inflation. A local expansion impulse would thus be favored if other communities were in a more dormant condition.

If thus local cycles are to converge into a national movement, they will encounter supply resistance. There must be a powerful influence at work or a set of "integrating factors," as Arthur Burns called them, or an "extraneous force of considerable magnitude"—such as would be represented by "wars, inflation, or structural transformation,"—to "bond together local cycles." It was tempting to invoke the "extraneous factors," since these historically could be dated so readily and since they were known to be associated with backlogged need and surges of building. I, too, tended throughout the early phase of the present investigation to rely on these "extraneous forces."[9]

The "extraneous forces" unquestionably affect the long-wave process. But other bonding forces are available to integrate local cycles. These bonding forces spring from the local movements themselves, as soon as these movements are regarded not as oscillations around a stationary process but as a wavy form of growth. For as a form of growth, local cycles involve concurrent fluctuation in industrial building and the rate of labor-force inflow or immigration. The local boom in building then becomes a response to enlarged demand for shelter generated by expansion in local income, employment, and production. This has been satisfactorily demonstrated in many contexts and in many different historic environments by the statistical and descriptive materials assembled in the preceding chapters.

Where does this local expansion in income, employment, and

production in a given community come from? It can only arise from an increase in local primary employment, which, in turn, will correspond to expanded demand in other localities for goods produced or services rendered by the given community. This expanded demand in other localities may arise from improved terms of service or from displacement of other products and production centers. Or expanded demand may involve all products and centers. Local industrial expansion, in turn, generates expansion elsewhere; and each local contraction tends to generate a counterpart contraction in other urban centers. Concurrent urban expansions thus occur under unfavorable supply conditions; but when supply conditions are most favorable the demand impulse is lacking. We now see why extraneous forces of considerable magnitude are not needed to integrate local cycles. These cycles are bonded together by the industrial interdependence which forces all urban communities with a diversified base to fluctuate in unison.

The tendency of local cycles to coalesce into a common typical pattern is, in its way, similar to the tendency of national business cycles to coalesce into a common international movement. Any domestic expansion, through the force of the import propensity, tends to generate counterpart expansions in trading partners at the same time that the impulse for domestic growth is scaled down. These counterpart expansions will of course generate some export "seepage," as it is called, or induced exportation, which, considering the likely scale of the parameters for an international economy, will be of much smaller magnitude than the originally induced importation. The tendency to produce a common movement out of the disparate impulses of the individual countries will be greater the higher the average level of import propensities and the more sensitive credit facilities are to shiftings in the current account of the balance of payments. Other countries had to "keep in step" which requires, as Keynes once wittily noted, that "everyone must conform to the average behavior of everyone else" [154, II, p. 286].

Local urban communities are much more closely bonded together than the national economies of the Atlantic community. The import propensity, so to speak, is much higher, and a larger fraction of productive output is channeled for sale to outside markets. Under these circumstances it would be very difficult for an urban community with a diversified industrial base to take off on special tangents of growth that vary significantly from the predominantly national movement. Urban areas that face comparative disadvantage in attracting new or in keeping old industry will, of course, lead at downturns and lag at the upturns. Urban areas that are favored by comparative advantage and in which, accordingly, nationwide industrial growth is concentrated will tend to lead in upturns, to rise at higher annual velocities, and possibly to lag at peaks. Otherwise lags and leads will grow out of "overshooting" induced by the process of rise or fall and exemplified excellently by the behavior of the vacancy series. But the extent of overshooting will itself be constrained by shifts in demand impulses growing out of the rise or fall in demand for industrial products locally produced. Communities with a nondiversified industrial base, in which an important role is played by industrial products serving special markets at home or abroad, could more readily exhibit a particular nonconforming reference pattern. It is striking that a collection of small neighboring urban communities—such as was drawn together in some of our Ohio groups—conformed to the national and regional movement. Indeed, our Ohio groups, down to the lowest degree of urbanization, conformed closely to the statewide movement, while the still more comprehensive and closely interlocked Australian regions disclosed an almost perfect synchronization of regional and national patterns. A similar synchronization of regional patterns was established by the early work of Riggleman [222].

So too, we are not surprised at the relatively low level of the mean deviations found by Long to coexist between the median yearly turning point and his individual city turning points.[10] But we now see that dispersion was held in bounds by the powerful forces which balance income accounts and impose a common rhythm of movement on industries, regions, and cities.

E. NATIONWIDE WAVE MOVEMENTS: REVIEW

We have found that there are good reasons why local and nationwide cycles in building should coalesce and conform as they do to a common typical pattern. On the same grounds we should expect a similar reproduction on the national scale of features which we found to play an important role in local cycles. Our investigation showed that nonresidential building swings in cycles comparable to residential building, though with a tendency to lag; that industrial building should exhibit a marked short or major decennial rhythm which also responds to residential long-swing rhythms with a tendency to lead; and that total building should, accordingly, fluctuate in long swings. We would also expect that the urban labor force would be mobilized nationally as they are locally in long swings, and that marriage rates should reflect long-swing rhythms though perhaps only in very mild form.

To these manifest rhythms exhibited on the local scene there would correspond other rhythms more likely to become recorded and statistically identified on a nationwide basis. Thus, if input resources of labor and real capital are drawn into the industrial economy in long swings, there should be corresponding fluctuations in total gross capital formation and the flow of final output or at least in the rates of growth of capital formation and final output. So too, we would expect long rhythmic swings in the composition of gross capital formation and in the modes of its financing by domestic or foreign sources or through profit or credit inflation. A rhythmic fluctuation would be expected in at least the rates of growth of total money stock, for otherwise price levels of output would fluctuate inversely to output. We know that this pattern of inverse fluctuation did not characterize the behavior of an important segment of the price level of output, namely, the cost of new building.

The field of investigation before us has widened considerably. It now encompasses all systematic influences that affect economic progress and industrial growth. This field of investigation is evidently too wide and too difficult to be pursued rigorously with the intensity of effort that has characterized our local investigation or our efforts to analyze nationwide patterns of urban building. Nor is this effort necessary. For at least two countries—the United States since 1870 and Great Britain —informed investigators have ransacked available historical and statistical information and their pioneer work has already attracted considerable research support. For the United States I refer to the work of Simon Kuznets, Moses Abramovitz, Richard Easterlin, Jeffrey Williamson, Burnham Campbell, who together have thoroughly treated long swings in American aggregative development since the Civil War in many of the collateral fields of behavior we have noted. See [161, 1, 78, 126.]

Our particular research effort has added to this recent work three important additional nationwide nonfarm measures of new residential construction and the annual value of residential and total building both available since 1850.[11] (See Chart 7-6.) These series exhibit the same long swings with slight variations in turning points as the number of residential units built. More interesting is the implied relationship between residential and nonresidential building inherent in the estimated series. Both types of building fluctuate in the same rhythm, but the timing relationship is subject to drift. In the first long swing nonresidential building leads in the downturn and upturn; in the second timing is uniform. In the three succeeding swings nonresidential building lags appreciably at the peak. This drift in timing is clearly indicated in the succession of reference patterns shown in Chart 7-7, and is exhibited by Long's estimates for the latest prewar swing (closing in 1918) [1, Table 4].

The somewhat divergent tilt of the average patterns for residential numbers and residential values corresponds to the secular growth of per unit values in residential building. Thus the

CHART 7-6

Patterns of Average Long Cycles, Specific and Reference, Value of Residential Building and Total Building, Nonfarm, U.S., 1843–1933

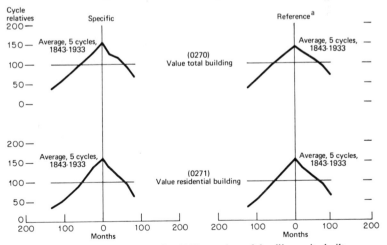

[a]Reference chronology is from series 0155, number of dwelling units built.

CHART 7-7
Patterns of Successive Specific and Reference Long Cycles, Value Nonresidential Building Nonfarm, U.S.

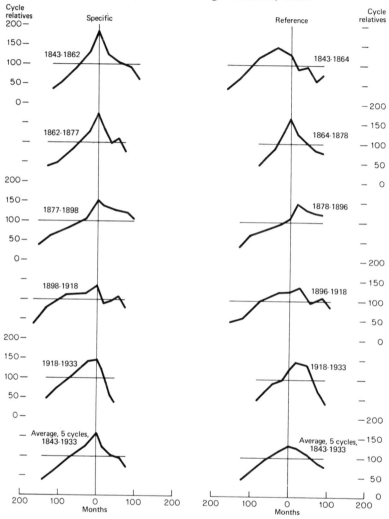

annual growth rate of residential numbers, 2.977 per cent per year, contrasts with 3.783 per cent per year for the value of residential building. A detailed examination of the trend rise in residential per unit values was attempted in earlier publications, and it is believed that the trend rise of the order of magnitude specified is amply supported by independent data, by the upward drift of real per capita incomes, and by known propensities for housing expenditure out of income [108, pp. 268–276].

The other major country that has been the subject of extended inquiry into long swing movements is Great Britain. Here the pioneer work was by A. K. Cairncross and Brinley Thomas whose impressive investigations published nearly at the same time in the early fifties [46; 245] have set off a flurry of research and debate regarding long wave experience in Britain, especially the relation between waves of domestic activity and migration of labor force or export of capital during the six decades preceding World War I [284; 66; 117; 167; 47]. Study of the long-swing process in British economic development has now been pushed back to the first decade of the eighteenth century by new revelations about economic development and population growth during that century and especially by the publication in 1959 by the distinguished historian of the industrial revolution, T. A. Ashton, of a new work on "economic fluctuations" during that century inclusive of fluctuations in building and real estate [11]. Ashton assembled time series of building materials used, including imported fir timber (graphed in Chart 7-2), window glass and wallpaper output; and he showed from contemporary evidence suggestive snatches of patterns of behavior characteristic of the more familiar contemporary long-swing movements. Though Ashton himself interpreted his materials in terms of short-term business fluctuations and financial crises, the longer rhythm of building and urban development stood out both from his account and from his time series. That rhythm was independently brought to light by two major students of London economic life and building during that century, one noting that the "records of population and the number of houses . . . show London expanding irregularly from its centre . . . in a succession of waves" [100, pp. 98, 99–111], the other asserting flatly that London's growth "has not been a matter of gradual and even incrementation but of distinct waves of activity at intervals roughly of about fifty years" [243, pp. 24, 25, 98, 292]. A corresponding growth pattern in industrial output exhibited four major growth surges between 1700 and 1810 [129, Diagram P]. With this supportive background J. Parry Lewis in his recent monograph on British building cycles had little difficulty in recognizing the same long swings marked out in our chronology of the eighteenth century except for his classification of a "halting, gentle, barely perceptible rise" in timber imports between 1727 and 1733 as an expansion phase of a new long swing while our statistical analysis treats this "rise" as only a phase of a twenty-year-long decline [167, pp. 17 ff.]. A corresponding decline in rates of domestic economic growth over the two decades in question seems well established [71, pp. 5 ff., 61; 243, p. 111; 100, pp. 21–62].

While these long swings in urban growth and building in the eighteenth century appear well established and with many of the characteristics of those occurring in the next century, in one crucial respect they differ with regard to causation. The contraction phases of three out of four eighteenth century swings are associated with wartime periods of what we would now call "tight credit" marked by high levels of consol yields (1700–1711, 1740–49, 1756–63, 1776–85). These were periods when public debt was being rapidly increased to finance wartime expenditure and the rising yields which made public stock attractive to investors drew loan capital away from mortgage markets, hampered by an interest ceiling fixed by the usury act at 5 per cent. Ashton rightly insists that the "existence of this upper limit is of the utmost importance to an understanding of the fluctuations of the period, since beyond the usury limit further mortgage borrowing "might become impossible" [11, p. 86; 57, I, p. 348; 154, I, pp. 186 ff.].

As the pace of economic development accelerated with the industrial revolution and as usury restrictions were eased, the character of the long-swing movement appeared to change. The wave process became more intense, the per year amplitudes of both rise and fall increased while the durations shortened (see Chart 7-2) and especially during the decade of the 1830's there was a full coalescence of a "long swing" in building with the business cycle proper. After 1860 durations were more extended and amplitudes became more sluggish. The relationship between American and British building cycles shifted at about the same time and the migration of both capital and labor took on greater importance.

Besides the United States and England, the Canadian experience has been subjected to intensive analysis, with regard to both adequacy of statistical measures and substantive wavelike movements. The Canadian series on transportation and population that can be carried back to 1820 and annual estimates for GNP that go back to 1870 "display seven and a half long swings of an average length of seventeen and a half years over the period ending in 1950.[12] The fluctuations closely parallel the related American series.

With regard to other countries that have been less intensively studied, no effort was made to compile a complete set of long nationwide time series. The respective statistics are in process of development and the work involved in the evaluation and processing of such data exceeded the bounds of our investigation. We did, however, collect and analyze long nationwide time series that seemed particularly suitable—as was the case for Australia and Italy—or, as in the case of Germany, involved a country which through its major cities had loomed large in our investigation. The Italian patterns show the same degree of conformity between residential and nonresidential building as was found in America over a similar time period. The Australian patterns indicate that the different industrial and product sectors of the economy will develop a wide variety of timing relationships. The activities which show the lowest degree of participation in nationwide wave movements are mining investment (possibly reflecting the fortuitous character of mineral discoveries), investment in shipping, and investment by local authorities. Railway and commercial investment exhibit marked swings, as in the United States, and the reference patterns for industrial investment show clear-cut participation with a tendency to lead at upturns, as did our Ohio patterns of industrial building. It is noteworthy that agricultural reference patterns of investment, dominated by investment in livestock, are not inverted.

F. SUMMARY

Our study of nationwide patterns of urban residential building utilized twelve series for seven countries. The long-swing experience of two countries, Sweden and France, was not included in our formal tabulations because our available time series did not go back far enough to cover two or more long swings. Six of our series related to building in the United States and in the United Kingdom, two of the series related to Canada, and one each related to building in Australia, Argentina, Germany, and Italy. We surveyed 28.5 long specific cycles in residential or total building in seven countries.

This formidable body of long-cyclical experience was studied with regard to patterns of movement in absolute values and in rates of change. Absolute values were reduced to cycle relatives, smoothed, and averaged, as in the usual National Bureau procedure. Rates of change were computed from first differences of these cycle relatives expressed on an annual basis and then averaged. Cyclical experience in both the absolute values and rates of change was found sufficiently homogeneous to warrant consideration of the "average" as the representative form. The tests for homogeneity related to sign of secular movements, predominance of phase, sign of stage movements, and secular trend in amplitude or duration.

The average rates of change from stage to stage of building cycles reproduced in their pattern of movement many of the characteristic features found running through rates of change during short business cycles. There was experienced the same diversity of forms of movement with early and late peaks and early and late troughs. In building cycles the peak and trough in the rate of change tends to be reached later—and often at the close of the phase—both in expansions and in contractions. Building cycles thus appear to be characterized by greater intensity of spirit. Both the rise and fall take more time to reach their climactic rate of change. This appearance of greater intensity was produced by some combination of real movements and by a smoothing procedure bias which tended to magnify up and down rates of change at peaks and troughs.

Comparison of mean durations of local and national building cycles disclosed nearly the same duration in both. Our local series including 81 cycles averaged 19.7 ± 5.0 years per cycle; our national series with 30.5 cycles averaged 19.0 ± 4.4 years per cycle. But on virtually the same durations, total amplitudes of the nationwide movements were scaled down by some 30 per cent in the process of aggregation. Mean, median, and extreme range values for nationwide amplitudes were appreciably less than for local amplitudes.

This erosion of amplitude in aggregation was found whenever our investigation uncovered both aggregates and their components. Degree of erosion generally ranged between 30 and 40 per cent. Erosion of amplitude grew chiefly out of variations in local timing around national or regional reference turning points. The mean lead-lag, signs disregarded, varied around 1.35 years, but the mean deviation at turning points was nearly twice this, 2.61

years. Rarely did a local series persist in an offbeat course after four years. Of the nineteen local communities surveyed that could be related to a nationwide or reference frame, only one showed characteristic inversion. The larger and more important the local communities, the greater the synchronization with the national movements.

This synchronization was partly induced by major wars, which are known to generate concurrent waves of building in the various communities of a nation. But synchronization will also be generated in the peacetime economy by the normal tendency of matured local communities with a diversified industrial base to grow in integrated fashion. Any prevailing national rate of growth will be translated into a counterpart local rate of growth of demand for industrial products produced in any particular locality. Communities that are innovating or that are favored by comparative advantage will grow at a faster than average rate; and conversely for the retrogressive communities. Any local domestic expansion generates expansion elsewhere by reason of the import propensity and export multiplier. Convergence is thus forced upon local communities; as Keynes says of nations under a gold standard, they "must conform to the average behavior of everyone else."

Since local and national cycles converge, we should expect features found in local cycles to show up on the national scale. Many of these features for the United States, the United Kingdom, Canada, and Australia have been detected and analyzed by other investigators. New evidence was presented showing that the value of American nationwide nonfarm building, both residential and nonresidential, fluctuated with near corresponding amplitude. Nonresidential building tended to lead before the 1870's and thereafter to lag, particularly at peaks. Our new estimates showed that residential building values grew at a yearly mean rate of secular growth nearly 0.8 per cent greater than the corresponding rate for residential numbers.

NOTES

1. The French series exhibits a clear-cut long swing from 1886 through to 1901; the character of the movement thereafter is ambiguous. Kindelberger found no reliable measure of nationwide building activity for any stretch of years before 1914 and thus exaggerated the extent to which patterns of building

activity in France "remains shrouded in mystery" [155, p. 304]. On Sweden, see Chapter 2.

2. Canadian building permit data are evaluated in Appendix I.

3. For analysis of the bias in question, see [193, pp. 199 ff.].

4. For a more detailed exposition see [41, pp. 30–31; 193, pp. 296 ff.; 2, pp. 350–358].

5. The exceptions are:

Series	Stage	Series	Stage
0140	VII–VIII	0145	VI–VII
0155	IV–V, VII–VIII	0147	VII–IX
0016	VII–VIII	0049	VI–VII, VIII–IX
0018	IV–V		

6. The wholesale price level was for imported and domestic commodities 1792–1850. Nineteen specific cycles were analyzed, having timing I–V with eleven leads, ten lags, and three concurrences; the mean lead at peaks was 0.4 months, at troughs 0.2 months. The cyclical variation in the pig iron price level should have conformed closely to pig iron output. The series runs from 1795–1803 to 1817–43 and involves 8 specific cycles with II–V timing [97, pp. 814–815].

7. Most of the comprehensive series analyzed by Mitchell showed a retardation between I–III and "a goodly proportion of the series show a partial recovery from the retardation" [193, p. 299].

8. To illustrate, the total mean specific amplitude of our five Ohio sample groups involving twenty counties was 227.28. In the process of aggregation of sample group returns, 42.2 per cent of local mean amplitude was lost.

9. The "extraneous forces" hypothesis has been given its fullest published defense in [62]. Drawing upon the "variety of demand" (p. 36 ff.) and the "influence of localism" (p. 51 f.) Colean and Newcomb noted certain "general movements, in which the normal diversities of construction demand according to type and locality were forced into a general coincidence" (p. 54). Such "forced coincidences" were found in the twenty years following the Civil War and World War I and were thus located in "special circumstances among which war obviously plays a crucial part" (p. 57). In a more guarded way, Long [173, p. 162 f.] merely observed "that wars have had far-reaching effects on cycles in the building industry"; they intensify the severity of cycles "and determine when at least some cycles occur." A leading study of the role of war and associated disturbances in "long waves" has marked out the periods, 1816–41, 1872–97, as most peacelike or free from warlike activity. See [56, p. 370]. Yet each of these periods spanned one or more building waves.

10. See Long's interesting account of dispersion in timing in [173, Chap. VIII]. He reported that all the local series for detailed residential construction "agreed rather well" with the computed nationwide index (p. 133), that "troughs show high correspondence" rarely exceeding more than two years (p. 139), and that despite the "immobility" of the building industry and the potential "great individuality" of building activity, "long cycles do appear in

all cities and the agreement of the turning points of these cycles is surprisingly high . . ." (p. 145).

11. For full analysis and derivation of these three series see my [109], [110], [108]. In view of critical commentary on these series by M. Melnyk [187, pp. 485–486], note the following caution about the new series which "should not be regarded as embodying an independent set of measurements." The new series should, rather, "be regarded only as a relatively consistent set of estimates intended to reconcile and link together a conglomeration of independent annual or decennial measurements and primary estimates of building activity or stocks of wealth produced by many collecting agencies both in the State of Ohio and nationwide. Reconciliation at best is approximate and rests upon inferences from information which is often of uncertain quality or relates to relationships which are merely indicated but which cannot be conclusively proven. We can only link data of different character and scope by judgments which sometimes have a margin of error" [110, p. 418]. With these qualifications may I add that the new estimates are *much more reliable* and rest upon a broader base of tested information than any of the alternative series of nonfarm building. The total urban building series is derived from a set of decade nonfarm building aggregates for 1850–90 resulting from the application of Ohio building rates per unit of changes in wealth and nonfarm labor force to nationwide changes in the two measures which themselves were drawn from Census returns. Decade aggregates were then distributed annually for 1860–89 on the basis of decade indexes showing decadal movements as derived from our Ohio annual returns and from building permit indexes developed by Riggleman, Isard and Long, with Ohio returns weighted one-third, not one-quarter as Melnyk mistakenly asserts. See [187, pp. 485–486] and [109, p. 67].

12. [36]. See also [35; 90]. See, for brief review, our Appendix I. For the latest analysis using GNP estimates (of dubious acceptability before 1900) see [69, pp. 279–301].

CHAPTER 8

Demographic and Supply Aspects of Nationwide Building Cycles

A. MARRIAGE RATES

Fortunately for our study, marriage activity has been subjected to intensive analysis on a nationwide basis with regard to short- and long-swing movements. European students were attracted to the use of marriage rates as a significant business cycle indicator that would reach far back into the nineteenth century and provide for many countries comparable time series in standardized units of measurement. Highly formalized techniques of time series decomposition were used to extract long waves and short cycles from annual returns for twelve countries in the period from 1870 to 1913. Growth trends were eliminated by conversion to a per capita basis which, as was noted in our earlier discussion, results in a gross measure of marriage activity. Long waves were extracted by taking an orthogonal function of fifth or higher degree (yielding two or more turns) less a similar function of second degree (yielding one turn). The lower degree function approximated to the underlying movement of marital habits or shifts in age composition. The fifth degree function picks up any secondary waves if they are found in the original series.[1] Chart 8-1 illustrates the relationship between the original series and derived patterns for Great Britain and the Netherlands. In both instances it will be observed that the fifth degree function provided a very close fit; experimentation with functions of higher degree yielded only insignificant improvement [176, pp. 17f.]. The accompanying chart of the relationship of the difference between the values of the fifth degree trend and original values and unemployment rates indicates how accurately the short cyclical component has been isolated and measured apart from longer-wave movements. In some cases the functions were computed from time series pushed back to the

223

CHART 8-1

Marriage Rates, Netherlands and Great Britain, 1870–1913

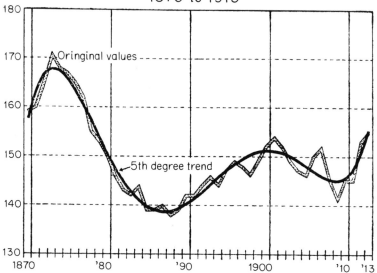

Marriages per 10,000 Population in the Netherlands
1870 to 1913

1850's; but only the segment of computed values for 1870 to 1913 is presented.

Being thus fortified as to the values of the statistical methods used, we present in Chart 8-2 the computed long-wave movements with superimposed short-wave oscillations for twelve countries presented separately and consolidated in three groups: industrial, agricultural, and mixed. The chart is clearly of exceptional interest because of the striking synchronization of wave patterns among the five "industrial" countries of Western and Northern Europe and among the agricultural countries which include the Balkans, Australia, and Italy. Of course the fifth degree function with its two generated long waves does not fit the original data equally well in all cases. Quite clearly the Nordic countries have only a slight tendency toward the "industrial" wave pattern; while the "fit" or dispersion of pattern from experience of the agricultural countries is much greater. However, the long-wave movements are more concordant than the short cyclic movements. Thus, the correlation of the long-wave values for the Netherlands and Great Britain yielded a coefficient of .83; but the short cyclical components were correlated

CHART 8-1
(Concluded)
Great Britain
Observed Values from 1870 to 1913

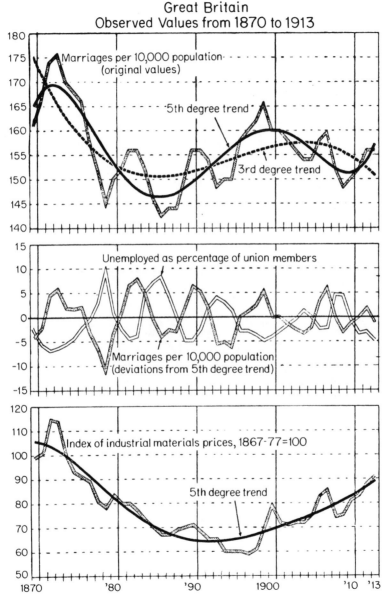

with an index of .29 [176, pp. 68f.]. There seems little doubt that a definite inversion characterized the relationship of marriage rates between agricultural and industrial countries. Precisely this fact may give the clue as to why the United States, which was

CHART 8-2
Long Waves of Marriage Rates: Twelve Countries and Country Groups,
1870–1913

━━━ Long waves
──── Deviations of observed values from 2nd (or 1st) degree trend

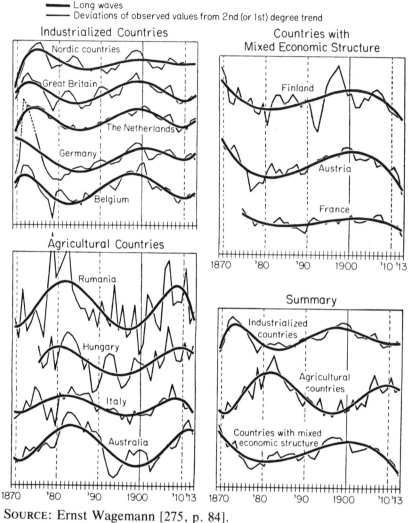

SOURCE: Ernst Wagemann [275, p. 84].

developing both its industry and its agriculture over the surveyed period, exhibits marriage series free from long swings of
any distinct character.

Since these marriage long waves were extracted by complex
mathematical methods, comparison with results reached by a
simple moving average—which leaves in long time trend but
excludes short fluctuations—may be interesting. Moving aver-

ages for five countries are shown in Chart 8-3. They show the same tendency to inversion between England and Australia, the same mild and ambiguous character of the French movement and the parallelism between the German and English movement. The wave patterns extracted by more complex methods are confirmed. We can then go on with the use of our standard techniques to determine amplitude, timing, and other characteristics of marriage wave patterns. The use of these techniques will make easier the comparison of wave movements in marriage

CHART 8-3

Marriage Rates: Five Western Countries, Per Capita Five-Year Moving Average, 1854–1913

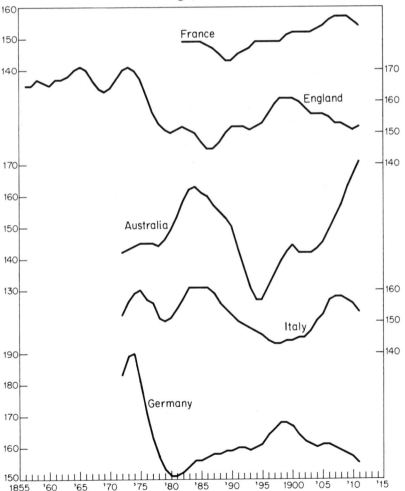

rates and other activities and will thus help to fit marriage wave movements into the complex of movements which make up the long-wave phenomenon.

Data on long marriage rate cycles for six countries are set forth in Table 8-1. Average cycle pattern charts are omitted since amplitude was so slight that patterns of movement are barely discernible. The correlograms are set forth in Chart 8-4.

For both America and England it will be noted that Table 8-1 contains two different sets of data. The English marriage time series runs without a break from 1785 through to 1913. Long-swing characteristics for two long waves after 1870 differ markedly from the two shorter waves between 1816 and 1843. The characteristics of the transition period are also ambiguous: hence separate presentation for the two sets of waves seemed indicated.

In the American case our statistical presentation reflects uncertainties about the validity of the underlying data. The act of marriage in the United States, as in other countries of European settlement, was enmeshed in documentation and ceremony arising from the Church prohibition of clandestine marriage in the Council of Trent and the 1754 English statutory requirement for standardized registry of marriage performances.[2] The tradition of church solemnization carried over to the New World but disestablishment of religion and secular attitudes fostered civil control over marriage. By the middle of the nineteenth century in nearly all of the states and territories a marriage could not take place except with a license issued for a fee by a local civil officer [293, p. 47]. In "nearly all states and territories," a written return of the marriage was required to be filed for legal recording purposes; and in twenty-one states an effort was made to maintain statewide registry or tabulation [293, pp. 61ff.].

Notwithstanding the requirement for written records in most states and territories by the middle of the nineteenth century, the first attempt in the late 1880's to measure marriage activity over a prior twenty-year period was unpromising. An attempt was made to canvass some 2,600 local centers of marriage recording or licensing activity over a twenty-year period, 1867–86. Returns for a third of the counties were not obtainable and there was evident confusion between returns of marriages consummated and licenses issued. Only for five states and the District of Columbia were the returns felt to be complete and fully satisfactory; in nine other states returns were felt to be reliable but were less complete and less satisfactory. The entire marriage report was characterized as "thoroughly incomplete and unsatisfactory" [293, pp. 18, 134–139]. The next attempt at record keeping for the following twenty-year period, 1887–1906, contained a report of the number of marriages by years that was "fairly complete" [264, p. 7]. Still, doubts as to the validity of the statistics carried over, especially for the three decades prior to 1900 when the crude marriage rate "never fell below 8.6 or rose above 9.3," a performance characterized by an outstanding student as "unbelievable" [145, p. 22]. It is presumably because of this haze of statistical doubt that, in his recent study of demographic processes in long swings, Richard Easterlin [78] almost completely neglected statistical analysis of marriage activity.

While the original 1867–86 survey did not produce the desired nationwide enumeration over the twenty-year period, still the returns should hardly be cast aside as unusable. There were, for most of the twenty years, nearly complete returns for eleven states and there were usable partial returns for particular counties in twenty-one additional states.

The present national marriage rates analyzed in Chart 8-5 are derived from these usable returns, reduced by the National Office of Vital Statistics to a per capita basis for the covered jurisdictions. It would have been desirable in extending the partial returns to a nationwide basis that allowance be made for special characteristics of marital behavior by race, region, and degree of urbanization. We doubt, however, that either the level of the estimates or the pattern of fluctuation would have been much affected, though it has already been shown that during the depression of 1873–77 marriage rates had a wider range of movement for areas of greater industrialization [288, pp. 83f., 135f.]. Some differences in marriage rates could well persist because of changes during this period in the character of immigration, as well as the intensification of industrialization, and the offsetting marriage patterns among the agricultural and industrial populations. A very striking correlation was achieved between marriage rate activities over the years in question in a set of six states with preponderantly industrial populations and a suitable measure of business-cycle performance [248, p. 62]. A comparison of the two long-cycle patterns for the nationwide

TABLE 8-1

National Summary Measures, Long Cycles, Per Capita Marriage
Rates, Five Areas
(Series number given below area)

Item	Units	Total[a] or Mean	Italy (0280)
A. Totals			
1. Number of areas		5	
2. Number of specific long cycles		10.5	2.5
3. Number of turning points (TP):			
a. Matched		24	4
b. Unmatched		2	1
B. Mean values			
4. Full specific duration	Years	19.8	15.0
5. Specific cycle amplitude			
a. Full	Cycle relatives	36.52	35.0
b. Full per year	"	1.87	2.33
c. Fall per year	"	−2.30	−2.05
6. Full reference amplitude	"	16.70	10.0
7. Lead-lag (LL) TP:			
a. LL	Years	−1.07	2.25
b. Average deviation	"	2.02	2.75
8. LL reference pattern	"	− .20	3.80
9. Optimal serial correlation, trend adjusted			
a. LL	Years	−3.0	n.a.
b. Correlation coefficient		.716	n.a.
10. Per cent change Average annual rate successive average long cycle standings	%	− .9	−4.0

n.a.—not available.

[a] Exclusive of Ohio and counting Nationwide U.S. rather than 6 States where available.

[b] Reference cycles.

[c] For short specific cycles.

[d] Not marriage rates but number of marriages.

		England		United States		
Germany (0278)	Australia (0277)	1854– 1914 (0282)	1810– 50 (0302)	6-States (0281)	Nation- wide (0281-A)	Ohio[d] (0146)
2.5	1.5	2	2[b]	2	4[b]	3[b]
6	4	5		5		
0	1	0		0		
16.0	25.5	25.5		17.0		
21.2	57.7	28.7		40.0		
1.33	2.22	1.13		2.35		
−1.52	−2.74	−1.42		−3.76		
14.2	21.9	15.0	11.6	21.2	27.5	26.1
−1.33	−5.25	−1.80		.80		
2.00	1.75	1.76		1.84		
−2.30	−4.35	0	.90	.75		0
−3.00	−2.0	−4.0			−3.0	−1.0
.705	.855	.625			.679	.623
+2.1	+2.0	−4.7	−4.2	+3.5		1.427[c]

CHART 8-4

Correlogram of Marriage Rates, Five Countries (Trend Adjusted)

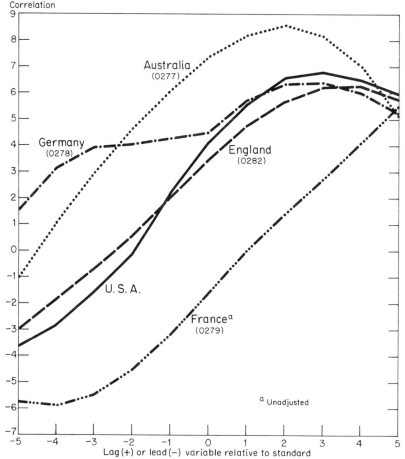

and six-state basis, as shown in Chart 8-5, shows nearly perfect stability in the nationwide index and a mild but clear-cut cyclical pattern in the six-state index. Other investigators, too, have noticed that in the more industrialized and urbanized regions a significant decline in marriage rates was exhibited during the 1870's [288, pp. 83f., 135f.].

On the agricultural side quite different patterns of movement were exhibited. So far as short cycles are concerned, investigators of the social effects on marriage and demographic phenomena have conclusively established that nuptiality rates of agricultural populations do not respond to short business-cycle

CHART 8-5
Patterns of Successive and Average Long Cycles, Per Capita Marriage
Rates, U.S. Nationwide and Six-State Composite

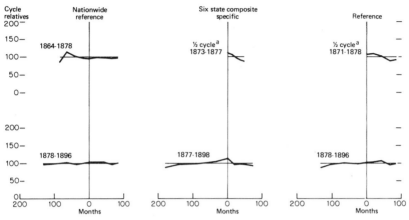

[a]Inverted base.

influences [275, p. 81; 249, pp. 107, 161; 125, p. 153, n. 5; 17, p.
100; 227, pp. 52–62; 76, I, pp. 282–285, 527–532]. So far as
long-swing movements are concerned, for non-American populations the tendency for divergent rhythms of countries predominantly agricultural and industrial was clearly demonstrated
for the period 1870–1914 in the data depicted in Chart 8-2. Over
the same period we can document on the American scene the
tendency for inverted movements in agricultural and industrial
activity. During the two nationwide reference
expansions—1878–92 and 1897–1909—agricultural rates of
growth of land enclosed in farms, physical capital increments,
and income increments were retarded; and during two nationwide reference contractions—the 1870's and the
1890's—agricultural growth was accelerated.[3] Ohio farmers responded positively in their mortgage takings and building to long
waves (see Chap. 4, section D, p. 104). But nationwide agriculture
responded inversely. Patterns of farm agricultural activity must
have extended to vital processes of population composition and
renewal and thus been reflected in corresponding patterns of
marriage activity. The relatively large role of American farm
population even during the closing decades of the nineteenth
century—in 1870 and 1900 farm population amounted to 56.3 and
41.1 per cent of our total population and a higher fraction of

marriageable youth—would thus have ensured the near erasing in the nationwide index of marriage activity of any tendency to long-swing fluctuation exhibited by the industrial population. Quite possibly, these divergent and neutralizing tendencies for long-swing movements in agriculture and industry respectively were perhaps responsible for the striking finding of Simon Kuznets that "the difference in timing between the long swings of population-sensitive components and of other capital formation, which prevailed until World War I, resulted in so much cancellation that the comprehensive capital formation totals fail to reveal distinct long swings" [161, p. 351].

Our nationwide marriage rates were not only affected in all countries by the mixture of agricultural and industrial populations but also by the scale and nature of migratory movements. We have previously noted that migrating individuals increasingly through the nineteenth and twentieth centuries were in the main young unmarried adults (see Chapter 5, p. 114). As a migratory wave swept into a country it would enrich marriage potential. Conversely it would depress per capita marriage rates in the sending countries. A migratory wave thus shifts the locations of the marriage event even when it does not affect true marriage activity and dislocates the marriage patterns of two countries. Since migration tends to generate sex disparities in both sending and receiving countries, it would tend to reduce international net marriage rates; but by optimizing the fit of job opportunities and labor power it tends to increase net marriage rates. Perhaps the two "net" effects cancel off; in any case they have varied in importance over time and place. Certainly the magnitude of the effect of migration on gross rates will greatly overshadow the more variable influence of migration on net rates.

An effort was made for the United States and for Great Britain to gauge the quantitative influence of immigrant flow on marriage potential for the four decades between 1870 and 1910. The procedure of estimation differed with the two countries. For America it was convenient to attempt to estimate the relative contribution to the Census total population count at the 20–29 age bracket by persons arriving in the country by immigration in the particular decade.

Basic data were derived from the Census returns of the 20–29 age brackets adjusted to allow for aging and for distribution of foreign-born by decade of arrival. The form of the English data permitted a direct comparison of the relative proportion of unmarried adult net migration to the stock of unmarried adults between 18 and 44 years of age. Details of estimation are presented in Appendix G and relevant results of estimation are presented in Table 8-2.

The results, I believe, indicate that waves of migration left a small imprint on marriage potential in both countries but that both absolute level and variation of the influence of migration on marriage rates were greater in the United States than in England and Wales. Over the four decades net immigration to the United States amounted to 12.1 per cent of resident population in the 20–29 age bracket; the corresponding share of net emigration in England and Wales to unmarried adult class was much smaller, 2.7 per cent. The absolute level of migration is not, in this

TABLE 8-2

Estimated Migration Net and Marriage Potential England and Wales and United States 1870–1910

(In thousand persons)

		1870's	*1880's*	*1890's*	*1900's*
I.	England and Wales unmarried adults aged 18–45:				
	1. Total estimated net emigration[a]	78	296	32	221
	2. Mid-decade population[b]	4,345	5,219	6,275	7,239
	3. Ratio line (1/2)	1.8%	5.7%	0.5%	3.1%
II.	United States population 20–29 age bracket:				
	4. Estimated net new immigrant arrivals[a]	693	1,440	1,144	2,307
	5. All other U.S. population[a]	8,475	9,985	12,661	14,848
	6. Ratio line (4/5)	9.6%	15.6%	10.0%	16.8%

[a] See Appendix G.
[b] Compiled from General Register Office [99, Summary Tables, pp. 126–127]. The returns for the 15–20 year bracket were distributed 3/5 to under 18 and 2/5 to 18–20.

context, important; important rather is the variation in the level. In the case of England and Wales variation in migration from one decade to another affected between 2.6 and 5.2 per cent of marriage potential. In the American case the range was somewhat greater, between 5.6 and 6.8 per cent. Since the total reference amplitude of English gross marriage rates was only 15.0 per cent, the influence of migration would appear to be limited to a fourth of reference variation. And this influence would be felt only if variations in emigration would induce proportionate changes in gross rates of marriage.

In the American case the relative influence of migratory waves on long-swing amplitude of marriage rates was greater both because the percentage range of decade fluctuation in migration was greater and because specific amplitude, so far as this is indicated, was less than in the British case. If we take the only two reference long swings unaffected by a major war and substantially coterminous with the migration waves with which we are here concerned—1871–1909—the indicated specific and reference amplitude of 23.0 and 12.2 respectively are appreciably less than corresponding English amplitudes. Recorded fluctuation in net migration additions to the most eligible age-brackets would have accounted for one-half the reference, and for a good third of the specific, American marriage rate amplitude.

While it was not feasible to attempt to gauge the quantitative importance of immigration flows in marriage rate long-swing amplitude for other countries, for both Germany and Australia an appreciable influence is indicated. This means that true amplitude of long-swing variation in marriage rates would be scaled down by some 10 or 20 per cent from the magnitudes shown in our table.

While scaled down in amplitude the variation in marriage rates over long swings tells an extremely significant story. Marriage rates are sensitive to changes in work and earning opportunities for dependent populations. Within a limited range, impairment of these opportunities leads to deferral; improvement, to acceleration of marriage decisions. Continued deferment over an extended period, such as the full length of long-swing contractions, would require an unusually strong impairment of living conditions and income deterioration. Hence even a slight persistent decline in marriage rates over a period as long as our reference contractions, with a mean duration of nearly eight years, gives witness that these reference contractions have been associated with a significant impairment of mass urban opportunities for work and welfare.

B. MIGRATION

We have seen that nationwide marriage rates respond only slightly in absolute terms to the long-wave movement that runs through the industrial economy of the nineteenth and twentieth centuries. It is quite different, however, with migratory flows. As was the case in local cycles, these fluctuate in prominent long swings which develop extraordinary amplitude, rivaling that of building activity. The role that these migratory flows play in long swings has been intensively investigated in the work of Cairncross, Brinley Thomas, Kuznets, and Abramovitz. We seek to extend these investigations at this point in our study by bringing under formal analysis the migration experience of Germany, England-Wales, and the United States.

These countries were selected for detailed study partly because data for these countries is more readily available and partly because the real estate and building experience of these three countries has been consulted so frequently in this study. Two of the countries illustrate the way migration influences "senders" or countries of emigration; the other country, the United States, illustrates the way migration influences "receivers" or countries of immigration.

The English migration experience is grouped in two sets of years. During the first set, 1816–49, all outgoing passengers to extra-European countries leaving from all ports of embarkation in Great Britain including Ireland were included in the statistical returns, thus providing an all-British emigration series. From 1853 onward accurate annual statistics became available of the outward movement of residents of England and Wales and these statistics are used in our analysis. It would have been more satisfactory to have analyzed English migratory experience on a uniform basis. However, this duality of treatment proved expedient for a number of reasons. First, identification of national origin was only attempted in migration statistics in 1825 and identification was very imperfect. Up through 1843 American reports indicate that the Irish provided somewhat over two-thirds of the over-all British outward migration.[4] But the pattern of movement of the Irish exodus paralleled that of the English.[5] Then, too, our reference cycle chronology for the earlier period closes with 1843, i.e., well before the burst of Irish emigration which would have grossly distorted our patterns. As it was convenient to use an all-British emigration series from 1816 onward so it proved convenient to shift to an English and Welsh emigration series for the period after 1854. The special secular drift of the Irish emigration in the last half of the nineteenth century would have impressed itself on our patterns though there was no corresponding influence felt in the English industrial economy. Our marriage and other data for the later years in Great Britain all referred to England in the narrower sense, including Wales but excluding Ireland and Scotland. For these reasons the less inclusive time series of British emigration statistics was analyzed for the second half of the nineteenth century.

The predominant receiving country for both the German and British emigration of the period concerned was of course the United States, which was, however, not the only area that attracted emigrants. As the nineteenth century advanced, other areas challenged the American lead partly through the aid of the mid-century Australian gold discoveries and the completion of the Canadian Pacific Railway in 1886 [254, pp. 178–192; 158, II, pp. 13, 95; 150].

In the earlier years of the nineteenth century, immigration not only responded to favorable industrial labor markets but also provided opportunities for experienced farmers to settle the fertile lands of the New World. Hence, Jerome found that before 1860 fluctuations in immigration were not "closely" aligned to changes in industrial conditions although there was "some tendency for the effects of a depression to be evident in immigration after a period of time somewhat irregular in duration" [146, p. 82]. His record of cycles in imports and immigration exhibits a wide range of relationships before 1870 ranging from the inverted to the positive [146, Chart 10]. We have calculated correlation coefficients by subperiods. It is indicated that before 1860 the correlation between immigration and imports was weak and inverted and involved immigration leading imports. After the Civil War timing increasingly became concurrent and quite strong.[6]

Using less comprehensive measures for a shorter period, Brinley Thomas also finds evidence of a "structural change" before and after the Civil War in the relation between immigration and economic conditions. Before the Civil War immigration lagged behind building and railway construction and was heavily influenced by conditions in Ireland and Germany as well as by the famous California gold discoveries.[7] Manifestly, before the Civil War the "pulling power" of America on immigration did not so closely correspond with changes in industrial labor markets as after 1870.

In any case American "pulling power" was supplemented by gravitational force exerted by internal conditions in migrating countries.[8] If these influences corresponded—so that the migrating country tended to expel at the same time that America attracted—then building and economic growth movements in the two countries would become inverted. Under such conditions reference cycle patterns of migration—analyzed on chronologies of the sending country—will be inverted, i.e., migration will fall in (domestic) reference building expansions and rise in (domestic) reference building contractions. The same migration, showing up as an in-migrant wave in the receiving country, would exhibit positive cycle patterns.

But if long-wave movements of countries of emigration and immigration are not inverted but are in phase then the gravitational field of migrational flows will be dispersed. When migrants are needed at home emigration signals will be favorable. And when conditions are more deteriorated at home, they may also look less favorable abroad. Under such conditions migratory movement will be governed by the relative strength of the respective pulls and pushes, by the momentum of past movements, by structural disparities in levels of living, and by special circumstances or events. There is no reason why these forces should be distributed over the decades according to a set pattern. Hence, when phase movements of building and growth waves of centers of emigration and immigration correspond, then actual migratory flows are likely to become irregular in behavior. This tendency to irregularity will be greater with regard to the considerable migration oriented to farm settlement or to exploitation of new mineral discoveries. Precisely this tendency toward aggravated irregularity was found by Allen

Kelly in his regression measure of the influence of unemployment conditions in England and Australia on Australian net immigration during 1865–1935.[9]

For the three countries—Great Britain, the United States, and Germany—for which detailed migration experience was analyzed, a comparison of in-step and out-of-step phase movements is provided in Table 8-3. To make this comparison, the all-construction U.S. chronology was utilized and the English chronology for the gap between 1843–57 was filled in by an estimated peak in 1852. Use of turning-point zones would have rendered the pattern of movement more accurately but delimitation of these zones involved questionable judgments and the simplest procedure seemed indicated.

Year-by-year phase comparison indicates that at no time were movements completely inverted or completely parallel. Divergences in timing and "extra cycles" generated by special conditions would produce out of phase alignment even for corresponding movements. German movements were shorter, since her ten turning points covered only 73 years, while the ten American and English turning points covered 91 and 87 years,

TABLE 8-3

Number of Years German and English Long Swings Were in Phase
with American—1821–1912

	1821–61		1862–1913	
	No.	Per Cent	No.	Per Cent
1. England:				
a. Years in phase	23	56.1	19	37.3
b. Years out of phase	18	43.9	32	62.7
c. Number of turning points used	6[a]		4	
2. Germany:				
a. Years in phase	7	31.8	24	47.1
b. Years out of phase	15	68.2	27	52.9
c. Number of turning points used	3[b]		7	
3. U.S.:				
Number of turning points used	5		5	

SOURCE: Chronologies listed in Chapter 1, Table 1-1, with British peak estimated for 1852. Tabulation was cut off with 1912 rather than 1913.

[a] Beginning with 1825.

[b] Beginning with 1840.

respectively. There was a tendency for shorter German waves *after* and shorter British waves *before* 1861 while American waves ran a more steady course.[ ]

But while conforming and opposing tendencies were intermixed there was a considerable shift after 1861 in both English and German patterns. Before 1861 English waves tended on balance to conform with the American and the German tended more nearly to invert.[10] After 1861 the German rhythm followed the American more closely while the English shifted to the predominantly inverted status. These long-wave synchronizations bear little relationship to short cyclical synchronizations in which for the post-1870 period extraordinarily close German-English solidarity is indicated with divergent U.S. timing.[11]

Our tabular results confirm the well-established pattern of inversion between building and growth waves in the United States and the United Kingdom between 1870–1914 and a lesser degree of inversion and a more confused relationship for 1820–60.[12]

C. MIGRATION PATTERNS

We now examine the three sets of migration cycle patterns and associated tabular measures (Table 8-4). The British experience is detailed in Charts 8-6 and 8-7; the German and American experience, in Charts 8-8 and 8-9. As expected, the patterns indicate a disturbed field of long cyclical experience, especially for the earlier cycles. The British building boom and growth wave that came to a head in 1836 and reached a trough in 1843 found little reflection in records of American immigration, though there was some retardation with a quick pickup (Chart 8-9). So too the British migration patterns through the 1860's exhibit considerable diversity of form (see the cycle patterns in the charts for 1816–32, 1832–43, and 1854–73, and 1861–77). The tendency to inversion is predominant in British reference patterns but more consistently in domestic reference contractions than domestic reference expansions. In only three out of sixteen reference contraction stages did emigration turn down. If we had analyzed the 1843–59 transition with a likely cycle chronology, the whole of what would have been reference contraction would have shown a steady rise in emigration, which of course is the mark of an inversion pattern. But reference expansion periods

TABLE 8-4

Summary Measures, National Long Cycles, Migration

Item	Units	Total or Mean	Germany (0310)	U.S. (0312)	Great Britain (0301)	England and Wales (0311)
Totals						
Number of series		4	4	5	2	3
Number of specific long cycles		14				
Number of turning points (TP):						
a. Matched		25	5	11	5	4
b. Unmatched		5	2	2	0	1
Mean values						
Full specific duration	Years	17.2	12.5	22.0	15.0	19.3
Specific cycle amplitude:	Cycle relatives					
a. Full	"	273.5	212.3	361.2	309.9	210.5
b. Full per year	"	16.61	16.98	16.42	22.13	10.89
c. Fall per year	"	−15.92	−14.58	−18.19	−22.71	−8.21
Full reference amplitude		155.2	120.6	177.5	173.7	149.1
Secular weighted average growth per year[a]	%		−3.329	−1.723	8.880[b]	n.a.
Lead-lag (LL) TP:	Years					
a. LL	"	−.41	−1.2[c]	−.90[c]	1.20	−.75[b]
b. Average deviation	"	2.03	2.16	2.08	2.64	1.25
LL reference pattern	"	.93	−.85[c]	−.75[c]	−.90	6.20

n.a.—not available.

[a] Per year change in mean annual standings long cycles, mean of positive and inverted bases.

[b] Taken from [97, p. 943].

[c] The correlogram with inverted timing optimized at zero lead-lag. r = .600.

CHART 8-6
Long Cycle Patterns, Migration to Non-European Countries, Great
Britain, 1816–1843

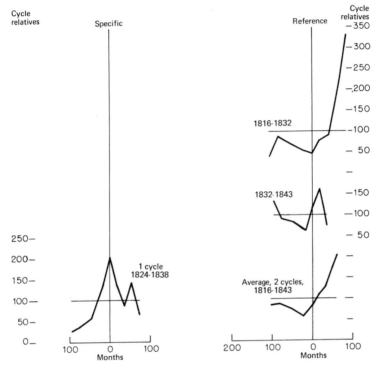

were not so consistent. In only six out of fifteen stages was
behavior conforming as it would have been through part of the
expansion period of an 1843–59 chronology. This indicates
possibly that in reference contractions domestic expelling influence is potent but that in reference expansions attractive power
is less potent and easily offset by overseas opportunities. The
one reference expansion that ran most of its course in opposition
to the American movement—1886–99—readily exhibits a truly
inverted emigration cycle pattern.

The German patterns (see Chart 8-8) also exhibit a disturbed
course of migration experience with a predominant tendency to
inversion. The locus of disturbance seems to fall more in
reference contractions than expansions. In only four out of
twelve expansion stages was there a conforming movement;
while there were conforming movements in seven contraction
stages. Apparently domestic expansions exerted attractive

CHART 8-7

Patterns of Successive Specific and Reference Long Cycles and Their
Averages, British Emigration Overseas, 1859–1913

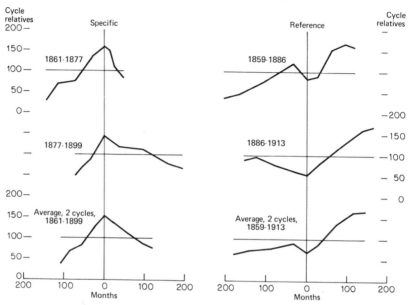

power while domestic reference contractions had relatively
weak expelling power. These inferences regarding primacy in
migration experience of Germany and England are made on the
basis of simple rankings of stage directions of movement.
Possibly, influence could be more successfully decomposed by
multiple correlation.

The wide diversity of shapes assumed by the American
reference—and even the specific—patterns illustrates the disturbed field of migration experience as it impacts on a receiving
country with mixed agricultural and industrial growth trends.
We note the very short decline in the first cycle pattern, the long
lead both at peak and trough of the second pattern, and in
general the individualized character of all the patterns. Some
remnant, however, was preserved of that marked decennial
rhythm which bifurcated our local and citywide reference patterns, particularly between 1878 and 1918 (see pp. 117 ff.).
The average six-cycle reference pattern is consequently very
unrepresentative.

CHART 8-8
Patterns of Successive Specific and Reference Long Cycles and Their Averages, German Overseas Migration, 1862–1913

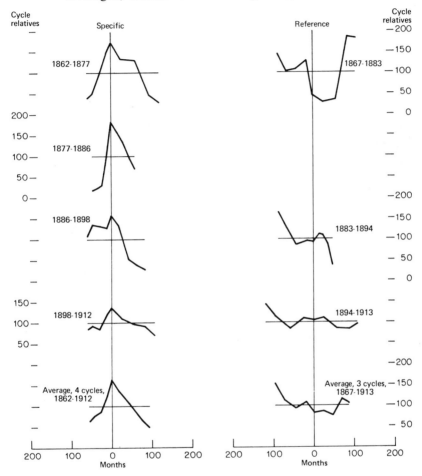

D. SUMMARY

Rates of per capita marriage for twelve countries between 1870 and 1914 were found in 1931 by Ernst Wagemann to exhibit in systematic clear-cut form our long waves in positive form for predominantly industrial, and in inverted form for predominantly agricultural, countries. His technique of time series decomposition—by use of orthogonal functions—was confirmed by use of other techniques including correlogram and National Bureau nine-stage cycle patterns. Specific total amplitudes were

CHART 8-9
Patterns of Successive Specific and Reference Long Cycles and Their
Averages, U.S. Immigration, 1823–1933

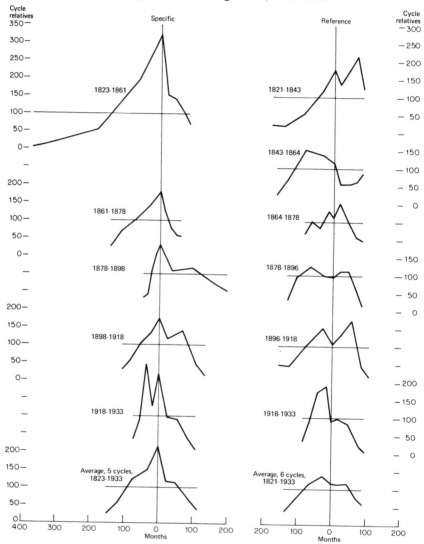

exceptionally low, averaging only 36.5 relative cycles for 10.5
long specific cycles, and due to timing variability this amplitude
eroded by more than half, to 16.7 cycle relatives on a reference
basis. Except for an agricultural country such as Italy the
tendency to lead between two to four years was exhibited by all
the surveyed areas.

The low amplitude is in part the result of elimination from the marriage series of the upward trend resulting from population growth; and in part it reflects the influence in the nationwide aggregate of the agricultural populations. Changes in agricultural conditions dominated nationwide marriage rate statistics for all major countries at the beginning of the nineteenth century and were important factors for America, France, Italy, and elsewhere at the close of the century. Economic advance in American agriculture on a nationwide basis was retarded when industry spurted ahead and vice versa. Hence, any mixture of agricultural and industrial influences would dampen American amplitudes.

Some of the marriage amplitude is derived from the migration of young unmarried adults seeking improved conditions of life. Analysis of the interplay of migration and marriage behavior for the United States and England and Wales between 1870 and 1910 indicated that perhaps one-half and one-quarter, respectively, of the total reference marriage amplitudes could be traced to migration. Because of the resistance to continued deferment of marriage even this slight sensitivity of marriage rates in our industrial-agricultural composites is significant.

Nationwide migration, unlike marriage rates, exhibits long-wave movements that developed extraordinary amplitude rivaling that of building activity proper. Domestic building expansions are associated with growing cities and expanding employment opportunities. Hence, it was assumed that in reference expansions industrial emigration is discouraged and immigration attracted and vice versa in reference contractions. If countries invert in their building patterns, then "push" and "pull" are synchronized; if countries move together in their building cycles, then "push" and "pull" conflict and the resultant net flow will measure the stronger influence on industrial populations. Migration oriented to agricultural settlement will respond to other influences including crop conditions, land distribution programs, and land settlement facilities. Before 1860, American immigration was predominantly oriented to agricultural settlement; after 1860, the industrial influence became paramount.

Our analysis of gravitational influence of "push" and "pull" for the United States, United Kingdom, and Germany was made partly by counting the years of corresponding phase. Taking the American chronology as standard, between 1821 and 1861

English long swings were out of phase with the American swings 44 per cent of the time; and German long swings, 68 per cent of the time. After 1860 tendencies to inversion became more important in England and less important in Germany. Since long swings both before and after 1860 ran separate courses with different durations in the three countries, they were never completely in or out of phase and gravitational influence on migration was usually more or less dispersed. In English or German cycle phases where dispersion was minimized the reference cycles showed a clear-cut inverted form with near concurrent timing or a short lead. At stages or in phases where dispersion was maximized, the tendency to inversion was impeded and our cycle patterns became irregular in timing and form. So also the American reference patterns for immigration responded weakly to our first reference contraction during 1836–43 because the course of agricultural settlement and immigration oriented to it was not adversely affected. Because of these composite irregularities, total reference amplitude for our three countries was only 57 per cent of its total specific amplitude. Also one turning point out of six was unmatched. However, despite disturbance, a primary tendency to lead shows up on most of our measures.

NOTES

1. The technical methods used to extract the short and long patterns were set forth in [176]. On orthogonal functions generally, see [68, pp. 434 f.].
2. See [92, 229ff.; 160, p. 384].
3. I cite the following decade increments collected from Alvin S. Tostlebe [255, pp. 50–51, 101, 135].

	Unit	*1910*	*1870's*	*1880's*	*1890's*
1. Additions to physical capital, real estate	billions of dollars	10–14	8.1	5.9	6.6
2. 5-year average gross farm income	billions of dollars		1.30	.98	1.25
3. Land in acres	million acres		128.4	87.1	40.2

4. British statistics did not distinguish nationality of passenger regardless of port of embarkation but before 1850 between 71 and 72 per cent of American immigrants of British nationality were of Irish extraction. This percentage shows up by annual count from 1820 to 1843 of incoming passengers to the

United States [see 262, p. 57]; for the distribution of foreign-born counted in the 1850 Census, see [250, p. 96].

5. See charts of emigration from the United Kingdom and separately from England and Wales in [51, Diagram B, C, pp. 21, 22].

6. *Coefficient of Correlation Immigration and Commodity Imports (Standard Deviation Units from Trend):*

	1823–60	1866–1900	1901–23
Concurrent timing	.108	.755	.670
Immigration leading 1 year	.373	.557	.000
Immigration lagging 1 year	.254	.124	.000
Regression coefficient highest correlation	−.297	.767	.826
	(.115)	(.113)	(.188)

7. [245, pp. 93 ff., 116 f., 159 ff.]. Timing relationships at turning points (p. 93 f.) was confirmed by lead-lag correlation analysis (p. 159 f.) which clearly showed the 1870 breaking-point (really 1864–90 zone). (See his detailed Appendix 2, pp. 253–262.)

8. [278, p. 198]. For a generalized evaluation of "push" and "pull" in international migration, see [237, pp. 45 f.].

9. [150, p. 342.]. W. D. Borrie in his illuminating report noted that "until about the 1860's the "push" of land scarcity in Europe was strongly reinforced by the "pull" of cheap land in the New World . . . " [26, p. 4].

10. This burst of German migration in three years alone, 1853–55, carried almost half a million persons out of Germany annually. In some regions of the Rhineland, population diminished (Hesse, Würtemberg, and Baden). The German migration wave took off in 1843 and reproduced the pattern of the U.S. growth wave of that period. See [88, II, pp. 334ff., 347f.]; German building waves before 1867 are only tentatively suggested on the basis of behavior in Berlin, Bremen, and in the price series.

11. See on this score the intensive investigation of Oscar Morgenstern [194, Chap. 2]. He found that in 90.2 per cent of the 419 months between September 1879 and August 1914 German and English short cycle phases were in unison while each was in unison with the American phase 64.9 per cent and 62.3 per cent, respectively (p. 49). For interest rates short and long the phase coordination is more equal (see pp. 113, 456). If interest rates are not merely compared at turning points but over their full range by correlation analysis, German-English solidarity and American "isolation" is again indicated (pp. 165, 395); for comparison in "share" prices, see p. 533.

12. Though this inversion was indicated by Cooney and Cairncross, it was classically elucidated by Brinley Thomas [245, Chap. 11]. Thomas thought that inversion could be traced back to 1847 and other writers have suggested it goes back to the 1820's. For discussion of these claims see [117; 66]. Our tabulation suggests, however, that a degree of inversion and convergent movement persisted and that only the relative balance shifted. The pattern of experience between 1832 and 1850 was generally shared. Since Britain experienced three wave movements between 1816 and 1859 while the United States experienced

only two (1821–1861), tendencies to overlap and inversion shifted. Then, too, in the 1850's a plateaued movement developed in both countries. Thus we agree with Habakkuk that "there was no regular alternation between British and American building fluctuations" [116, p. 204] before 1870 but with Lewis we shy away from finding in Britain only standard business cycles and not long swings.

Appendix A

Text, tables, and chart appear on microfiche. See inside back cover.

Note: All Appendix notes are to be found immediately follow-ing Appendix J.

Appendix B

Series Number	Title and Source

0001-
0009
Number of houses erected or for which building plans were approved: for various municipalities, Great Britain.
Source: Basic work sheet of B. Weber of annual entries for number of residential houses "erected" or "planned" in thirty-four cities. For description of sources and methods used see [284, pp. 107–8, 129 f.]. The annual entries are the original crude data adjusted to a calendar year basis and made available for this research by A. K. Cairncross.

0010
Percentage of Unoccupied Dwelling Houses, London.
Source: Calculated by J. C. Spensley, as given in [46, Table 32, p. 153].

0011
Value of Plans Passed for Warehouses, Stores and Workshops, Glasgow, Great Britain, 1873–1936.
Source: From NBER file 2,71b; Office of Public Works, City Chamber of Glasgow. Memorandum of Linnings Granted by the Dean of Guild Court.

0012
Permits Granted for New Streets, Glasgow, Great Britain.
Source: From NBER file 2,71c; same as for 0011.

0013
Percentage of Unoccupied Dwelling Houses, Glasgow, Great Britain.
Source: [46, Table I, p. 16].

0014
Average Cost per Room, Residential Building, Glasgow, Great Britain.
Source: [46, p. 16].

0015
Number (in thousands) of Houses Erected in Great Britain, 1856–1950.
Source: [284, Appendix, p. 131, col. 2].

Series
Number   Title and Source
0016   Brick Production, Great Britain.
        Source: From NBER file 2,72; [231, pp. 316–17].
0017   Imports of Deals and Fir Timber, Great Britain.
        Source: [11, Table 10, p. 188].
0018   Urban Residential Building Index (1890 = 100), Germany.
        Source: See Appendix H.
0019   Building Materials Price Index (1913 = 100), Germany.
        Source: [144, p. 82].
0020   Index of Cost of Building (1890–99 = 100), Germany.
        Source: Unweighted average of index relatives (1890 = 100) of our series 0019 and average hourly wage rates of building workers (three cities) 1871–1913 [34, p. 335].
0021   Net Change Mortgage Holdings Prussian Urban Savings Banks (Sparkasse) and All-German Mortgage Banks (Hypothekenbanken).
        Source: [136, p. 61, cols. 2, 9]. Hunscha data extended only to 1870. The series was extended back to 1864 on the basis of a mortgage lending series in [219, Table XXII, p. 143].
0022   Net Construction Dwelling Units, Berlin, Germany, 1841–1894 (new construction minus demolition).
        Source: [219, Table XIII, pp. 134–35]. From 1896–1909, linked (in NBER file 2,81) to comparable series from [15, p. 303].
0023   Number Vacant Dwelling Units, Berlin, Germany.
        Source: [219, Table III, p. 126 for years 1841–95; Table V, p. 128 for years 1896–1910].
0024   Net Annual Migration, Berlin, Germany.
        Source: [219, Table I, p. 124, col. 3, "Mehrzuzug"].
0025   Average Annual Rental per Occupied Dwelling Unit, Berlin, Germany.
        Source: For the years 1841–95 Total Rent Income (Mietwert) was divided by number of occupied dwelling units [219, Table II, p. 126, cols. 2, 4]. The division was performed by Reich but inaccurately (see her col. 6 "Mietwert einer Wohnung"). Rents were extrapolated to 1909 on the basis of index relatives

Series Number	Title and Source

derived from a related series [219, Table V, p. 128, col. 4, "Nutzertrag der im Laufe des Jahres benützt. Wohn. und Gelasse"].

0026   Fire Insurance Values as Per Cent of Selling Price of Sold Properties, Berlin, Germany.
Source: [219, Table XVIII, p. 137].

0027   Mortgage Loan Recordings, ("Eintragungen") Berlin, Germany.
Source: [219, Table XX, p. 139, col. 1].

0028   Forced Sales, Berlin, Germany.
Source: [219, Tables XVII, XVIII, pp. 137–38]. From 1867 to 1906 series represents the number of forced sales in improved property ("Zwangsversteigerung," col. 4). To this was linked in 1868 by use of index relatives an overlapping series of "Subhastationen" (sheriff sales) (col. 3) for 1843–68.

0029   Number of Vacant Dwellings as Per Cent of All Dwellings, Hamburg, Germany.
Source: [136, p. 60, col. 7, "Anzahl in v.H. Aller Lokalitäten"].

0030   Net Annual Change Dwelling Stock, Hamburg, Germany.
Source: [136, p. 60, col. 14, "Lokalitäten überhaupt"].

0031   Average Annual Occupied Dwelling Rental, Hamburg, Germany.
Source: [136, p. 60, col. 9 "je Lokalität in Gebrauch"].

0032   Average Annual Rental of Unoccupied Dwellings, Hamburg, Germany.
Source: [136, p. 60, col. 10, "je Lokalität leerstehend"].

0033   Number of Non-Residential Buildings Constructed, Hamburg, Germany.
Source: From NBER file 2,81e; [121, 1890, p. 87; 1920, pp. 131–32; 1925, p. 114; 1935/36, p. 70].

0034   Number of Residential Buildings Erected in Bremen, Germany.
Source: From NBER file 2,81h; [30]. The years 1855–1911 and 1902–35 are from two different official agencies, both segments being simultaneously re-

Series
Number   Title and Source

ported. Years 1855–1911 are new buildings (residential) erected; 1902–37 are new residential buildings inspected and approved. For 1902–27, second segment also in [29, p. 31]; for 1932 see [31, Dec. 1932, p. 345]; for 1933–35, see [32].

0035   Building Activity Index (1909–13 = 100), Paris, France.

Source: [93]; supplemented by private communication to M. Gottlieb supplying index numbers. The index was derived from building materials used.

0036   Real Estate Price Index Residential Property, Net of Depreciation (1939 = 100), Paris, France.

Source: Index derived from index relatives of price change for structurally identical residential properties sold twice or more within a set of successive 20-year periods. The individual indexes for a given year were lined up in an array from which was selected the median of the interquartile range. The medians were joined by a three- to five-year moving average. Allowance was then made for depreciation calculated from prices of property per square meter sold in 1939, classified by period of construction. This yielded a value shrinkage per decade of 23.08 per cent though a more "moderate" decade allowance of only 16.7 per cent was finally used. As presented here, the gross index of sale price was adjusted or "rectified" by allowance for depreciation. For details see [75, pp. 170–79].

0036-1   Residential Vacancy Rate, Paris, France.

Source: Statistical estimates on the percentage of vacant to total dwelling units were available between 1879 and 1913 for six years from census surveys, for 22 years and 10 years, respectively, by two types of property taxation, "la contribution foncière" and "la contribution mobilière." Using estimates from "la contribution foncière" as a base, an index of uncertain quality was pieced out. Data was graphed in the article by Flaus [93] and actual data communicated in a letter to M. Gottlieb.

Series
Number | Title and Source
0037 | Annual Tax on Number of New Residential Buildings, Paris, France (Fluctuations du principal de l'impot foncièr relatif aux maisons nouvellement construites). *Source:* Albert Aftalion, by private communication, from tax administration as disclosed in [6, p. 13]. Series extended to 1914 on the basis of a parallel series of number of new buildings constructed, NBER file 2,77.
0038 | Number of Marriages, Stockholm, Sweden. *Source:* For 1867–93, [264]; for 1894–1948, [241, Table 39, p. 41].
0039 | Permits Residential Building Rooms, Stockholm, Sweden. *Source:* [241, Table 132, p. 124, col. 9 (Summa eldstäder)].
0040 | Vacancy Rate, Stockholm, Sweden. *Source:* [241, p. 124, col. 28 (Ledighetsprocent. Eldstäder)].
0041 | Number of New Rooms Added, Sweden. *Source:* [139, Part II, Table 109, p. 340, col. 8, "The Statistically Recorded Production of Dwelling Houses"].
0048 | Number Permits New Building, Montreal, Canada. *Source:* [35, pp. 140–41].
0049 | Index Urban Building Activity, (1900 = 100), Canada. *Source:* [35, pp. 140–42].
0050 | Number Dwelling Units Completed, Canada. *Source:* [89, p. 299]. The years 1896–99 were developed by M. Gottlieb from Buckley (our series 0049), using Firestone's series with 1900 as index base.
0052 | Number Residential Buildings Authorized, Amsterdam, Netherlands. *Source:* Bureau of Statistics, Amsterdam; letter from Netherlands Central Bureau of Statistics, Dec. 30, 1960. Data from 1903–35 compiled by taking average per cent of residential to total (88.31 per cent for preceding four years).
0053 | Number Nonresidential Buildings Authorized, Amsterdam, Netherlands.

Series
Number   Title and Source

Source: Bureau of Statistics, Amsterdam; letter from Netherlands Central Bureau of Statistics, Dec. 30, 1960. Years 1903–8 estimated as 11.69 per cent of total authorized.

0054   Increments of Population, Amsterdam, Netherlands.
Source: Bureau of Statistics, Amsterdam; letter from Netherlands Central Bureau of Statistics, Dec. 30, 1960.

0055   Value of Building, Denmark, 1870–1913.
Source: Data communicated by letter May 28, 1953 from Det Statistiske Department, Denmark.

0056   Value of Building, Denmark, 1921–39.
Source: Same as for 0055.

0057   Private Nonagricultural Construction, Argentina.
Source: [12; years 1900–15 from Table V, p. 291, col. 2; years 1915–55 from Table IV, p. 290, col. 9].

0058-   Brick Production, States and Commonwealth as des-
0061   ignated, Australia.
Source: Before 1906 various state statistical registers; since 1906 Commonwealth Bulletins. Taken from [120].

0062-   Gross Private Capital Formation, by Category as des-
0074   ignated, Australia, (1936–39 prices).
Source: [44, Table II]. These figures were divided by cost index communicated by letter from Reserve Bank of Australia for the years 1861–1939.

0075   Brick Residential Rooms Added, Victoria, Australia.
Source: [43, Table L, p. 50]. Derived by Butlin from Building & Loan Societies, trade journals.

0076   Average Cost New Brick Rooms Built, Victoria, Australia (average of urban and rural).
Source: [43, Table L, p. 50].

0077   Residential Brick Rooms Added, Urban Area (Sydney) of New South Wales, Australia.
Source: [43, Table N, p. 56].

0078   Cost of Building New Residential Brick Rooms, New South Wales, Australia.
Source: [43, Table N, p. 56].

0079   Total Number New Rooms Added, Sydney, Australia.

Series
Number   Title and Source

Source: [43, Table O, p. 59, col. 3]. Derived by Butlin from metropolitan water receipts (flat charge per room).

0080   Vacancy Ratio, St. Louis, U.S.
Source: [224]; made available through M. Abramovitz' NBER series 000641.

0081   Number of Family Accommodations Built, St. Louis, U.S.
Source: [224]; made available through M. Abramovitz' NBER series 000621.

0082   Foreclosure Rate, St. Louis, U.S.
Source: [224]; made available through M. Abramovitz' NBER series 000632.

0083   Rent, Four-Family Flat, St. Louis, U.S.
Source: [224]; made available through M. Abramovitz' NBER series 000651.

0084   Value Building Permits, St. Louis, U.S.
Source: NBER files, 2,50.

0085   Value of Total Building Permits, Chicago, U.S.
Source: From NBER file 2,47. Original source: Building Department of Chicago *Reports, Chicago Tribune, Chicago Daily News Almanac,* as reported for years 1854–1933 in [134]; years 1934–43 from *The Economist, Annual Reviews.*

0086   Approximate Number of Acres Subdivided in 1931 City Limits of Chicago, U.S.
Source: From NBER file 2,67; [134, Table XC, pp. 479–80].

0087   Length of Pavements Laid (3-year moving average), Chicago, U.S.
Source: From NBER file 2,94b; for 1915–18 [53, p. 40]; for 1916–30, [54, p. 52]; for 1931–35, see [55, 1931, p. 272; 1932, p. 278; 1933, p. 223; 1934, p. 373; 1935, p. 364; 1936, p. 360]. Smoothed into 3-year moving average for this research.

0088   Increments Annual Population (3-year moving average), Chicago, U.S.
Source: [134, Table XCIII, p. 483]. Increments computed by M. Gottlieb and smoothed by 3-year moving average.

Series
Number   Title and Source
0089   Number Real Estate Instruments, Chicago, U.S.
            Source: [134, Table LXXX, p. 470].
0090   Value of Manufactures, Chicago, U.S.
            Source: [134, Table XCI, p. 481]; using figures ob-
            tained from the U.S. Census Bureau and the *Chicago
            Tribune.* These figures from 1879 onward were de-
            flated by Warren & Pearson Wholesale Price Index
            (1910–14 = 100) as given in [262, p. 231]. Years
            1872–78 were adjusted to currency from gold basis by
            using the Warren & Pearson index of gold discount
            [279, p. 351].
0091   Value of Building Plans Filed for Total New Building,
            New York City (Manhattan), U.S.
            Source: From NBER file 2,44. N.Y.C. *Record* for
            1868–80; for 1881–92, N.Y.C. *Annual Report of the
            Fire Dept.;* for 1893–1901, N.Y.C. *Record;* for
            1902–44, N.Y.C. (Manhattan) *Annual Report of the
            Dept. of Buildings* (esp. 1910, p. 6, which gives
            1868–1910); for Bronx data, 1902–20 from N.Y.C.
            (Bronx) *Annual Report of the President;* for 1936–44
            Records of the Dept. of Housing and Buildings. The
            entire series runs from 1868 to 1944, with the period
            1902–44 covering the area of Manhattan only. For
            1868–97 the data cover Manhattan and such portions
            of the Bronx as were annexed from time to time. For
            the years 1898–1920 data cover Manhattan plus the
            entire Bronx. (For the period 1898–1901 data were not
            separable for these two boroughs. Therefore for
            1902–20 data were here computed by adding figures for
            Manhattan to those for the Bronx to retain comparabil-
            ity.) In our present use of this series, the data for both
            Manhattan and the Bronx were used to 1918 for
            purposes of long-cycle analysis, and to 1920 for short
            cycles. Thereafter the data for Manhattan alone con-
            tinued.
0092   Value of Building Plans Filed for New Residential
            Buildings, New York City (Manhattan), U.S.
            Source: From NBER file 2,53. For 1868–80, N.Y.C.
            Record; for 1881–92, N.Y.C. *Annual Report of Fire*

Series
Number   Title and Source

Dept.; for 1893–1901, N.Y.C. *Record* and *Annual
Report of Building Dept.;* for 1902–35, N.Y.C. (Manhattan) *Annual Report of the Dept. of Buildings;* for
Bronx data, 1902–20, N.Y.C. (Bronx) *Annual Report
of the President;* for 1936–44, *Records of Dept. of
Housing and Buildings* (municipal building). Data for
residential were computed, NBER, by adding dwellings (detached), flats, tenements; frame and brick are
included and hotels and boarding houses are excluded.
The entire series runs from 1868 to 1944, with the
period 1902–44 covering the area of Manhattan only.
For 1868–97 the data cover Manhattan and such portions of the Bronx as were annexed from time to time.
For the years 1898–1920 data cover Manhattan plus
the entire Bronx. Figures for 1898–1901 are here
estimated: residential for 4 boroughs (excl. Brooklyn)
multiplied by the ratio of "Total New Building for
Manhattan and Bronx" to "Total New Building for 4
Boroughs." Figures for 1902–20 are here computed by
adding items for the Bronx and Manhattan in order to
continue first segment for overlapping purposes. In
our present use of this series, the data for both
Manhattan and the Bronx were used to 1918 for
purposes of long-cycle analysis, and to 1920 for short
cycles. Thereafter the data for Manhattan alone continued.

0093   Value of Building Plans Filed for New Commercial and
Industrial Buildings, New York City (Manhattan),
U.S.
Source: From NBER file 2,56. For 1868–80, N.Y.C.
Record; for 1881–92, N.Y.C. *Annual Report of Fire
Dept.;* for 1893–1901, N.Y.C. *Record* and *Annual
Report of Building Dept.;* for 1902–35, N.Y.C. (Man-
hattan) *Annual Report of the Dept. of Buildings;* for
Bronx data, 1902–09, N.Y.C. (Bronx) *Annual Report
of the President;* for 1936–44, *Records of Dept. of
Housing and Buildings.* Data for commercial and
industrial were computed, NBER, by adding stores,
office buildings, stables, manufactories and work-

Series
Number   Title and Source

shops, and beginning 1931, warehouses. The entire
series runs from 1868 to 1944, with the period 1902–44
covering the area of Manhattan only. For 1868–97, the
data cover Manhattan and such portions of the Bronx
as were annexed from time to time. For the years
1898–1920 data cover Manhattan plus the entire
Bronx. Figures for 1898–1901 are here estimated:
"Commercial and Industrial" for 4 boroughs (excl.
Brooklyn) multiplied by the ratio of "Total New
Building for Manhattan and Bronx" to "Total New
Building for 4 Boroughs." Figures for 1902–20 are here
computed by adding items for the Bronx to Manhattan
in order to provide an overlap. In our present use of
this series the years 1921–44 (Manhattan only) were
raised by the ratio of Manhattan and Bronx data to
Manhattan alone data for the year 1920 (1.0998 per cent)
so as to include the Bronx.

0094   Total Pavements Laid, New York City (Manhattan),
U.S.
Source: From NBER file 2,94a. For 1871–82, N.Y.C.
Dept. of Public Works, 1882, p. 18; for 1883–88,
1895–96, *Dept. of Public Works,* individual issues. For
1889–94, 1896–99, N.Y.C. *Annual Report of Dept. of
Highways.* For 1900–1935, N.Y.C. *Annual Report of
the President,* 1935, p. 38.

0095   Average Consideration per Conveyance, Manhattan
23rd & 24th Wards, U.S.
Source: [204, pp. 157–59].

0096   Value Real Estate, Manhattan Island, U.S.
Source: Lawyers Title Corp. of New York, from
assessment and sales records, as given in [262, Table
A100, p. 12].

0097   Building Material Prices (1910–14 = 100), New York
City, U.S.
Source: Warren and Pearson, as given in [204, Table
L1–14, p. 232, col. 10].

0098   Value of Building Permits, New Buildings, Detroit,
U.S.
Source: From NBER file 2,49a. For 1878–1907, City of

Series
Number

Title and Source

Detroit *Annual Reports, Fire Marshall Reports.* For 1908–44, correspondence with Detroit, Dept. of Buildings and Safety Engineering.

0099   Increase in Number of Lots in Detroit Area, U.S.
Source: From NBER file 2,68; [190, p. 43].

0101   Number of Deeds Recorded, San Francisco, California, U.S.
Source: Made available through M. Abramovitz' NBER series 000352.

0102   Number of Deeds Recorded, Alameda County, California, U.S.
Source: Made available through M. Abramovitz' NBER series 000372.

0103   Number of Lots Added Grand Rapids Area, Michigan, U.S.
Source: Made available through M. Abramovitz' NBER series 000522.

0104   Number of Lots Added, Milwaukee Area, Wisconsin, U.S.
Source: Made available through M. Abramovitz' NBER series 000542.

0106   Number of Lots Added, Ann Arbor, Michigan, U.S.
Source: Made available through M. Abramovitz' NBER series 000502.

0107   Number of Rural Residential Brick Rooms Added, New South Wales, Australia.
Source: [43, Table N, p. 56].

0108   General Economic Pattern, Ohio Valley, U.S.
Source: [16]; actual index relatives of "General Economic Pattern" given on pp. 409, 434, 470. Berry compiled a "general economic pattern" using the median link relatives of nine basic time series (described on p. 554). Three series wholly or primarily refer to western activity (nos. 1, 3, 6). Three series (nos. 4, 5, 7) are wholly nationwide in impact. The other three series are of mixed character.

0130   Number of Marriages, Cook County, Ill., U.S.
Source: [264, Part II]; [262].

0131   Number of Marriages, Paris, France

Series
Number   Title and Source

Source: [9, pp. 14–15].

0132   Rent Index Vacant Dwellings (1914 = 100), New York
          City, U.S.
          Source: [218, Table 32, "Rent Indexes for Six Cities,"
          p. 97; and Table 35, "Comparison of Rent Indexes,
          Three Cities," p. 101].

0133   Rent Index Vacant Dwellings (1914 = 100), Chicago,
          U.S.
          Source: [218, pp. 97, 101].

0134   Rent Index Vacant Dwellings (1914 = 100), St. Louis,
          U.S.
          Source: [218, p. 97].

0139   Gross Investment, Italy (1938 prices).
          Source: [143, p. 266, col. 4].

0140   Gross Residential Construction, Italy (1938 prices).
          Source: [143, p. 266, col. 1]. Only a general description
          of the sources and research methods used was pro-
          vided. See [143, pp. 99–102] (supplemented by a letter
          from the director of the research, Prof. A. Giannone,
          Sept. 3, 1960). It appears that from 1913 onward an
          index of residential building activity was constructed
          from building permit reports from a sample of leading
          cities (eight in number for the early years). Before 1913
          an annual series was constructed from decennial bench-
          mark returns of number of rooms interpolated by
          population and density coefficients (coefficienti di
          affollamento) into an annual series [143, pp. 100–3]. To
          this physical unit series there were applied estimates of
          per room value derived from "sporadic information"
          about average room prices and qualitative information
          from provincial towns (p. 102). Prof. Giannone advised
          in his cited letter that "data concerning building mate-
          rial and the number of those engaged in building activ-
          ity" was too fragmentary to permit a check on the
          estimates before 1917. Sources for total construction
          were somewhat more adequate, especially after 1896.
          Hence, it is not surprising that one well-informed
          Italian economist has seen fit to use the investment
          estimates only from 1895 onward [212, p. 477 and n.

Series
Number   Title and Source

17]. On the other hand, Italian scholars have begun to make use of the newly released statistics and a systematic investigation into "building cycles" was directly stimulated [244; 113].

0141   Total Nonresidential Construction, Italy (1938 prices). *Source:* [143]; the implicit price index of housing (pp. 264, 266) was computed and applied to construction values in current prices (p. 219).

0142   Value Gross Construction, Italy (1938 prices). *Source:* [143, pp. 266–67].

0143   Index House-Building (1901–10 = 100), South Wales Coalfield, Great Britain. *Source:* [169].

0144   Index House-Building (1901–10 = 100), Manchester Conurbation, Great Britain. *Source:* [169].

0145   Index House-Building (1901–10 = 100), Great Britain. *Source:* [169]. Years 1852–55 derived from unweighted index of nationwide building; thereafter derived from weighted index.

0155   Number Nonfarm Permanent Housekeeping Residential Dwelling Units Erected, U.S. *Source:* [109].

0156   Price of Pine Timber, 4-City Average, U.S., quarterly. *Source:* For New Orleans, yellow pine; Cincinnati, clear pine; Charleston, white pine; N.Y.C. and Philadelphia, mixed. From 1819 to 1824 based on Philadelphia, Charleston, and New York City; New Orleans included in 1825. From 1843–55 Charleston is excluded and Cincinnati is added. For 1856–60, based on Philadelphia, New York, and New Orleans, adjusted to 4-city average by use of 3-city index using Jan. 1856 = 100 [61, pp. 186 ff.]. The data for these cities were logarithmically averaged and the cities given equal weighting. An extension of three quarters beyond Oct. 1860, was made by extrapolation on the basis of building material price behavior in order to provide a long-cycle reference date.

0160   Population Growth, 17 Cities, U.S.

Series
Number   Title and Source
            Source: [206, Table X, p. 72].
0161   Building Permits Divided by Building Costs, 17 Cities
            (1913 = $1 million), U.S.
            Source: [206, p. 72].
0167   Building Cost Index (1913 = 100), U.S.
            Source: Computed by J. R. Riggleman from various
            sources and used in deflating building permit expendi-
            tures from 1830 to 1933. See [222, App. L, from 1830 to
            1851].
            Riggleman's building cost index 1913 = 100 was com-
            piled from the following:
            I. *1830–51.* Constructed by combining on the basis of
               equal weights an index of building trade wage rates
               with an index of average wholesale prices of soft-
               wood lumber.
               Wage rate 1840–51 = the average wage rate for
               bricklayers in New York state, carpenters in Mas-
               sachusetts and New York, masons in Mas-
               sachusetts, painters in New York, and plasterers in
               Pennsylvania.
            Source: Wage rate 1830–51. 1. [63, p. 86]. 2. [266, pp.
            57, 58, and 153–205].
               Lumber prices 1830–39. 1. From Department of
                                          Agriculture—prices
                                          of merchantable pine
                                          in the New England
                                          market.
               Lumber prices 1840–51. 2. From Department of
                                          Agriculture index of
                                          average wholesale
                                          prices of upper
                                          grades softwood in
                                          Eastern markets,
                                          converted to a com-
                                          parable basis.
            Source: Lumber prices 1830–51. 1. [267, pp. 119–23].
            2. "Timber Depletion, Lumber Prices," etc., [267, pp.
            40–48].

Series
Number   Title and Source
II. *1852–1903*. American Appraisal Company's cost
of industrial buildings in Eastern cities includes:
1. Indexes of frame building costs.
2. Indexes of brick mill costs.
added in 1890 3. Indexes of iron-clad buildings.
added in 1890 4. Indexes of steel iron-clad buildings.
added in 1890 5. Indexes of reinforced concrete
construction.
added in 1890 6. Indexes of concrete and steel
construction.
The above combinations were made on a weighted
average basis.
III. *1904–33*. *Engineering News-Record* construction
cost index with modifications for 1904–33 is com-
posed of four weighted components:

		Weights
	1. Structural steel at Pittsburgh	2500 lbs.
Materials	2. Cement at Chicago	6 barrels
	3. Lumber at New York	600 feet
Wages	4. Average for common labor in 20 cities	200 man-hours

Riggleman's reservations on the construction cost-
index in *Engineering News-Record,* pages 30–31:

In using the above index of construction costs, it is
recognized that its basis is limited to building material prices
and labor rates and that it may not represent any of the other
changes that take place in building costs, such as in
contractor's overhead and profits, financing charges,
architect's fees, technical improvements in machinery,
economy in design, greater prefabrication of materials, and
cyclical and secular variation in the efficiency of labor and
management. These factors may vary considerably from
time to time and changes may not correspond to the changes
in building-material prices and in total construction costs. If
a synthetic index of this type does not properly reflect the
changes in the efficiency of labor and management and the

Series
Number   Title and Source
improvements in the use of materials, its use may cause an
appreciable error in the secular trend, as discussed later in
the chapter.

Riggleman states that the slight upward trend in
building permits per capita for the whole period
1830–1933 may not really be significant but may be due
to the following:
1. The synthetic cost index based on fixed amounts
of labor and materials.
2. "It is probable that an extension of the period,
either backward or forward, or the addition of cities in
the earlier parts of the period, might cause some
changes in the slope. . . .
"If a cumulative upward bias does exist in the cost
index used, it would mean that the per capita trend
from 1830 would have a slightly greater upward slope.
"The above qualification applies to any interpretation that might be made of the secular trend. The
objective of this particular study, however, is to show
cycles, and the secular trend has been eliminated.
Since any trend that has been indirectly eliminated by
a steadily accumulating bias in the cost index simply
reduces the trend that is directly eliminated, the
cycles in as erratic a series as the one under consideration would not be affected to any practical extent by a
secular bias in the cost index."

0267   Differential Between Mortgage Rates (M) and Bond
           Yields (r), Germany ($M - r$, in basis points).
           Source: Mortgage yield in Germany was represented
           by the average interest rate for "Pfandbriefe"
           (interest-bearing depositor certificates issued by Ger-
           man mortgage banks). Bond yield was represented by
           yields on long-term securities (Rendite festverzins-
           liches Papiere) [73, pp. 98–99]; [136, p. 60].
0268   Differential Between Mortgage Rates (M) and Bond
           Yields (r), U.S. ($M - r$, in basis points).
           Source: [114, Table 0-1, cols. 1, 6].

Series
Number   Title and Source

0270   Value Total Nonfarm Building, U.S.
        Source: [110].
0271   Value Nonfarm Residential Building, U.S.
        Source: Same as for 0270.
0272   Value Nonfarm Nonresidential Building, U.S.
        Source: Same as for 0270.
0273   Price Vacant Land, Paris, France.
        Source: [75, pp. 184–88]. In 1939, 32,000 square meters
        of vacant land were sold for a total return of 9,250,000
        francs (p. 188). This return was the base of a series of
        index relatives of median prices for the sale of identical
        sites sold at different time periods. These index rela-
        tives were the smoothed 3- to 5-year moving average
        of the weighted mean indexes for sales of identical
        properties sold in different base periods (1939, 1920,
        and 1900).
0274   Unit Cost Standard Building (1910 = 100), London,
        England.
        Source: [148], as arranged in [46, p. 157].
0275   Index of Price Series of Building Materials (1910 =
        100), England.
        Source: Same as for 0274.
0277-   Marriages per Capita, for Designated Countries.
0280   *Source:* [275, pp. 404–5].
0281   Marriages per Capita, Six States, U.S.
        Source: [248, p. 189].
0281-A Estimated Number of Marriages per 1000 Estimated
        Midyear Population, U.S.
        Source: [262, Table C77, p. 49].
0282   Marriages per Capita. England.
        Source: [248, p. 189].
0300   Scotch Mortgage Yield Differential.
        Source: "Interest received on sums invested in landed
        securities" minus yield on 3 per cent consols. Both
        series were analyzed for cyclical characteristics by A.
        Gayer, W. Rostow, and A. J. Schwartz in [97]. The
        series were obtained from the manuscript tables and
        texts were kindly made available by Mrs. A. J.

Series
Number   Title and Source

Schwartz (Tables 190, 187, Part IV Typescript, p. 589). The "landed securities" rate is derived from Giffen [102, p. 136]. He quotes from a memorandum obtained by him on rates of interest on mortgages in Scotland:

> The Commissioners at Edinburgh are a body representing the Writers to the Signet, Solicitors before the Supreme Courts of Scotland, Chartered accountants, and Ministers of Scotland Widows' Fund. Perhaps there may, from the constitution of this body be rather a leaning towards borrowers, as the interest of the Lawyers is to cultivate that connexion [*Ed.:* i.e., the Commissioners are partial to borrowers in fixing the rate]. The Insurance Companies were at one time parties in fixing the rate, but from some cause or other ceased to be so. They, however, do lend on the terms fixed by the Commissioners, though wherever there is any specialty in the nature of the loan (such, for instance, as loans for drainage, farm-buildings, etc.), a somewhat higher rate is charged. It may also be mentioned that the large monied bodies, especially the Insurance Companies, now lend to Poor-Law Boards, School-Boards, Municipal Corporations, etc. a good deal of money which formerly would have been invested in loans on land. These loans are negotiated at higher rates.

Giffen concludes that the interest received by the Widows' Fund of Writers to the Signet is "a correct statement of the rate at which money was lent on first-class landed security for the time specified." The time specified, however, raises some difficulties. The Edinburgh Commissioners, who fixed the rate twice yearly, met regularly at Martinmas and Whitsuntide. One year the date of meeting occurred at Lammas. Giffen lists the interest rate as of these periods of the year. In converting the time unit of the data into calendar years, Martinmas was dated the end of November, Whitsun, the beginning of June, and Lammas, the beginning of August. In years when the rate changed an average of the monthly rates was computed.

0301   Migration to Extra-European Countries from United

Series Number	Title and Source
	Kingdom (includes Irish, Scotch, English, Welsh and aliens leaving from English ports). *Source:* Analyzed in [97, Table 255].
0302	Marriage Rate in England and Wales per 1000 Inhabitants. *Source:* Analyzed in [97, Table 279].
0310	German Overseas Migration. *Source:* [88, I, p. 697; II, pp. 333, 335].
0311	Outward-Bound Passengers, English and Welsh Nationals, to Extra-European Countries. *Source:* [51, Table C(1)]. Figures include migrants and transient passengers leaving for overseas ports excluding Europe. Before 1876 aliens other than Irish or Scotch are included in the returns.
0312	Immigrant Arrivals from Overseas, U.S. *Source:* [263, Series C88-114, pp. 56–59]. From 1820 to 1867 figures represent other passenger arrivals. In later years, variation is involved regarding minor classes of immigrants. Beginning in 1894, European emigrants who arrived at Canadian ports were included.
0313	Hourly Earning Differential, U.S. Building Trades and Manufacturing. *Source:* The series is a set of percentage terms expressing the value of hourly earnings of building trade workers as a percentage of hourly earnings of workers in manufacturing. The bases of the series were the percentage differentials derived from the Aldrich Report for 1860–1890 as reported by Clarence D. Long [175, Table A-10, p. 152]. This series was the longest continuous series and was free from questionable performance. Similar percentage differentials were then computed from the average hourly earnings series as prepared by Douglas for 1890–1926 [263, Table D, pp. 589–602]. The Douglas series for manufacturing workers was extended forward to 1939 by using a lower level set of earning figures (adjusted upward at the splicing point) for 1927–39 [263, Table D, pp. 626–34]. The Douglas hourly earnings for building trades was extended to 1939 on two bases: union wage rates between

Series
Number   Title and Source
1927 and 1934 and experienced hourly earnings 1934–39
[263, Table D, pp. 642–53, Table D, pp. 669–84]. The
whole set of extended 1890–1939 per cent differentials
was then reduced (by multiplying .89323) to adjust to
the lower Aldrich level, which unlike the Douglas level
was not primarily based upon union rates. If we accept
as rock bottom the Aldrich differential and that reported from BLS experienced hourly earning surveys,
which for the building trades commence in 1934, then
the union-based segment of our series (1890–1934)
gave it an upward bias of 14.2 per cent in 1939, i.e. our
terminal differential was that amount higher than the
differential reported by the BLS earning figures. Substantially this means that the differential end 1939 is
nearly at the same magnitude as between 1860–70.

0314   Consol Yields, England.
Source: Approximate yield on 3 per cent funds. Recip-
rocals of the average annual prices of the 3 per cent
stock [11, Table 9, p. 187].

Appendix C

OHIO SAMPLE GROUPS

Detailed information about the twenty sampled counties, returns for which were tabulated individually or in groups, may be found in Table C-1. The first ten counties listed were not, in the strict sense of the word, sampled at all. These ten were by 1920 standards the most highly urbanized counties of the state and were by 1950 the areas of highest urban density. Both the counties and the central cities involved are of highly unequal size. If they were dealt with as an aggregate, the smaller counties (and cities) would not have an appreciable influence; the aggregate would be dominated by such counties as Cuyahoga (containing Cleveland) and Hamilton (containing Cincinnati). To enable the different size groups to exhibit the peculiar patterns which may characterize their behavior, this large urban category is broken up into three subgroups, which are entitled: large metropolitan, large urban, and small urban.

In all of these counties, the urban influence dominates the county totals, though unevenly, according to the measures noted in Table C-1. As regards population by 1920 the counties were urbanized (defined as having incorporated municipalities of 2,000 or more) by at least 71 per cent (up to 95 per cent for the highest of the range). However, if we go back in time, the rural or farm influence becomes stronger. Thus, of total recorded mortgages in 1884 (which is near the center of our survey period) as much as 68 per cent by dollar volume for the ten counties was on agricultural lands. In all of the urban counties, real estate market activity as a per cent of sales of nonfarm property or platted property, was predominantly urban, with the farm component ranging from 11 to 58 per cent.

In terms of geographical location, the ten urban counties are distributed over the state and into widely differing resource layouts. Hamilton (containing Cincinnati) was from early days the leading commercial and industrial center of the upper Ohio valley. Two of the other counties, Lucas (Toledo) and Cuyahoga (Cleveland) are harbor ports on the Great Lakes. The other urban counties are interior, though most of these were tapped by

273

TABLE C-1
Ohio Building Study. Sample Counties and Their Characteristics

Areas	Sales of Farm Land as % of Sales of Town Lots, 1884	Urban Pop. as % of Total Pop., 1920	Nonfarm Value Mort. Recorded as % of Total Mort. Value, 1885	Value Total New Building, Unadjusted (Thousands of Dollars)			Population (Thousands)		
				1857	1884	1908	1860	1880	1900
Ohio total	107	63.8	51	5,150	16,300	45,541	2,340	3,198	4,158
Large metropolitan									
Cuyahoga (Cleveland)	12	95	90	260	1,609	9,823	78	197	439
Hamilton (Cincinnati)	11	91	86[b]	1,296	3,119	4,941	216	313	409
Total[a]	12	93	88	1,556	4,728	14,764	294	510	848
Large urban									
Franklin	31	83	32[c]	149	1,224	3,118	50	87	164
Lucas (Toledo)	22	89	84	108	435	2,100	26	67	154
Montgomery	35	77	67	192	713	1,144	52	79	130
Total[a]	29	83	61	449	2,372	6,362	128	233	448
Urban									
Mahoning	46	82	78	58	109	3,366	26	43	70

Summit	45	87	68	53	457	841	27	44	72
Stark	58	71	51	70	294	948	43	64	95
Butler	42	72	52	161	401	954	36	43	57
Clarke	51	75	63	59	323	427	25	42	59
Total[a]	48	77	63	401	1,584	6,536	157	236	353
Southeast small urban									
Jefferson	313	48	42	22	204	440	26	33	44
Belmont	63	44	50	74	213	423	36	50	61
Washington	151	35	—	61	99	129	36	43	48
Muskingum	111	51	73	45	138	472	44	50	53
Guernsey	164	35	8	31	101	241	24	27	34
Total[a]	160	43	43	233	755	1,705	166	203	240
Northwest rural farm									
Williams	84	29	12	18	71	58	17	24	25
Hardin	65	26	29	35	41	54	14	27	31
Wood	106	12	8	19	52	92	18	34	52
Henry	197	17	13	8	63	68	9	21	27
Wyandot	88	19	18	26	64	55	16	22	21
Total[a]	108	20	16	106	291	327	74	128	156

[a] Entries for first three columns are unweighted means.

[b] For 1880.

[c] For 1886.

the canal lines running north and south which were constructed in the 1830's to provide passage for bulk freight. Altogether four of the urban counties are on the border of the great iron and steel region which fringes the northeastern corner of the state and runs on into Pennsylvania. Two of these counties, Cuyahoga and Mahoning (Cleveland and Youngstown), are leading centers for the iron and steel producing industry. Except for these counties, industry is highly diversified.

Unfortunately, neighboring cities are not usually of the same size-class. Thus, the decision to group cities of similar size linked together, in one aggregate, cities which have little direct impact on each other, even though economic activity in the Ohio Valley and along the Great Lakes responded to a common set of influences. Since our principal Ohio results, so far as local cycles are concerned, involve the behavior of these loosely related groups of urban communities of like size, it is necessary at the outset to establish the degree to which behavior patterns of the aggregate reflected behavior patterns of group members.

To permit such a study, a complete analysis was made of cycle patterns for Cleveland and Cincinnati considered separately and together. Four sets of average patterns are shown in Chart C-1. The aggregate, as expected, cuts across the dissimilar patterns of the rapidly growing Cleveland and the more matured Cincinnati area. The form of movement and timing is affected by aggregation only in one of the four sets of reference patterns. Though located at opposite ends of the state, growth patterns of the two cities responded to wave movements of comparable force and timing. The average divergence in years between specific turning points in residential building was only 1.5 years (see Table C-2). Divergences in timing narrowed toward the end of the period. No growth waves are rubbed out by nonconvergence, though amplitudes are dampened and patterns are somewhat smoothed.

Similar conclusions are indicated by the comparison set forth in Chart C-2 of average patterns for Toledo and the composite of three counties in Group II including Toledo. The process of rubbing down and smoothing out was probably carried somewhat farther in Group III, which is made up of five counties, three of them located in the northeast Piedmont region and two in the western and southern areas. The divergence in cyclical timing was greatest for Group III (see Table C-2).

The surveyed materials reveal the hazard of treating even

CHART C-1
Average Long Cycle Patterns, Specific and Reference, Value of Total
Building and Number of Dwellings Built, 1857–1914, Ohio Sample
Group I and Its Component Countries

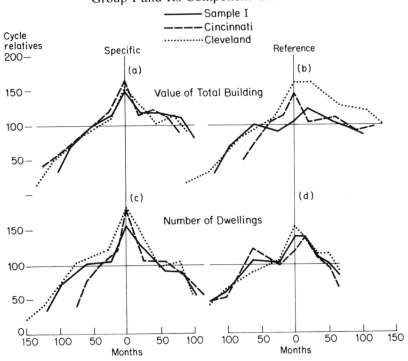

slight aggregation as trivial. Our first three sample groups are
themselves not representative or modal. Average group patterns
will thus understate the force of movement which swept through
the area. The group patterns do indicate the comparative behavior over the same time periods of city areas in different size
classes. To the extent that demand and supply for building work
was satisfied by shifting manpower throughout the area, the
aggregate pattern is more representative of the movement of
productive activity than city patterns taken separately.

The other two sample groups with five counties each are
sampled in the proper sense of the word. One group (labeled
southeast small urban) is made up of nearly contiguous counties
of nearly similar size. These counties are in the broken country
of the Appalachian plateaus draining into the upper Ohio. They
were all settled early in the nineteenth century. Four of them
have an active coal mining industry, and in the later years of our

TABLE C-2

Deviation of Individual Counties from Group Chronology,
Residential Building

(In years)

Group	Total Number of Years Deviation, All Turning Points	Average Deviation per Turning Point
I	18	1.50
II	18	1.27
III	74	3.20
IV	49	1.90
V	68	3.10

survey period were favored by exploitation of gas and oil deposits. The economic development of the region rested on exploitation, successively, of forests, fields, and mines. Of the twenty-four counties which make up the southeast region,[2] the five were selected with the requisite degree of urbanization, city size-class, absolute size, and contiguity. Contiguity played a role since it was felt that building-trades workers spread their field of employment over a wider area than a county, and that hence something like a regional resource pull would develop and give economic meaning to the group aggregates. No attention was paid to the kind of building pattern exhibited, to the movement of population, or to industrial characteristics. The sampled counties were characterized by the absence by 1900 of any large urban center of more than 25,000 population but involved a degree of urbanization which in 1920 ranged between 25 and 50 per cent. Whereas the simple average of urbanization for the ten urban counties is 82 per cent, for these counties the comparable simple average in 1920 was 43 per cent. In 1884–85 our two measures of real estate activity exhibited about the same proportion for nonfarm transactions by number and by value.

The other five counties were selected to represent the behavior of northwest Ohio with its flat drained farmlands devoted chiefly to corn and hog farming.[3] This area has a comparatively light density, averaging only 71 persons per square mile. The degree of urbanization is under 30 per cent, with no city over 20,000. It is hoped that this subgroup of counties will typify the

CHART C-2
Average Long Cycle Patterns, Specific and Reference, Value of Total
Building and Number of Dwellings Built, 1857–1914, Ohio Sample
Group II and Lucas County (Toledo)

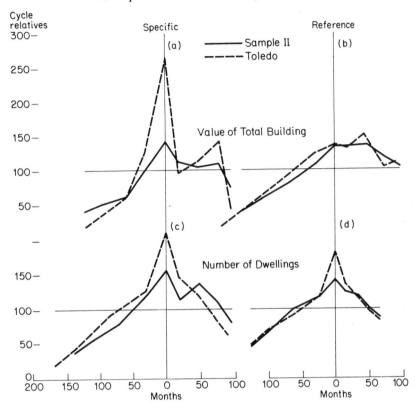

building and real estate behavior of the midwestern farm belt,
which stretches beyond Ohio to the Great Plains states. Corn
and hogs account (in 1950) for 26 per cent of total farm incomes,
dairying 16 per cent, wheat 14 per cent, and poultry 14 per cent.
This region was settled late. Population growth in these counties
was light after 1880, and after 1900 in most of these counties a
population decline, reflecting lighter farm density, set in. Of the
seventeen nonurban counties making up this region, five were
selected on grounds of contiguity, appropriate size, and degree
of urbanization.

Appendix D

SOURCES AND METHOD USED IN CONSTRUCTING SERIES 0186, U.S. NATIONWIDE ANNUAL INDEX (1855–60 = 100), PRICES OF BUILDING MATERIALS

Indexes for prices of building materials have been computed by different investigators for different building markets for varying periods in the past, as given below.

Area	Years	Investigator	Source
N.Y.C.	1800–90	G. F. Warren and F. A. Pearson	[279, pp. 11–13, 25–27]
Philadelphia	1800–61	Anne Bezanson; R. D. Gray; M. Hussey	[18]
U.S.	1890–1939	Bureau of Labor Statistics	[263, Table E-13-24]
Philadelphia	1852–96	A. Bezanson; M. C. Denison; M. Hussey; E. Klemp	[18]
Cincinnati	1844–1904	W. H. White	[286]
Vermont (rural)	1800–90	T. S. Adams	[4]
U.S.	1844–91	R. L. Falkner	[85]

While the original sources were consulted, it was found convenient to use the above series as compiled by E. D. Hoover [131, appendix tables for Cincinnati, New York, Vermont and Philadelphia]. The indexes were all reduced to a common basis in terms of an 1855–60 base period. The indexes for Philadelphia until 1860 for building materials were separately stated for wooden and nonwooden materials. These two subindexes were joined together, weighted 2 and 1, respectively.

It was clear that from 1890 onward the standard BLS index was to be used. Between 1870 and 1890 building price levels in our sampled building market areas exhibited a common cyclical pattern and secular trend. For these years different schemes of weighting would only slightly affect the average. But much more variation was found both during and before the Civil War. Chart D-1 shows that building material prices were falling in the half-century before the Civil War outside New York City but fluctuating in New York City around a stationary trend up to 1836, thereafter exhibiting a rising tendency. There was also a

CHART D-1
Annual Indexes, Prices of Building Materials, U.S., 1815–65

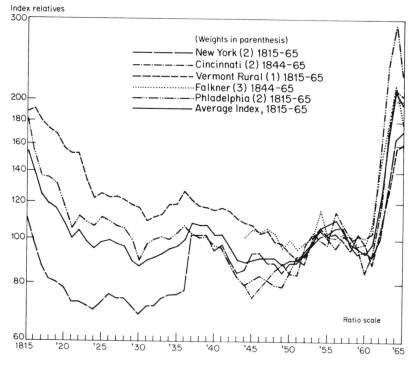

different degree of participation in the long-swing price movements of the period. The problem of weighting was complicated by the tendency of sampled areas to represent price movements over a wider region. Thus, price behavior in rural Vermont might well be indicative of New England farm markets. New York City and Philadelphia probably would typify price patterns in other northern seaboard cities (from Portland, Maine, to Baltimore). Cincinnati experience might typify price behavior in the trans-Alleghany Ohio and Great Lakes settlement. If the Falkner index were representative, it might have served as a basis for averaging after 1844. Unfortunately the Falkner index chiefly reflected price experience in the northeastern states and was probably heavily weighted by the easily available pricing records in New York City and Philadelphia, the two areas for which independent series are on hand. Hence, it seemed unwise to allow the Falkner index a very considerable weight. We accordingly decided on equal weights of two for Philadelphia,

CHART D-2
Annual Index, Prices of Building Materials, U.S., 1810–1939
(1855–60=100)

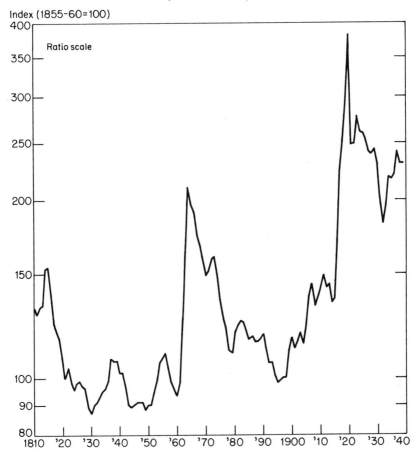

New York City, and Cincinnati, with weights of one for Vermont
and three for the Falkner index. The indexes were reduced to
logarithms, weighted, summed and averaged. The entire index is
shown in Chart D-2.

Appendix E

Included in this Appendix are fifteen master tables listing the annual Ohio series analyzed in Appendix A with a detailed record of all adjustments practiced on the raw data as extracted from Ohio documents and a full account of sources used. The Ohio statistics were inaugurated by statutes which in April 1857 established an Office of Commissioner of Statistics and which a year later made the office permanent and specified a plan for statistical reporting. A bureau of statistics had been contemplated by the new constitution adopted in 1851.[4] Impetus for the creation of a bureau was given by the distinguished Salmon P. Chase in his gubernatorial message of 1856.[5] Once the office had received legislative sanction, Chase appointed to it one of the few representatives of a vanishing type, a man of letters, active in public affairs, knowledgeable about agriculture, industry, and trade.[6] The appointee, Edward D. Mansfield, was doubtless infected with the scientific virus by his professor father, who was singled out for his scientific interests by President Jefferson and appointed to the staff of West Point and to the office of surveyor-general of the northwest territories. Despite young Mansfield's many-sided schooling in Eastern institutions, he settled and made his home in the state early. From 1836 to 1852 he edited various Ohio newspapers and for eighteen years thereafter he published a journal on railroading. He participated for ten years in educational institutions and published works on biography, current events, social topics, and short manuals on mathematics, politics and education [181; 19, I, p. 162]. He learned about statistical methods the hard way, as Census taker for Cincinnati in 1825 and as field researcher in marine statistics at the behest of a Secretary of the Treasury.[7]

Mansfield began his work as Commissioner of Statistics in 1857 and in the years following produced eleven memorable reports. In 1868 he retired from the office, which was abolished

Note: Tables for this Appendix appear on microfiche. See inside back cover.

as a separate agency and, in the form of a statistical bureau, was placed under the general supervision of the Secretary of State, an elected officer of state government, who in the early years frequently complained about the assumption of duties for which he was unfitted and which were meagerly funded as well.[8] However, the statistical system developed by Mansfield had become sufficiently routinized so that it was possible for the bureau, staffed by only a few persons and headed by a person serving as "statistician" to compile and issue an annual statistical report, though without the commentary or explanation previously provided. In this form the bureau functioned for the next half-century.[9]

The bureau not only continued the system but twice carried through major expansions in the reporting network by arranging for a more detailed breakdown of classes of building annually erected and for a separate reporting of conveyances of real estate on a farm and nonfarm basis and for nonfarm lands on a platted or unplatted basis. Visible through most later reports was evidence of perfunctory interest. No attempt was made to make up for omitted county returns or ever to call attention to questionable items.

The statistical plan of Chase and Mansfield was embodied in an 1858 document included in this Appendix (see pp. 298–300). Local officers of local government were required to keep records of, and to report on, their own ministerial or executive actions. Thus county coroners were to report violent deaths, sheriffs were to report prisoner confinements, probate judges who issued marriage licenses were to report the number of licenses issued, welfare officers were to report the number of "paupers" assisted, recorders of documents were to report on the number, consideration or acreage of basic deeds and mortgages recorded, district attorneys were to report on prosecutions and convictions, clerks of courts were to furnish information on civil actions, naturalizations, and judgments, and auditors who supervised the preparation of local budgets and who managed the property tax rolls were to report on government expenditures, taxable property of various types, and agricultural production. The auditors carried out their duties through a network of elected part-time township or ward personal property tax assessors who conducted in the spring of each year virtually an annual census enumeration of households and establishments, using forms printed by the state and distributed in early spring through county auditors. The core of the duties of these assessors was (a) to obtain from each head of household or establishment a sworn detailed statement of personal property by type and value and (b) to prepare from his own knowledge a detailed list of newly built nonexempted structures or improvements worth over $100 or loss of the same by fire, destruction, or demolition, with the value estimated in line with valuation of realty already assessed and reappraised for tax purposes by special district assessors and equalization boards elected in 1846, 1853, 1859, and thereafter decennially to 1910. Along with these two operational reports was a third which asked for an enumeration of crop production, acreage allotted, and certain husbandry productions for the preceding year. By the third Monday of May, the ward or township assessors were to deliver to the county auditor the requisite listings with sworn affidavits of honest fulfillment and with proper footings for the different columns of the lists. The law provided for penalties for willful violations and auditors were enjoined not to approve payment to assessors unless the lists were satisfactorily made out.[10] For purposes of property taxation the assessors would not need to collect crop and acreage data. However, collection of that information for wheat and corn had been undertaken before the statistical system was installed and under that system it was merely extended to include all varieties of farm products.

Certain kinds of information, e.g. meteorological, were systematically collected from a handful of private or quasi-public primary collectors; while banks and railways were separately enumerated from time to time. Intermittently, attempts were made to collect statistics on births, deaths, and industrial production, but local officials were neither empowered nor enjoined to set up the necessary data-collection procedures and these classes of statistics were dropped. Under Mansfield and for a few reports after him, annual reports were usually commemorated by special statistical collections but these special reports soon disappeared. Once routinized, local officers of government considered data collection and reporting as a secondary function of the job. As this was not their primary function and as no compensation was allowed for the work, a tendency to neglect and carelessness came to the attention of central compiling officers, and hence recommendations for compensation to local reporting officers were frequently made [10, 1880, p. 194; 1881, pp. 6f.; 1888, pp. 16f.].

There were three separate classes of time series for Ohio utilized in the present investigation: (a) building of different types by number and/or value; (b) recorded conveyance information regarding deeds and mortgages by number and value; (c) marriages by number. Since statistics were collected and published chiefly in the form of county returns, we had, besides statewide aggregates, separate tabulations for the three highly urbanized counties with the largest central cities—Hamilton (Cincinnati), Cuyahoga (Cleveland), and Lucas (Toledo)—and for twenty sampled counties collected into five groups, selected to exhibit both degree of urbanization and location. The basis for selection of the sampled counties and general information about them is provided in Appendix C.

All the Ohio data were collected by local officers of government and consolidated at the county level into county totals. It was found possible to test the validity of other Ohio series by independently derived annual series for (a) building permit data, (b) marriages, (c) mortgages and deeds by number and value in Franklin County for 1900–1920, and (d) mortgage recordings by number and value annually by counties between 1880 and 1889 [38; 214; 265; 264]. Comparison of building permit data available for four central cities from 1900 to 1912 and for one central city back to 1888, with corresponding assessor data for the counties involved, showed the expected order of magnitudes and parallelism of pattern. Cumulated into decade totals, our Ohio series were checked against decennial benchmark measures derived either from state or nationwide Census counts. All comparisons, both annual and decennial, showed divergences, partly traceable to variations in coverage and definitions and partly due to other causes. However, these divergences did not impair broad comparability for level and pattern even on the county level, and were reduced to minor proportions for county returns consolidated into group or statewide totals. A detailed presentation of this evidence is reserved for a later publication.

In my work of 1964 [109, pp. 19–34] a full presentation was made in both tabular and graphic form of the economic and demographic characteristics of Ohio as related to that of the nation as a whole. The course of Ohio residential production both by decades and on a year-to-year basis was related both to year¹y variations in residential building elsewhere and to decade shiftings in net dwelling stocks in Ohio as disclosed by decennial Census benchmark counts. A detailed report on Ohio building statistics may be found in my paper of 1966 [108].

Conveyance Statistics

Our Ohio statistics include conveyance as well as building records. Conveyance statistics are those on the number and value of real estate instruments designed to convey or affirm title (deeds) or to borrow money on the security of a mortgage instrument. These instruments are filed, or "recorded," in public records maintained by a local county "recorder of deeds." Both internal and external checks indicate that the work of compiling the recorders' reports was generally performed conscientiously, though it was necessary to scrutinize statewide collations carefully for lapses and irregularities. It is worth noting that on two occasions independent tabulation of recorders' annual mortgage recordings for all counties between 1880 and 1889 and for Franklin County between 1900 and 1920 confirmed the general validity of the countywide totals listed in the published returns [38; 265].

The earliest conveyance reports merely listed the number of deed instruments, mortgage recordings, and the "amount secured." Since mortgage instruments must specify unambiguously the sums borrowed and payable, an accurate comprehensive return of dollar value liability would not be difficult to render. Leases were included in the deed totals until 1867, but since they numbered only 3 or 4 per cent of deeds, allowance for them could be made. Liens were specifically included with mortgages for only a few early years; they were dropped explicitly in 1864 without affecting the trend. From the beginning, railway mortgage recordings were separately noted, though formal exclusion from the totals and separate tabulation did not begin until the 1868 report. Since railway mortgages ran to immense sums, relative to other recordings, it seems likely that our series from 1858 to 1868 did not include them.[11]

Conveyance statistics were made much more usable in 1877 with major increases in detail reported. Reporting on deeds was amplified by the separation of nominal from bona fide deeds. The latter were reported for three categories of transactions:

deeds for farmlands, deeds for unplatted lands ("town acres") sold by the acre but included within municipal boundaries, and deeds for platted or subdivided land within municipal boundaries ("town lots"). Later a fourth class of deeds, entitled "complicated" or "mixed" conveyances, was added. These soon came to number less than 3 per cent of town lot deeds. Their money values were highly uneven, since they included many very small and some large transactions. In this fourth category were, evidently, transfers of parcels of property located both within and without corporate boundaries and conveyances for mineral and oil-bearing lands (formally so designated in the 1903 and following reports). Our tabulations were confined to town acres and town lot transactions. These deeds were reported both by number and "amount of consideration"; while deeds in town acres were also enumerated with regard to number of acres (as were farmlands). When reporting for consideration began, only 6.85 per cent of the deeds were for nominal consideration. The practice of recording only nominal values slowly spread until, by the end of the period, 71.8 per cent of all recorded deeds were nominal. Hence it was clear that trends for bona fide deeds by number or total value would be biased downward. Our records of bona fide deeds were accordingly tabulated by computing per deed values, providing some indication of the movement of realty price levels, complicated by shifts in the mixture of sales for different classes of property. Though recording of consideration was voluntary, there seems little grounds to dispute the validity of the consideration for bona fide deeds. Buyers and sellers of real property could oftentimes benefit by recording contract of purchase. In Chicago, Hoyt reported that true consideration was usually given in deeds from 1830 to 1890 "or later."[12] In legal proceedings, however, little credence is given to consideration "expressly cited in deeds" [25, p. 482]. Certainly even without desire to hide disclosure of terms of sale, a legitimate motive for recital of nominal consideration would be present in the case of deeds executed by trustees, by administrators or guardians, or for conveying of gifts and inheritances. More disturbing is an Ohio report which found that practice varied with regard to inclusion in consideration of value of mortgage assumed [38, Table 16, pp. xxii, 32 ff.]. Since between 10 and 20 per cent of deeds in this Franklin County study involved assumption of mortgages, variation in practice in this respect was important. In the same study, a tabulation was made by years, from 1917 to 1937, of the amount of consideration stated in bona fide deeds and assessed value for the same property. The assessed value is shown in Chart E-1 as a per cent of stated consideration. In the early 1920's assessed value should have fallen to perhaps two-thirds of true consideration, and should have risen as a fraction of consideration in the Great Depression. The erratic behavior of the chart indicates that in the later years of our survey, movement of per deed value became unreliable, at least according to one investigation. On the other hand, recorded deed values for farmlands exhibited a

CHART E-1

Ratio of Assessed Value to Consideration Given, "Other Than Dollar Deeds," Recorded in Franklin County 1917–37

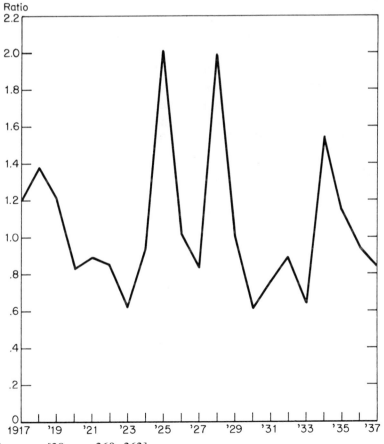

Source: [38, pp. 360, 363].

rational and orderly character throughout most of our surveyed period.

With the indicated caution, we analyzed per deed values for town lots and town acres, yielding respectively a per deed value for platted town property and a per acre value for undeveloped town acreage. A series for aggregate town acres sold and total consideration was then checked for pattern of movement against a series of amount secured by mortgages of town acres. The patterns were congruent, indicating that deed consideration data is worthy of close scrutiny. These series plus one on total deeds, bona fide and nominal, were tabulated and analyzed.

Adjustments on grounds of deficiencies or errata were most easily handled in the series for total deeds. There were eighty deficient counties over the sixty-three reporting years; some twenty-two of these deficient returns were in one year, 1864. Returns for the year 1888 were not published and were interpolated linearly; while for two years the number of nominal deeds was estimated.

Few adjustments were needed for the sample deeds data. For the years 1858–67, deeds and leases were reported in a single category. The number of deeds alone was then estimated, using the ratio for 1867–72 of deeds to deeds and leases (88 to 98 per cent), and applying it to 1858–66. The sample groups included twenty-six deficient returns throughout the sixty-three-year period. These were adjusted either on the basis of their own behavior or that of their group in adjoining years. Linear interpolation was used for the six years for which Group I and the two years for Group II were absent from the returns. From 1895 to 1920 the total number of deeds was taken from the sum of nominal and bona fide deeds, rather than from the "grand total" reported, as the latter seemed unreliable.

The "town lot" data was in poorer shape. Except for the years 1882 and 1900, published summary totals were accepted subject to two adjustments: any unmatched report for number or values for a given county and any outlandish or extreme entry for numbers and value were deleted. Altogether, eighty counties were deleted from the numbers count and twenty-seven from the values count. More difficult to allow for was absence of value reports for Hamilton between 1883 and 1893 and 1897 and 1898. Since differentials between Hamilton and the rest-of-state levels per deed were declining, we adjusted statewide value levels per deed for the absence of Hamilton by a sliding scale.

Adjustments for the sample groups were more complicated because of the numerous (sixty-one) deficient and erratic returns. Per deed values for Group I were adjusted for the absence of Hamilton for 1883–95 by a sliding scale, similar to the statewide adjustment, on the basis of Cuyahoga per deed values. For 1899–1900 per deed values for Cuyahoga alone were used. For sample IV unmatched reports in number or value in a given county for the years 1879–87 were deleted, and group per deed values included only those counties reporting both number and value. The same procedure was used for sample V from 1877 to 1893, with only two exceptions (1883, 1887). All omissions for Groups II and III were adjusted by a "group method" which was also used for Group IV after 1887 and for Group V after 1893. Through the group method the group total, rather than an individual county, was estimated on the basis of group behavior in an adjoining year.

Town acre statistics were difficult to correct for deficient returns since coverage of sales of town acres was spotty for the smaller counties. Counties reporting acreage sales varied between thirty-eight (1919) and fifty-eight (1884). Deficiencies in acreage or consideration were made up in the following manner: if the county reported only the acreage and not the consideration, the acreage report was subtracted from the audited statewide total. The resulting total was then divided into the consideration total, yielding an average value per acre. This average value was then applied to the reported acreage figure for the deficient county, giving an estimated consideration for that county. The same procedure was followed in estimating the number of acres when only consideration was given. In this case, the amount of consideration for the deficient county was divided by the average value, rendering the estimated number of acres. When an urban county was deficient, the same procedure was used except for the derivation of the average value. An urban average value was used, based on the average values of ten urban counties (composing the first three sample groups) for the year in which a county was deficient in acreage or consideration.

There were many cases where either numbers of acres or total

consideration was reported alone. Altogether, of the ten urbanized counties there were 22 omissions, and of other counties,
121 omissions, over the forty-two-year period. Particular county
returns, which by reason of abnormally high or low acreage
values seemed aberrant after special examination, were dropped
from the returns in ten cases. Because of the unevenness in
returns and difficulty in checking for deficiencies, all final
acreage returns were adjusted by a three-year moving average.
Of the statewide totals, there were analyzed total consideration
for town acres, number of acres sold as recorded in bona fide
deeds, and consideration per deed. For the sample groups, only
the number of acres and per acre value were analyzed.

The more detailed reporting of mortgage data commenced
only with 1885 and ran to 1920. In 1885 mortgage returns by
number and value were separately presented for farmland, town
lots, and town acres. Fortunately, it was found possible to
extend our town lot series back to 1880, based on a census
investigation of mortgage recordings for each year of the 1880's
[265]. Adjustments of mortgage returns for statewide and group
tabulations were carried on at four levels: (a) use of Census
returns between 1880 and 1884; (b) exclusion of oil and mineral
mortgages especially enumerated after 1885; (c) adjustment for
absence of Hamilton county mortgage value figures between
1883 and 1900; (d) adjustment for deficiencies either of number
or value or both.

Census values for town lot mortgages between 1880 and 1884
were scaled down by 10 per cent to exclude town acre mortgages
and to allow for varying coverage.

A special check was made of per deed value mortgages for all
counties in which gas or oil activities were involved. Mortgage
values for four counties between 1881 and 1885 were found
abnormally high and were scaled down to statewide levels.

The adjustment for Hamilton had to make allowance for its
heavy weight in statewide totals and for the trend of its performance as well. From 1883 to 1889, use could be made of Census
enumeration. From 1890 to 1899, Hamilton mortgage returns
were estimated on the basis of the average of four large urban
counties.

Adjustments for deficiencies were relatively few in all the
mortgage series. Thus town lot mortgages recorded seventy-
eight deficient returns for a thirty-five-year period. Between

thirty-one (1919) and forty-nine (1893) counties reported mortgage recordings on town acres. Adjustments for sample groups were scrutinized with special care. Only in ten instances were particular sample county returns for total mortgage number and value modified because of assumed error. Throughout all mortgage series, Stark County was excluded from sample Group III because of its irregular behavior.

All deed and mortgage returns from 1858 to 1920 were for a fiscal year ending June 30. To avoid further smoothing of our material, the fiscal year was treated as equivalent to a calendar year. This tended to cause conveyance data to lag slightly in our timing calculations.

Since mortgage and deed values were in current dollars, it was necessary to consider adjustment to some standard of defined purchasing power. Chart E-2 shows the value of mortgages per recording in current dollars (series 0170) and as adjusted by the Riggleman index. The contrast with the set of corresponding charts on residential and total building before and after adjustment for appraisal shifts is striking. Application of the Riggleman index to the 1858–65 mortgage values results in a very questionable level of per-unit value recordings not reached again until the 1910's. There is little doubt that the sudden rise of per-unit mortgage values in 1917–20 and the doubling of the value and volume of mortgage recordings in 1920 do reflect wartime inflation. However, these peak values were not included in our main tabulations, which ran, so far as cycles are concerned, from trough to trough. Hence systematic price adjustment of our mortgage values until after World War I did not seem called for. Unlike the per-unit building values, undeflated mortgage recordings between 1858 and 1905 fluctuated around a stationary level. The influences which were working to boost average values of transactions—higher levels of income, higher land values, and use of larger and more expensive buildings—were apparently offset by extension of the facilities of mortgage lending to smaller classes of dealings or to lower-ranking home and farm buyers.

Marriages

Responsibility for tabulation of marriage licenses was centered on probate court judges who were required to make an

CHART E-2

State of Ohio: Per Unit Value of Mortgages (Original and as Modified by Cost of Building Riggleman Index)

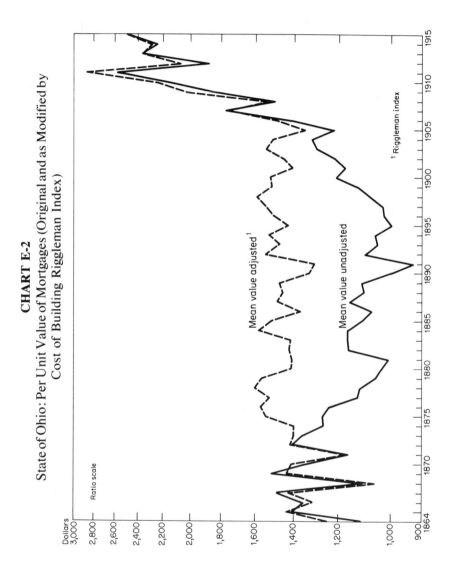

¹ Riggleman index

annual report on them to the statistics commissioner, along with statistics of wills, births, and divorces. The first three reports merely enumerated "marriages," but the 1861 report distinguished between marriage by license and by banns, the latter accounting through the years for less than 4 per cent of total marriages. Between 1887 and 1906 there is an independent Census enumeration, which, both on a statewide and sample level, approximates closely the magnitudes enumerated in state statistics. Differences in annual returns could grow out of errors of enumeration and divergent fiscal years. The respective totals are shown in Chart E-3.

CHART E-3
Comparison of Ohio Marriages as Compiled by Ohio Officials and Census Bureau, 1887–1906

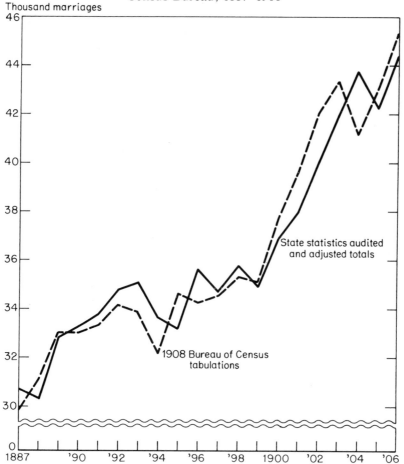

Adjustments for deficient returns of counties presented few problems. For the entire period there were only fifty-one deficiencies, concentrated in the reporting years 1858, 1868, 1869, 1875. The first fourteen reports were based on a fiscal year ending July 1. Thereafter, reporting dates were March 31. Rather than adjusting returns to a neat calendar-year basis, we preferred to predate the marriage series on substantially the same basis as our residential building chronologies.

Plan of A Bureau

"Plan Of A Bureau" Prepared By the Commissioner of Statistics, February 1858. Report to Governor and Legislature*

1. A commissioner of statistics, and one clerk; the commissioner to be charged with the supervision, arrangement, compilation and report of all the statistics now or hereafter to be obtained; and, for this purpose, all statistics, not necessary to the auditing of public accounts, or to the duties of their respective offices, be transferred from the offices of the Auditor and Secretary of State to that of the Commissioner of Statistics.

2. That the laws relative to the duties of assessors, auditors, clerks, recorders, &c., be amended in these particulars.

1. The ASSESSORS to report, in addition to crops of corn and wheat now obtained, the crops of oats, barley and hay, to be obtained and reported in the same manner as heretofore in regard to corn and wheat. The assessors of cities, towns and villages, in the same manner as they now return carriages, watches and pianos, to ascertain and return the number and kind of manufacturing establishments, the number of hands employed, and the value of the manufactured products.

These duties are all performed in Massachusetts and New York by the township assessors, and very well performed. When it is considered that these officers have to visit every house, and ask numerous questions, it will be seen that no more locomotion, and very little additional trouble is required by the additional questions.

3dly. That the auditors, recorders, clerks of courts, and clerks of towns be required to report to the Bureau of Statistics, any matters of fact to be found in their office, relating to the subjects

* [208, 1858, II, pp. 547–49]. See p. 286 above.

of his inquiry, and to be allowed the usual fees of office, from the county.

4thly. The canal collectors throughout the State be required to report, as far as they can ascertain these facts, the commerce of the ports where they are stationed, with their exports and imports.

5thly. The officers of Railroad Companies be required to make to the Commissioner of Statistics an annual report, at the time he may specify, in reply to the questions he may ask, of the condition, cost, machinery, and business of said road, in the same manner as banks, insurance companies, and other corporations are now by law required to do.

This provision will be all that is necessary to secure what has been much demanded, an official supervision of Railroads, in regard to a large number of which the public has no authentic information. The States of Massachusetts and New York have made very strict regulations, in regard to reports of Railroads, the result of which is, that in those States every material fact, in relation to the cost, safety, and management of Railroads is fully known.

6thly. In relation to births, marriages and deaths, a much simpler and less expensive plan may be adopted, than is now in force. The marriage licenses now issued by the Probate Court, is the nearest approach to accuracy, which has yet been obtained in the U. States. It is defective, however, in one particular, that some small societies, and some individuals choose to publish the *bans* of marriages, as it is termed, before a religious society. The number is small, but a defect may be easily supplied. Let the law require the clergymen to report the number, name, and condition of those whose *bans* they published, and the parties who obtained a *license* furnish the Probate Court with all the particulars which is now required. In this way an accuracy may be had in relation to marriages, not to be obtained any where. In regard to BIRTHS, there seems to be no way to arrive at them, but through the means heretofore employed. But the assessors, physicians, and those who obtain these facts should report them to the Probate Court, there to be embodied. In regard to DEATHS, there is one certain and perfectly accurate mode of obtaining them, and only one mode. This is by the *Interments.* In New York, Boston, Cleveland, and many other places, the deaths are obtained more accurately than any other class of statistics. All who die must be buried, and when buried in fixed places, the burial is always known. The State has a right to know, for purposes of justice and police, as well as statistics, the burial place of every one who dies. The want of that knowledge has sometimes defeated justice. It is absolutely necessary to prove a marriage or a death to establish just rights. The law should require a *permit* from the Probate office for each burial made, and this should show the age, name, and disease of the party buried. This permit should be recorded in the Probate offices. Thus the entire record of births, marriages, and deaths, will be like mortgages and judgments, recorded in each county. The expensive polls, and printing now required will be done away with, while the statistics will be more perfect and the ends of justice better answered.

In the information I have obtained, much has been got, by my solicitation, of private individuals, who alone possessed the power to give it. This has been particularly the case in relation to coal, iron, and manufactures. Even if perfectly willing to furnish it, the State should be equally willing to offer them some slight compensation. I suggest that the Bureau of Statistics, be allowed a small contingent fund, to be used for such purposes, and accounted for by sufficient vouchers, furnished the Auditor of State.

In the plan of a Bureau of Statistics here suggested, it is quite probable that the saving of labor, in other public offices, and in the statistics of births, marriages, and deaths, will be quite equal to the cost of the Bureau to the State, while the local statistics will cost only a small additional fee paid by the counties for their own local statistics. While the cost on one hand is so small, the value to the State, to each county, and to the whole people will be very great. Bankers, merchants, railroad companies, insurers—have all learned so well the value of this species of knowledge, that they have all paid high to obtain it, while the Government of the U. States, and the enlightened governments of Europe are using all proper means to advance the science, the study and the utility of statistics.

Appendix F

The determination of specific and reference chronologies makes possible a simple yet precise measure of timing for all corresponding series. One need merely count off the years of lead or lag, if any, and compute a mean lead or lag with an average deviation as a measure of dispersion. This is one of the standard cyclical timing measures worked out and used by the National Bureau of Economic Research in previous investigations.[13] The measure is derived from a direct comparison between matching or "corresponding" specific and reference peaks and troughs, i.e., between turning points for selected activities and residential building. The specific chronologies of a local residential building series are related, as we have previously stated, to reference chronologies of the corresponding larger regional or national aggregate. Altogether some 661 specific turning points, about 85 per cent of the total available, were matched for 118 series, involving, all told, some 260 long reference cycles. The results are set forth in Table F-1. The 119 unmatched turning points represent "extra" specific cycles or "skipped" reference cycles. Nearly two-thirds of the unmatched turning points relate to Ohio experience; non-Ohio reference and specific cycle patterns are more synchronized. In the great majority of cases, turning points were more easily matched than was indicated in the case of national business-cycle chronologies. The heterogeneity of the series there dealt with, measuring against a single reference scale all phases of business life analyzed on a sensitive monthly or quarterly basis, made the operation of "matching" specific with business cycles "very hazardous" [41, p. 117]. The greater homogeneity of our series and predominant use of local reference chronologies simplified the task of judgment. Nearly half the unmatched turns were found in "irregular" series—nearly four-fifths of which were in Ohio—with only slight apparent relation to building cycles. In a small minority of cases, the scope for judgment was wide and the resulting measures were unreliable.

Even when turns are successfully matched, the resulting leads

TABLE F-1

General Characteristics of 169 Analyzed Series

	Building Series			Other Series			Total
	Ohio	Non-Ohio	Total	Ohio	Non-Ohio	Total	
1. Number of series with:							
a. Matched turning points	34[a]	24	58	33[a]	34[a]	67	125
b. Reference cycle only	0	0	0	32	3	35	35
c. Specific cycle only	0	4	4	0	5	5	9
Total	34	28	62	65	42	107	169
2. Number of turning points:							
a. Matched	180	131	311	148	202	350	661
b. Unmatched	53	27	80	22	17	39	119
3. Number of long reference cycles included in:							
a. (1a) above	84 1/2	32	116 1/2	66 1/2	89 1/2	156	272 1/2
b. (1b) above	2	0	2	67	7	74	76
Total	86 1/2	32	118 1/2	133 1/2	96 1/2	230	348 1/2

NOTE: This table includes all local building series analyzed on a nationwide reference chronology.

[a] Contains one series which was noncorresponding by turning points.

or lags must be used with caution as a measure of structural temporal relationship. In the first place, the practice of setting reference dates at the close of a flat or double peak or trough produces a bias. Secondly, the temporal relationship holds only for turning-point years themselves. But even a long time series running over three long cycles will yield only seven eligible turning points; a two-cycle series will yield only five eligible turning-point years. Not all eligible turning points will be successfully matched. The use of unsmoothed annual returns allows what Mitchell once characterized as the "cloud of random happenings" to affect chronology when operative in the turning-point zone [193, p. 98]. In addition structural changes are at work—and more potently in long than in short cycles. Temporal relationships may well vary with the strength of influences which expand or contract durations. For these reasons, it has always been indicated that they were "highly variable" in the business cycle [42, p. 179]. It was just this high variability in temporal relationships which the Harvard research group found so disconcerting when an attempt was made to estimate them among covarying time series.[14] The tangible measure of this high variability is taken by our mean deviation from the mean lead-lag and the ratio of the mean lead-lag to its average deviation. For fifty-seven building series, the mean lag was .19 ± 1.51 years. The mean deviation for the same measure was 2.06 ± .96 years.

Because of this high variability, our lead-lag measure at turning points was supplemented by two alternative measures. One is another NBER standard timing measure, derived directly from review of reference cycle patterns. The procedure of determining lead-lag from reference cycle patterns is comprehensively described in [41, pp. 185 ff.]. On the basis of successive and average reference cycle patterns, each series was classified as either positive, inverted, neutral, or irregular. Classification was carried through on the basis of six rules crystallized along lines previously developed in the National Bureau:

A. Neutral Series
 1. Expansion segment covers two reference expansion phases and two reference contraction phases.
B. Postive and Inverted Series
 2. Must generally rise for at least two but not more than six

consecutive stages or fall for at least two but not more than six consecutive stages.
3. More than half of the phase movements are conforming (positive) or more than half are nonconforming (inverted).
4. The selected expansion must contain more stages of expansion than contraction.

C. Irregular Series
5. All patterns are irregular if they do not meet A and B above or if successive cycle patterns diverge essentially from the average pattern.

D. Trend
6. Leveling off in a phase is only considered a movement if it is in clear contrast with a trend of the opposite phase.

The most unambiguous is rule 1. It indicates that specific turning points will tend to be placed at nearly the center of reference cycle phases.

The effect of rules 2 and 4 is to screen out irregular series. Under rule 2, a series is considered irregular if its reference cycle pattern over the eight cycle stages moves continually in the same direction or continually changes direction. Under rule 4, a series is considered irregular unless the selected expansion segment contains more stages of expansion than contraction. If, for example, it seems that expansion runs from II-VIII, then at least four of these stages must involve expansion.

Rule 3 provided the basis for characterizing a given series as positive or inverted. Patterns with five or more phases which conform to standard (rise during reference expansion I-V and fall in reference contractions V-IX) are positive; and vice versa for the inverted.

These rules were chiefly used to evaluate a time series as reflected by its average and successive reference cycle pattern. If these successive patterns were themselves irregular, or fluctuated excessively in form, then regardless of the behavior of the average pattern the series was classed as "irregular." Usually irregular series were so exhibited both in their individual and average versions. Discretion in classification was exercised chiefly when use of the rules yielded a different outcome with individual cycle patterns and their average.

The results of this allocation into classes of 160 reference series are summed up in Table F-2. It is interesting to compare this pattern of distribution of building cycles with the analogous pattern of distribution of 794 American series for business cycles. The respective per cent shares for each class are set forth in the following tabulation:

Cycle Class	794 Series Analyzed for Short Business Cycles	160 Series Analyzed for Building Cycles
Positive	76.5	71.3
Inverted	9.8	10.0
Irregular	10.7	16.3
Neutral	3.1	2.5

SOURCE: [193, pp. 53-56].

We see that the distribution of building reference cycle patterns by type closely resembles the analogous distribution of business-cycle reference cycle patterns. The principal pattern divergence is the larger number of irregulars in building cycles. Most of these are found in Ohio and include few series measuring building activity directly. The more common types are series relating to activities only slightly affected by waves of building, e.g., manufacturing value, mortgage lending series, sluggish series such as marriages, or average value series. The last are affected by a crisscross of influences, including price movements proper, as well as shifts in distribution by type of deed (purchase or mortgage) or size of instrument. Over half of the Ohio irregulars were found in the sample group made up of counties with a low degree of urbanization, heavily dependent upon farming. It is a measure of the diffuse quality and lack of

TABLE F-2
Classification of Local Reference Series by Type

Classification of 160 Reference Series	Building			Other			Total
	Ohio	Non-Ohio	Total	Ohio	Non-Ohio	Total	
Positive	25	22	47	44	23	67	114
Inverted	2	0	2	8	6	14	16
Irregular	7	2	9	12	5	17	26
Neutral	0	0	0	1	3	4	4
Total	34	24	58	65	37	102	160

coherence in realty and building markets of such areas that seven out of sixteen reference cycle patterns in this area were irregular, while in other sample group areas no more than three patterns were found to be irregular.

It is curious that inverted series among business and building cycles should crop up with a frequency so nearly identical, at 10 per cent. Among business cycles, inverted series chiefly record unfavorable business developments like unemployment, commercial failure, or activities with negative income elasticities, or buffer stock inventories maintained to absorb sales instability [193, pp. 62 ff.]. Among building cycles, the same classes tend to invert, such as vacancies (a kind of unemployment of shelter facilities), and foreclosure (which falls into the class of unfavorable business developments). Only rarely will a nonresidential building series become an inverter, though long leads or lags or irregular behavior is common.

Positive and inverted patterns can have a variety of characteristic expansion phases depending upon relative duration and lead or lag. The number of reference patterns in each type is listed by our four-way breakdown in Table F-3. Because of the longer duration of building cycles it seemed advisable in twenty-four cases to recognize two-stage contractions, though this class was not recognized for business cycles. Hence, our list of possible expansion stages is more extended than was the business cycle list.

Despite this variance in classification, the distributive patterns of leads and lags at the peaks or troughs, as detailed in Table F-4, closely resemble the analogous pattern for business cycle series. There are more coincidences of timing in short cycles and there are fewer longer leads and lags. As with business cycles, leads preponderate at troughs; but at peaks, building cycle lags outnumber leads though business cycle leads and lags balance [193, pp. 73 ff.]. This greater preponderance of lags at peaks is owing to the tendency of many real estate and other building-related series to have relatively short contraction periods. These contractions come late and do not last long. Since reference chronologies are not adjusted to the predominant cluster of specific turning points but to one basic activity, other activities less strongly attuned to the predominant rhythm would tend to lead at troughs and lag at peaks.

To a degree, the phase lead-lags of reference cycle patterns

TABLE F-3
Classification of Reference Cycle Averages by Series, Ohio and Non-Ohio, Building and Other

Reference Cycle Stages with Expansion	Building		Other		Total
	Ohio	Non-Ohio	Ohio	Non-Ohio	
V-VIII (inverted)			2		2
V-IX			1		1
V-II					
V-III					
VI-IX					
VI-II					
VI-III	1		1		2
VI-IV	1			1	2
VII-II					
VII-III (neutral)			1	1	2
VII-IV (positive)			1		1
VII-V	1				1
VIII-III			2		2
VIII-IV	2	2			4
VIII-V	2	4	5	3	14
VIII-VI	1		5		6
VIII-VII	2				2
I-III			1	1	2
I-IV				3	3
I-V	9	6	10	6	31
I-VI	4	2	6	3	15
I-VII	2	3	5	1	11
II-V	1	4	2		7
II-VI			2	1	3
II-VII			4	4	8
III-V		1		1	2
III-VI	1		1		2
III-VII (neutral)				2	2
III-VIII (inverted)				1	1
III-IX			1		1
IV-VII			2	1	3
IV-VIII			1	2	3
IV-IX				1	1
Irregular	7	2	12	5	26
Totals	34	24	65	37	160

TABLE F-4

Leads and Lags, 134 Long Building and 709 Business Cycle Average
Reference Cycle Patterns

	Building Series Analyzed		Business Series Analyzed (Per Cent)
	Number	Per Cent	
Behavior at trough			
2-stage leads	7	5.2	5.3
1-stage leads	34	25.4	18.7
Coincidences	65	48.5	66.1
1-stage lags	18	13.4	5.8
2-stage lags	8	6.0	4.1
3-stage lags	2	1.5	–
All leads	41	30.6	23.9
Coincidences	65	48.5	66.1
All lags	28	20.9	10.0
Behavior at peaks			
2-stage leads	8	6.0	1.5
1-stage leads	15	11.2	14.6
Coincidences	59	44.0	66.7
1-stage lags	29	21.6	13.0
2-stage lags	23	17.2	4.0
All leads	23	17.2	16.1
Coincidences	59	44.0	66.7
All lags	52	38.8	17.1

NOTE: In addition to the series analyzed, there were twenty-six irregular building series and eighty-five irregular business series.

SOURCE: Data for business cycles taken from [193, p. 53]. Mitchell's schedule of percentages were adjusted to exclude per cent of irregular series, making analyzed series equal to 100 per cent.

are free from some of the biases which affect turning-point lead-lags. Thus, irregular or short-cyclical influences which accentuate peak or trough values are smoothed in reference cycle patterns. The reference cycle phase leads or lags may be converted into years by average cycle duration and then may be used to check turning-point lead-lags.

The mean and median lead-lags by reference cycle and turning-point analysis are set forth for all of our building and nonbuilding series in Table F-5. From this table, it appears that computation of lead-lags by reference cycle patterns in building activity comes out with appreciably longer lags (.41 over .19 years) but that the reverse occurs with nonbuilding series. Reference cycle results for building series are more concentrated than the distribution of lead-lags on a turning-point basis. Scatter diagrams of paired observations exhibit a relatively wide variance with one quarter of all observations falling outside a three-year range around the central tendencies. Uncertainty thus remains regarding our lead-lag measures, and to allay this uncertainty a third test was developed by pairing smoothed specific and reference series over the lead-lag spectrum and determining optimum lead-lag by the highest correlation coefficient.[15]

Before correlation, it was necessary to remove the role of short cyclical or irregular movements from the data. We experimented at first with interpolated overlapping average specific short cycle standings. But since short cycles overlapped very often during contractions with long-swing movements, use of a moving average of three to five years was found preferable. The correlations were carried out for eleven different time-period pairs (five-year lag to five-year lead). Trend was not removed from the series before the correlation but was removed from the correlation coefficients by a conversion formula.[16]

This permitted account to be taken of the effects in each case of removal of trend from the pattern of the correlation coefficients. The resulting set of correlation coefficients was graphed on standard scales, with serial lags for the X axis and the correlation coefficient on the Y axis, making up a "correlogram." As computed, the reference series (residential or total building) is treated as the dependent variable with fixed timing, while the other correlated variable is given variable timing from plus five years to a serial lead of minus five years. Only for a few series with extreme leads (such as vacancies) was the serial order high enough to disclose two turns for the mean period of fluctuation. For a few series with a long duration and long lead-lag, the serial order was too low to permit the optimum correlation clearly to emerge (as was true of Stockholm vacancy, series 0040). But in all cases the level of the correlogram at or near the optimum lead-lag provided an independent measure of the amount of variation in the reference variable "explained" by

TABLE F-5

Means and Standard Deviations of Timing Meaures, Ohio and Non-Ohio, Building and Other

	Average Lead-Lag, Turning-Point Method (1)	Average Deviation, Lead-Lag, Turning Point (2)	Average Lead-Lag, Reference-Phase Method (3)	Average Lead-Lag, Correlation Method (4)
		Building		
Ohio				
Mean	.16 (1.62)	1.97 (.71)	.53 (1.53)	−.138 (1.8)
Number of series	33	33	27	18
Non-Ohio				
Mean	.24 (1.34)	2.20 (1.18)	.25 (1.76)	.500 (.50)
Number of series	24	24	22	4
		Other		

			Total	
Ohio				
Mean	.78 (1.66)[a]	2.12 (1.18)[a]	.27 (1.78)	.786 (1.82)
Number of series	32	32	53	28
Non-Ohio				
Mean	−.34 (2.08)	1.96 (.83)	−.12 (2.31)	−.733 (2.21)
Number of series	33	33	32	30
Building				
Mean	.19 (1.51)	2.06 (.96)	.41 (1.63)	−.022 (2.17)
Number of series	57	57	49	22
Other				
Mean	.21 (1.97)[a]	2.04 (1.02)[a]	.15 (2.00)	0 (1.66)
Number of series	65	65	85	58

NOTE: Figures in parentheses are standard deviations.

[a] Uses inverted measure for 0232.

a linear regression on the correlated variable. The optimum correlation coefficient thus may serve as a crude measure of covariation between cycles of the reference series and of the "specific" series. Unlike other measures of synchronization or conformity, the correlation coefficient allows for covariation in form or magnitude of movement as well as in direction of movement.

Of course the correlation coefficient for a sample of observations is subject to sampling variation. However, the reliability of the observed correlation coefficients must be estimated by complex methods. See [84, pp. 293 ff.].

The form of the correlogram may point to disturbance in the serial correlation. It does not however directly indicate the source of this disturbance, which could be due to timing or amplitude irregularities or variation in allocation by phases of cycle duration in successive cycles either of the reference series or of the "specific" series. The fact that only comparatively few long cycles were available for tabulation meant that the five-year segments dropped from the correlation at either end of the serial order could exert an influence on the correlogram. In general, the sinelike form of the correlogram can be affected by random factors when only a short term of experience of two serially correlated autoregressive series oscillating irregularly around the same mean period are available for scrutiny [151, p. 406]. If a sufficiently long segment of experience were available for analysis, the form of the correlogram (if extended over advanced serial orders) would have provided a method of determining the underlying character of the temporal relationship [151, p. 404].

Comparison of different correlograms for the same reference series or local area or aggregate, however, points to characteristics of the relationship which are obscure in the original time-series or which are only weakly exhibited in the contrast of specific and reference cycle patterns. The correlograms therefore are serviceable for more than measuring optimum lead-lag. They supplement our exhibit of reference and specific cycle patterns. We have accordingly presented correlograms along with cycle patterns whenever the need arose.

The general level of lead-lags for building and other series in Ohio and elsewhere was presented earlier in Table F-5, col. 4. The mean level of lead-lags can be compared by the three different measures. For building series, reference cycle methods tend to lag and correlogram analysis to lead, with turning-point methods in between. For nonbuilding series no uniform tendency stands out. All three methods yield essentially the same result, since all three point to very short leads or lags, less than one year, on the average.

To permit divergencies in methods of estimation to stand out more clearly, the spread between high and low measures of lead-lag by the three methods was tabulated. One hundred and eight local series were analyzed where at least two alternative timing methods were practiced; in four cases out of five the three methods were utilized. We excluded the eight residential building series of England, for which no correlogram analysis was prepared. The results are as follows:

Spread Between High-Low Lead or Lag by the Three Estimation Methods (Years)	Number of Series		
	Ohio	Non-Ohio	Total
0– .99	18	16	34
1.0–1.99	21	19	41
2.0–2.99	14	5	19
3.0–3.99	7	5	12
4 and over	1	2	3
Total	61	47	108

The three instances of four and over years involve a volatile Berlin migration series (0024) and two unsystematic Ohio series—mean value of town (nonfarm) lot mortgages for group V (0241) and number of town acres sold for group IV (0305). Two series with very large gaps, the value of commercial building, Ohio, group I (0187) and the number of town lot mortgages, Ohio, group IV (0232), were excluded because the basis for classification (positive and inverted) diverged, depending on analysis of turning points, reference cycle patterns, or correlograms. The table indicates that in seven cases out of ten the highest spread between alternative timing measures was less than two years; and that only in 13.8 per cent of the cases was the spread over three years. Considering the diversity in methods of smoothing employed (between reference cycle stages and moving average), divergencies of coverage (complete series with correlograms, corresponding turning points or characteristic stage phases) and divergent methods of handling extreme values (by least squares or simple averaging), the diversity in results achieved is understandable.

Appendix G

REGRESSION ANALYSIS, THIRTY LOCAL RESIDENTIAL BUILDING SERIES

Four basic long cycle measures for all local residential series are listed in Table G-1. Bivariate cross-relationships were exhibited in scatter diagrams to test the hypothesis that total amplitude is significantly influenced by either total duration, rates of secular growth, or fall rate per year. The scatter is wide and any correlation, if present, is of low degree. For areas of very high amplitude, excepting only Detroit, there was a clear tendency for growth to be inversely associated with amplitude. For the next ten cities on the amplitude scale, the same tendency for correlation is indicated but with more scatter and another structural set of coefficients. For areas of moderate to low amplitude, including Paris, London, and the Ohio sample groups, little systematic relationship of growth rates to amplitude is indicated. It will be noted that all amplitudes below 250, including London, Paris, the Ohio rural group, and three English cities, fall within a low and narrow band of growth rates. The three exceptions to this are the other Ohio sample groups, whose amplitude, it may be assumed, has been cut down by inclusion of farm building or by aggregation. If these three observations are adjusted up to their presumed individual city or county levels, then it would appear that our thirty urban areas subdivide into three basic types:

(a) a group of high-amplitude (350 and higher) central cities for whom growth rates are linearly and inversely related to amplitude with relatively high coefficients of relationship;

(b) a larger group of central cities at a lower amplitude level (280-350) with a clear linear inverse relation of growth rate to amplitude and reduced slope terms:

(c) a group of cities of mixed character—including metropolitan capitals like Paris and London, rural Ohio counties, and South Wales coal mining areas—with lower amplitudes (below 250) and very moderate growth rates.

The relation between amplitude and duration seems to involve

315

TABLE G-1
Array of Thirty Local Residential Building Series, Mean Amplitude, Growth, Duration

Residential Building Series	Mean Amplitude Specific		Mean Average Specific Long Duration (Years)	Secular Weighted Average[a] (% Per Year)
	Total (+)	Fall Per Year (−)		
1. Sydney	551.9	16.10	29.0	.023
2. Detroit[a]	482.0	41.31	27.5	8.131
3. Glasgow	453.0	21.82	24.0	−2.790
4. Victoria	445.6	21.38	33.0	−1.229
5. Stockholm	421.9	17.41	23.3	1.630
6. Chicago[b]	407.5	26.21	17.8	3.890
7. Hamburg	363.6	29.35	16.0	9.489
8. Swindon	350.3	40.45	10.5	−1.106
9. Montreal[b]	347.0	19.44	20.5	3.527
10. Exeter	334.0	19.08	19.0	1.167
11. Birmingham	316.4	18.79	26.5	1.856
12. St. Louis	314.8	13.88	16.5	2.757
13. Manhattan	304.5	17.51	18.4	1.154
14. Berlin	296.1	17.87	16.3	3.566

15.	Amsterdam	290.9	22.46	15.3	3.391
16.	Cleveland	284.1	15.46	20.5	5.557
17.	Liverpool	282.8	14.03	18.5	.517
18.	Manchester	273.4	12.22	28.0	1.304
19.	Cincinnati	271.2	13.22	16.0	4.213
20.	Bremen	266.4	17.02	18.4	1.459
21.	Bradford	254.8	13.51	17.3	.462
22.	Hull	232.2	14.23	19.3	.981
23.	Ohio Sample V	225.6	12.90	17.0	1.745
24.	South Wales House Building	223.6	27.53	18.5	1.800
25.	Newport	210.9	11.82	12.5	.474
26.	Ohio Sample IV	205.1	14.96	15.3	3.797
27.	London	201.8	9.06	19.3	.557
28.	Ohio Sample II	196.5	9.71	19.5	4.614
29.	Paris	191.9	12.05	20.8	1.144
30.	Ohio Sample III	181.2	11.33	16.0	4.177

[a] Per cent change in secular weighted average growth per year, successive short cycle standings.
[b] Total building activity.

a corresponding set of boundaries. For the middle group of amplitudes—between 290 and 360—the higher the amplitude the shorter the duration. But with the high amplitude group above 350, the higher the amplitude the more extended the duration. Below 290 no relation seems indicated. Why relation should shift in character at a size breaking point is not clear, though the breaking point is common to both growth and duration measures. Apparently structural relationships change in character or intensity as an amplitude boundary line nears 350 in magnitude.

A corresponding change in boundary behavior seems to hold for amplitude fall per year when related to total amplitude. Within the enclosed boundaries, rate of fall to total amplitude shows a very consistent and positive linear relationship. A freehand regression has the form $X = 25 + 15.5\ Y,$ where $X =$ total specific amplitude percentage fall per year. Here again, the regression holds up to a total amplitude value of around 350 and a rate of fall of 21 per cent per year. Beyond these boundaries an inverted relationship appears to set in.

The appearances may of course be deceptive, as in all cases of simple bivariate correlation in a system of intercorrelated variables. Clearly, in this case we need to sort out the influences of duration, total amplitude, and growth rate through multiple regression, using the 350 amplitude boundary line to separate a group of "high" and "low" amplitude urban areas. In two successive regressions total amplitude was regressed separately against fall rate and growth rate and duration. The principal results are set forth in Table G-2. They may be summarized as follows:

1. The relationship between fall rate and total amplitude differs strikingly between the low and high amplitude groups (referred to hereafter as L and H). In the L group, fall rate is substantially and steadily associated with total amplitude. Each per cent change in fall rate is associated with a 4.7 ± 1.9 per cent change in total amplitude. The relationship is more scattered with the H group, but the tendency is for a reverse association, with negative correlation and statistically unreliable regression coefficients (-2.9 ± 2.5). Causation may be indicated by the simple correlations of fall rate of growth and duration (Table G-2, lines 11 and 12). The H fall rate is negatively associated with H duration $(-.454)$ and just as strongly associated with H

Summary Results of Correlation Analysis: Thirty Local Building Series, Total Amplitude Fall per Year. Growth Rate per Year, and Duration

Line	Item	*Eight High Amplitude Cities from 350.3 to 551.9*		*Twenty-Two Lowest Amplitude Cities from 217.0 to 347.0*	
1.	X1 Mean total specific amplitude	434.5	(60.73)	266.7	(42.23)
2.	X2 Mean specific amplitude per year fall	−26.88	(9.00)	−15.80	(4.42)
3.	X3 Mean duration	22.38	(7.21)	18.58	(4.16)
4.	X4 Per year growth rate	2.896	(3.65)	2.260	(4.53)
	Correlation coefficients				
5.	$R_{1.2}$ (norm.)	−.2291		.4461	
6.	$R_{1.3}$	.8173		.0342	
7.	$R_{1.4}$	−.2303		.2015	
8.	$R_{13.4}$	.806		.0706	
9.	$R_{14.3}$	−.0303		.2104	
10.	$R_{1.34}$ (norm.)	.7318		.000	
11.	$R_{2.3}$	−.4539		.2418	
12.	$R_{2.4}$	.4635		.0257	
13.	$R_{3.4}$	−.2611		−.1685	
	Slope coefficients				
14.	Simple bX2	−2.924	(2.48)	4.654	(1.87)
15.	Multiple bX3	6.837	(2.25)	.7119	(2.30)
16.	Multiple bX4	−.30	(4.43)	5.879	(6.27)

NOTE: Figures in parentheses are standard errors or deviations.

growth rate (.464). But whereas H duration dominates total H amplitudes both on the simple and multiple regression ($R_{13.4}$ = .81) and emerges with statistically significant regression coefficients (6.8 ± 2.2), H growth rate emerges with zero influence on H total amplitude ($R_{14.3}$ = .03) and with a statistically unreliable regression coefficient (−.30 ± 4.43). The hypothesis is thus suggested that H fall rates influence total amplitude inversely through an inverse influence on H duration. The L fall rate has simpler relationships at lower amplitudes. It is strongly associated with total amplitude ($R_{1.2}$ = .45) but weakly with duration (R_2 = .24) and is dissociated with growth rate ($R_{2.4}$ = .03). Whatever causes more violent rates of fall will generate higher total amplitudes without significantly affecting growth rate or duration. But at the critical amplitude boundary, the higher fall rate recoils and reduces amplitude by shortening duration. This conclusion seems to be indicated by the regression.

2. Growth rate per se exerts little influence on total amplitude, as indicated by low partial correlation coefficients ($R_{14.3}$ = −.03, .21) and unreliable net regression coefficients.

3. The influence of duration is more complex. Whatever it is that shapes duration exerts little influence on total amplitude because of an implicit inverse association of duration and per year rates of change. Longer durations do not cumulate more amplitude but result in slower movements up to the critical boundary. Thereafter, rates of movement are nearly constant and whatever stretches out duration builds up amplitude. For this reason, the duration variable is strongly associated with H total amplitude ($R_{13.4}$ = .806), with a reliable and high-valued net regression coefficient (6.8 ± 2.2), while L durations bear no influence on total amplitude ($R_{13.4}$ = .07) and emerge with a weak and unreliable net regression coefficient (.71 ± 2.3).

Appendix H

URBAN RESIDENTIAL BUILDING INDEX, GERMANY:
Series 0018 (1890–1900 = 100) 1867–1913

The materials out of which this series was constructed consisted of a number of measures of varying origin concerning urban residential building in Germany between 1867 and 1914. The various measures are listed below, with source identification, and are graphically reproduced in Chart H-1.

Measure	Our Series Number	Years	Source
1. Net Annual Change Supply of Residential Dwellings:			
a. Berlin	0022	1841–1909	See Appendix B, p. 254.
b. Hamburg	0300	1875–1913	See Appendix B, p. 269.
2. Number of Main Buildings Constructed, Baden		1871–1908	NBER Series File 2,81b.
3. Number of Residential Buildings Constructed, Nine Cities *a*		1867–1913	Derived from [239, p. 23].
4. Dwellings Erected, Forty-two German Cities (Medium and Large)		1896–1913	[136, p. 59].
5. Net Adjusted Annual Growth, Number Residential Buildings, Prussia, All Urban Communities (3-Yr. Moving Average)		1869–1908	[87, p. 36].

a From 1867 to 1873 based on only four cities (Bremen, Köln, Breslau, Duisberg); Kiel and Aachen added in 1874; Gladbach, Dortmund, Freiburg added in 1880; Köln was dropped out in 1880 and restored in 1896. The series was crudely adjusted to uniform coverage by use of weights obtained from average population standings as of 1910 and estimates for earlier benchmark years. Returns for 1867–73 and 1874–95 were raised by 1.6 and 1.4 per cent, respectively, to adjust to a nine-city basis. The nine cities had in 1910 a total population of 2,210 thousand persons, while Berlin with suburbs had 3,730 thousand persons.

The basic data for measure number 5 above, presented by Feig and Mewes as a "limited if defective" (gewisser, wenn auch

CHART H-1

Measures of Urban Residential Building, German Cities
and Regions, 1867–1913

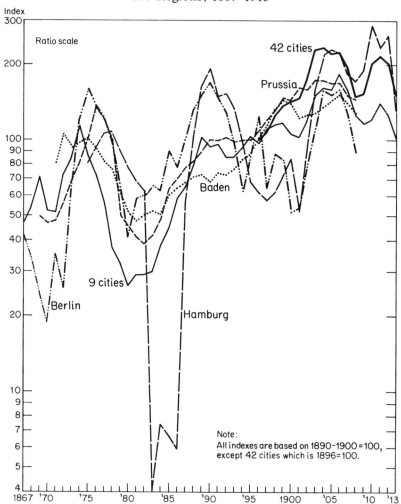

mangelhafter) substitution for building statistics, was provided
by the Prussian tax administration, which made available to the
authors an annual listing from 1870 to 1910 of the number of
taxable residential buildings in Prussia ("Anzahl der . . .
steuerpflichtigen Wohngebaüde . . . Preussen"). The authors
adjusted the increments (or first differences) to allow for
variation in reporting lags and fiscal year; and as adjusted the
increments correspond to completions within the calendar year
[87, pp. 31–33]. From 1870 to 1879 only total building reports

were available; for 1880 and later separate totals were provided for residential buildings located in cities ("Städte") and the rural communities ("Auf dem Lande").

In order to derive from these data a usable index of urban residential building, three sets of adjustments were made. First, the urban series was extended to 1868 on the basis of index behavior (1878 = 100) of total buildings. This seemed acceptable, since urban building accounted for all the net growth in later years and for most of the yearly variation. Secondly, some smoothing seemed indicated to offset yearly variations which creep into a flow series that would be affected by fiscal year variations, by variations in classifying buildings or by conversion of rural villages to city status. Hence, we applied a 3-year moving average. Finally, adjustment seemed desirable to offset the downward bias of a count of residential structures rather than of dwelling units. True, total structures over the period 1868–1908 increased by some 276 per cent, while Prussian urban population between 1870–1910 rose at nearly the same rate, 263 per cent [291, pp. 139–40]. However we know that during the period there was an increase in building density (number of dwellings per building), which in Berlin rose from 11.2 in 1867 to 19.77 in 1905 [219, p. 130]. Between 1897 and 1904 the average number of dwellings contained in apartment structures in 42 German cities rose from four to seven and maintained the latter level through to 1913 [136, pp. 60–62]. Moreover, there probably was some decrease in the number of persons per dwelling, which in Prussia in 1851 was 8.13 persons per dwelling, one of the highest for the period in Europe [70, p. 100]. In view of these facts it seems likely that our series has a sizable understatement of the secular drift; and to put the series on par with our other series of dwellings, adjustment seems indicated. For this purpose we computed an annual steady rate per cent factor $(1.005756)''$ which yielded a 25 per cent growth over a 40-year period.

The pleasing degree of similarity of pattern between these six divergent measures of residential building gave assurance that a satisfactory index measure could be derived by various weighting schemes from our assembled measures. Between 1896 and 1913 the superiority of the 42-city index over all competing measures seemed clear. Before 1896 we experimented with a number of weighting schemes which included the all-Prussian index. It was finally decided to drop this index, since it over-lapped to a high degree with our other measures. Between 1875 and 1896 the index measures for Hamburg, Baden, Berlin, and nine cities were averaged with weights of 2, 2, 3, 3 respectively. Since half of the index (Hamburg and Berlin) are on a *net* change basis, amplitude tends to be exaggerated. However, inclusion of Baden which covers both rural and urban building tends to offset this. The weights were arbitrarily assigned to avoid giving Hamburg and Berlin more than 50 per cent of the influence on the total. We extended the series back to 1867 on the basis of partial city coverage (Berlin and nine cities for 1867–70 and Baden between 1871 and 1874). We could not readily have used the all-Prussian index because of its later peak (1877). In Chart H-2 we compare our all-German urban residential building index and the independent Prussian series. The fit is close, and we may, accordingly, feel that our contrived index faithfully represents the main contour lines and trend movements of German urban residential dwelling production.

Also shown on Chart H-2 is a graph of a new estimate for German residential construction which became available after preparation of the contrived index. The new estimate was prepared as one of a comprehensive set of national income and expenditure estimates for Germany from 1851 onward. See [130]. For Prussia the estimate was derived partly from Prussian tax returns without indication that numbers or values were utilized, and also without benefit of differentiation between urban and rural building available from our sources since 1880. As rural buildings were allegedly declining in relative importance, Hoffman believed that the tax return data was subject to an expansive bias. Hence he averaged them with another source with what was believed to have a contrary bias, namely, net annual differences in insured values for residential properties insured in Prussia through public carriers, though these carriers insured a falling fraction of eligible property relative to private nonreporting carriers [130, p. 220 f.]. For non-Prussian states Hoffman used available insured values of public carriers, who were given by law a legal monopoly of insurance operations. Insured values were believed to be based upon the original cost of construction or so-called *Anschaffungspreisen*. From time to time, however, these were reappraised ("Allerdings ist zu berücksichtigen, dass fast alle Anstalten von Zeit zu Zeit

CHART H-2

Urban Residential Building Indexes, Annually, Germany 1867–1913 (1890–1900= 100)

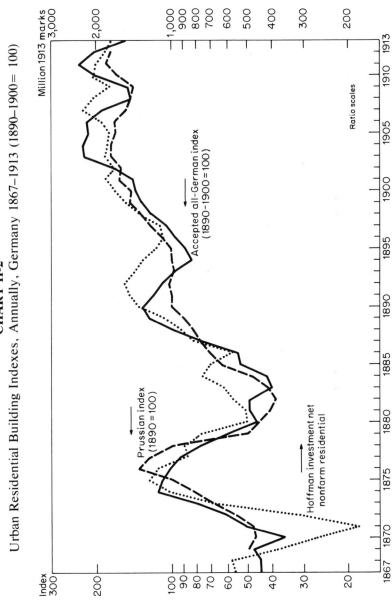

sämtliche Immobilien neu taxieren''). Hoffman believed that by careful review of carrier reports the distorting effects of reappraisals had been eliminated, though he recognizes that the elimination may not be complete (''. . . est es trotzdem möglich dass Neutaxierungen, die nicht zu ausgesprochenen Sprüngen in der Entwicklung der Versicherungswerte führen, übersehen werden''). From the year 1873 onward, the scope for revaluations would appear to be limited, as indicated by the congruence of the new estimate with direct measures of urban building activity for sampled urban populations. But it appears to us that revaluations were probably responsible for the rather wild movements of the Hoffman series between 1868 and 1871, since the fall by two-thirds in that period seems unlikely. Likewise the range of fluctuation from 1851 onward seems improbably wide. The annual estimates for the first seven years of the new series from 1851 onward are as follows in million marks: 200, 460, 360, 90, 110, 60, 120 [130, p. 257].

Appendix I

CANADIAN BUILDING INDEXES

There are two available indexes which reflect urban building: (a) The National Index of Urban Building from 1867 to 1946 by Buckley; (b) Dwellings Completed 1900–53 by Firestone. These are graphed in Chart I-1. The one index is residential and the other covers all urban building. Nonetheless, any index series for urban building will conform closely to a comparable index for residential building for the same area. The indexes however behave quite differently. For the period after 1920, the divergent behavior is plausible and consists merely in the greater amplitude of rise and fall during the twenties and thirties. Likewise during the first ten years of the century—1900–1910—the indexes harmonize in their movement, the Buckley index again showing greater amplitude. However, the next decade is full of problems. The upper turning point for the expansion movement varies by two years—1910 in the Firestone index and 1912 with the Buckley. Then the Buckley index shows a marked downsweep to 1918, which is not at all mirrored in the Firestone index. Moreover, in the Buckley index the boom of the twenties begins in 1918, while the Firestone index begins to rise in 1921. Yet during 1910–20 the Buckley index reflects building patterns of a large sample of cities, at least 35 from 1915 onward and perhaps more between 1910 and 1915 [35, p. 122]. At the same time Firestone asserts that the figures for 1900–1920 are "preliminary since the method yields only a rough approximation of the trend of housing completions." Firestone feels that the index report may understate completions in the 1910's and that building materials may have been used to a greater extent than allowed for nonresidential purposes induced by the war [89, p. 302]. Wartime building for nonresidential purposes probably distorted the estimates of wartime residential building.

The Buckley index lacked adequate coverage in the early years; it is based on two cities in 1886 and on three cities in 1890. The pattern of the movement of the Buckley index—when cumulated for the decades of the 1880's and 1890's—compares

327

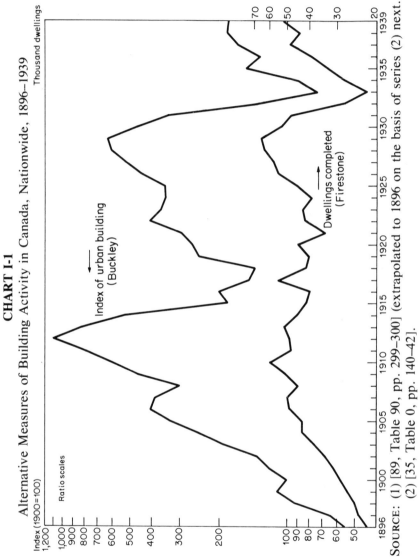

CHART I-1

Alternative Measures of Building Activity in Canada, Nationwide, 1896–1939

SOURCE: (1) [89, Table 90, pp. 299–300] (extrapolated to 1896 on the basis of series (2) next. (2) [35, Table 0, pp. 140–42].

favorably with the *pattern* of the Firestone benchmark figures for decadal production of housing.

Years	Urban Building Index Cumulated over Decade and Averaged[a]	Firestone[b]
1881–91	74	15
1891–1901	90	21

SOURCE: [a] [35, p. 141].
[b] [89, p. 299].

The pattern of the Firestone benchmark estimates for 1867–81 runs counter to the pattern involved in the Buckley index (when compared with the succeeding decade). The Firestone ratios are 24/15, while the Buckley index averages are 53/74. Moreover, the Firestone net value-added construction for 1880 and 1890 shows very little of the extreme rise projected in the Buckley index. If the Firestone benchmark construction estimates are sound (for 1870, 1880, 1890) then the urban building index becomes highly implausible both in its dive (or low of 1881) and its high in 1890. The Buckley construction estimates allow for a nearly constant fraction of housing to construction quadrennially for a 30-year stretch [35, p. 10].

Both Buckley and Firestone derive estimates of total construction expenditures for the years 1900, 1910, and 1920 by the Kuznets method of "blowing up" estimates of materials used. The allowances for materials used and values of total construction are as follows in million dollars:

	Gross Construction Value Current Prices[a]		Materials Used Ratios (Current $)	
	Buckley	Firestone[b]	Buckley	Firestone[c]
1900	119	128	49.8%	51.6%
1910	453	386	45.6%	51.6%
1920	986	852	48.3%	51.6%

[a] Based partly on letter from T. R. Vout, Economist, Office of the Prime Minister, Ottawa, Canada, February 7, 1961.
[b] Computed from [89, pp. 268, 296].
[c] Computed from [89, p. 294].

The values obtained are discrepant, as are likewise the underlying estimates of materials used and the "blowup" ratio which results from various statistical manipulations. One reason for the discrepant estimate is Firestone's assumption (based on 1934–51 operating experience) that materials used (in current dollars) will be 51.6 per cent of construction expenditures, while Buckley used a 43.21 per cent ratio (in real 1913 dollars) based on the 1921 Census.

Divergence between the Firestone and Buckley versions of urban building are thus in part similar in character to the divergent picture of building activity yielded by a Kuznets index (based on materials used) and a Riggleman index based upon building permits issued by central cities. The American experience with comparable statistics has indicated that the one method tends to understate, while the other method overstates, amplitude. Trend will be biased with both statistical methods, depending upon changing allowance made for repair, use of building materials, degree of reliance upon older permit-issuing cities and other factors.

Appendix J

RATES OF MIGRATION AND MARRIAGE, 1870–1910: U.S., U.K.[17]

U.S.

The broad problem was to investigate the effect of international migration on marriage rates. We would expect a net immigration into a country to swell its marriage rates and a net emigration from a country to dampen these rates, since a large fraction of the migrants are single and of prime marriageable age. To answer this problem fully for a given country, we would need to know the age distribution and marriage status of its immigrants, emigrants, and native-born population. Unfortunately, for the period under consideration (1880–1910) this data is not available. Thus, we were forced to narrow the scope of our investigation and estimate only the percentage of migrants in the nation's marriageable stock. Due to further limitations of the data, we defined this marriageable stock as individuals between the ages of 20 and 29, disregarding their marriage status at the time.

We were able to compute from the U.S. census data the number of immigrants in this age bracket for 10-year periods in the United States, and dividing this figure by the native-born Americans in the 20–29 age bracket we obtained the percentage of immigrants to the native-born Americans in the 20–29 age bracket. (See Table J-1.) This percentage gives a rough estimate of the contribution immigrants made to U.S. marriage rates in the latter part of the nineteenth century.

United Kingdom

Our inquiry into U.K. relationships of emigration to marriage rates concentrated on the unmarried component of British emigration and marriage time series. Our basic data was obtained from [51].

Carrier presents the per cent and total number of married

TABLE J-1

Foreign-Born and Immigration by Decade Totals, U.S., 1870–1910

Item	Decade Ending				Average
	1880	1890	1900	1910	
A. Foreign-born, 20–29 age bracket (Census)	1,199,000	1,990,000	2,017,000	3,093,000	
B. Estimated net new arrivals, 20–29 census age bracket	693,321	1,440,060	1,143,596	2,306,934	
C. All other U.S. population, 20–29 age bracket (Census)	8,474,679	9,984,940	12,661,404	14,848,066	
Decade averages	7,206,839	9,229,810	11,323,172	13,754,735	
D. Estimated net new arrivals, 20–29 as per cent of native white, 20–29 (B/decade averages)	9.6	15.6	10.0	16.8	
E. Unadjusted increment total foreign-born	1,068,000	2,537,000	1,092,000	3,130,000	
F. Estimated net new arrivals, 20–29, as per cent of unadjusted increment total foreign-born (B/E)	64.9	56.8	104.7	73.7	75
G. Kuznets and Rubin estimates of net immigration into U.S.	2,143,000	4,263,100	2,426,400	5,024,200	
H. Estimated net new arrivals, 20–29, as per cent of total net immigration (B/G)	32.4	33.8	47.1	45.9	39.8
I. Total gross immigration into U.S.	2,812,191	5,246,613	3,687,564	8,795,386	

NOTE (by lines):

A. [250, p. 146].
B. [250, p. 146]. New arrivals refer to immigrants entering the U.S. in the intracensal period. For example, new arrivals in the decade ending 1880.

(a Census year) include immigrants who arrived between 1870 (a Census year) and 1880. The detailed adjustments of the data presented by Thompson and Whelpton are presented herewith for the first decade, 1880.

705,000 foreign-born age 5–19 in U.S. Census 1870
84,000 foreign-born age 0–4 in U.S. Census 1870

To obtain an estimate of those immigrants who remained in the 5–19 age bracket in the U.S. Census of 1880, we performed the following computation:

$$\frac{1/3 \text{ of } 705,000 + 84,000}{2} = 159,500$$

159,500 of the 705,000 in the 5–19 bracket in the 1870 Census remained in this bracket in 1880. Therefore, 705,000 minus 159,500 = 545,500 left the 5–19 bracket and moved into the 20–29 bracket of the 1880 Census. By applying survival ratios* this figure shrinks to 505,679. The number of new arrivals (entering U.S. between 1870 and 1880) in the 20–29 bracket in the Census of 1880 is computed by subtracting 505,679 from the foreign-born 20–29 age bracket in the 1880 Census.

1,199,000 Foreign-born age 20–29 in U.S. Census of 1880.
−505,679 Foreign-born age 20–29 in 1880 Census who
            were in U.S. at the time of 1870 Census.
693,321 New arrivals, entered U.S. between 1870 and
            1880, in the 20–29 bracket in 1880 Census.

C. All other U.S. population 20–29 includes native white 20–29, Negroes 20–29, and foreign-born 20–29, who have resided in U.S. for at least 10 years [250, pp. 145, 146, 152].

E. [250, p. 146].

G. [162, pp. 100–101]. These estimates were computed by applying survival rates to the foreign-born white population in census data.

I. [272, p. 56].

---

* Five year survival ratios for five year age brackets were obtained from [162, p. 97]. To apply this data for 10-year age brackets over 10-year periods, the following adjustments were made:

1870–80. 10-year survival ratio = .927, obtained as follows:

$$\frac{.969 \text{ (5-yr. s.r. for } 10–14 \text{ to } 15–19 \text{ age bracket}) + .964 \text{ (15–19 to 20–24)} + .956 \text{ (20–24 to 25–29)}}{3}$$

= .963 (average 5-year. s.r.), and therefore, $(.963)^2 = .927$.

1880–90. 10-year survival ratio = .939.
1890–1900. 10-year survival ratio = .941.
1900–1910. 10-year survival ratio = .953.

TABLE J-2

Distribution by Sex or Marital Condition of Adult Passengers from England and Wales, 1877–1907

Year	To U.S.				To British North America				To Australia				To British South Africa			
	MM	MF	SM	SF	MM	MF	SM	SF	MM	MF	SM	SF	MM	MF	SM	SF
1877–80	16.5	18.7	49.7	15.1	11.3	16.6	59.1	13.0	17.0	17.2	47.3	18.5	24.8	15.3	47.4	12.5
1881–90	13.6	18.1	50.6	17.7	13.3	15.8	55.3	15.6	15.4	17.7	47.4	19.5	21.7	15.6	48.7	14.0
1891–1900	16.4	20.9	44.7	18.0	13.1	16.8	52.8	17.3	17.3	19.5	42.9	20.3	18.0	15.7	53.3	13.0
1901–7	18.3	23.3	42.0	15.4	16.1	17.7	53.2	13.0	20.6	23.0	38.3	18.1	20.6	21.3	40.3	17.8

NOTE: MM means "married male"; MF means "married female"; SM means "single male"; SF means "single female."
SOURCE: [51, p. 104].

adults (over 12 years of age) migrating from England and Wales to the U.S., British North America, Australia and British South Africa.[18] We cannot directly apply the per cent of unmarried or married to the various totals because the per cent refers only to those emigrants over 12 years of age. Hence, we must make some estimation of the age structure of British migrants. This was made by applying 1912–13 age distribution totals of English and Welsh migrants to the years 1870–1910. This approximation would be valid if the age structure of English migration was relatively constant in the years 1870–1913. Evidence in support of this supposition is given by data on English and Welsh emigration to the U.S. [88, I, p. 444], which shows a relatively constant yearly per cent of emigrants in the 0–14, 14–44, and over 44 age brackets for the years 1899–1910. Tables J-2 to J-4 present data as given by Carrier; Tables J-5 to J-8 show the various adjustments necessary to obtain the number of unmarried emigrants to all extra-European countries.

In Table J-8, col. D, we have extended the coverage of emigration from four major countries to all extra-European countries and we have reduced the age limit estimate to 40 years of age. We should like to have, however, figures that are net for returnees and in-migration into the U.K. Decade estimates of net migration have been prepared from periodic census and other data and these estimates have been found reliable. (See [245, pp. 123–25].) These estimates are presented in col. B of Table J-8. We list in col. A gross decade emigration, and the corresponding rate of net to gross emigration in col. C, Table J-8. We then assume that net migration rates for all migrants are applicable to unmarried migrants aged 18–40; estimates for net unmarried 18–40 migration are then listed in col. E.

This estimation presupposes that marital and age characteristics of *immigrants* was similar to those of *emigrants*. For the

TABLE J-3
Per Cent Distribution of English and Welsh Migrants, 1912–13

Year	Under 12	12–17	18–30	31–45	46 and Over
1912–13	17.6	6.1	47.2	22.9	6.1

SOURCE: [51, p. 106].

TABLE J-4

English and Welsh Migration, All Ages, to Four Major Countries, and Extra-European Totals

Year	U.S.	British North America	Australia	British South Africa	(E) Total to 4 Countries	(F) Extra-European Totals	Per Cent (E/F)
1871–80	549,756	126,381	200,353	44,172	920,662	970,365	94.9
1881–90	909,189	222,222	272,281	68,888	1,472,580	1,548,965	95
1891–1900	600,232	159,747	103,198	136,728	999,905	1,095,891	91.2
1901–10	649,721	623,585	187,785	223,335	1,684,426	1,875,534	90.0

SOURCE: [51, pp. 92–93, 95–96, 99–100].

TABLE J-5
English and Welsh Migration to Four Major Countries, over Age 12

Year	United States	British North America	Australia	British South Africa
1871–80	452,999	104,138	165,091	36,398
1881–90	749,106	183,111	224,360	56,764
1891–1900	494,591	131,632	85,035	112,664
1901–10	535,370	513,834	154,377	184,028

SOURCE: Computed by applying 1912–13 age distribution per cent (82.4%) to totals given in Table J-4.

TABLE J-6

Unmarried English and Welsh Emigrants over 12 Years of Age to Four Major Countries

Year	United States	British North America	Australia	British South Africa	Total to 4
1871–80	293,543	75,083	108,630	21,802	499,058
1881–90	511,639	129,826	150,097	35,591	827,153
1891–1900	310,109	92,274	53,742	74,696	530,821
1901–10	312,656	340,158	87,069	106,920	846,803

SOURCE: Computed by applying marriage-rate figures (Table J-2) to English and Welsh migration to four countries over age 12 (Table J-5).

TABLE J-7
Unmarried English and Welsh Emigrants to Four Major Countries,
Ages 18–45

Years	
1871–80	437,674
1881–90	724,586
1891–1900	463,938
1901–10	746,033

SOURCE: Figures for unmarried in Table J-6 refer to adults over the age of 12. We assume for this table that those between 12 and 17 were all unmarried; thus to eliminate this group from Table J-7 we used age distribution percentages of Table J-3, adjusting the percentages upward because totals in Table J-6 already exclude the under 12 class. Eliminating from the totals in Table J-6 unmarried persons over 45 was more complicated. This was computed in the following manner:

(A) Total to 4 Countries, 18	(B) Unmarried, 18	(C) Per Cent (B/A)
702,465	462,128	65.8
1,123,579	765,944	68.2
762,928	530,821	69.6
1,285,217	782,446	60.9

Col. A was obtained by applying age distribution percentages (Table J-3) to col. E, Table J-4. Col. B was obtained by excluding from Table J-6 totals individuals between 12–17 years of age by applying adjusted percentage of Table J-3 age distribution totals (12–17 bracket in Table J-3 comprises 6.1 per cent of emigrants while the adjusted percentage,which is applicable to Table J-6 totals, is 7.4 per cent). To exclude unmarried persons over 45 we applied percentages in col. C (above) to the adjusted percentage of emigrants over 45 (Table J-3; the 6.1 per cent figure in Table J-3 must be adjusted upward also because Table J-6 totals already exclude persons under 12) and then deducted these figures from col. B (above).

TABLE J-8
Net Unmarried Migration, 18–40 Years of Age, 1871–1910

Year	*(A)* Emigrants to Extra-European Countries	*(B)* Net Loss by Migration	*(C)* Per Cent (B/A)	*(D)* Emigrants to Extra-European Countries, Unmarried 18–40	*(E)* Net Unmarried 18–40 [(C) × (D)]
1871–80	970,565	164,000	16.9	461,198	77,942
1881–90	1,548,965	601,000	38.8	762,722	295,936
1891–1900	1,095,891	69,000	6.3	508,704	32,040
1901–10	1,875,534	501,000	26.7	828,925	221,322

SOURCE: Col. A from Table J-4, col. F.

1912–13 period, the mean age of immigrants over 18 was 33.7 compared to 30.5 for emigrants, a nearly comparable figure. Among emigrants over 18 years of age, 47.2 per cent were between 18 and 30, while 38.4 per cent of immigrants were in the same age class [51, p. 106]. American data for the 1908–10 period showed that 36.1 per cent of all English returnees were females, that only 14.9 per cent were over 45 years of age and that 83.3 per cent of returnees had resided in the country less than five years [272, pp. 113–16]. Then, too, European immigration into England may have brought into England adults with age and marital characteristics similar to British emigrants. There probably was a net tendency for overseas returnees to concentrate on older and single adults. However, our estimates are probably biased by less than 10 per cent by assuming homogeneity in emigration and immigration with regard to marital and age class.

NOTES TO APPENDIXES

1. Series 0018 and 00186 are fully described in Appendixes H and D, respectively.

2. On the southeast region and its ecological, demographic and industrial characteristics see [292, pp. 17–19, 35–42, 161–85].

3. On this region and its characteristics, see [292, pp. 21, 186–207].

4. For a record of constitution making, see [225, pp. 126 ff., 131 ff., 142 ff.].

5. "The Constitution authorizes the establishment, in the Secretary of State's Office, of a Bureau of Statistics. Some provision for the collection of statistical information is already made. The Township Assessors are required to make returns of the quantity of wheat and corn produced in their several Townships each year. The District Assessors are required to report, under a certain classification, once in six years, the number of acres of taxable land in the different counties. Various acts require the collection of other statistical information, more or less specific, in relation to production, education, population and crime. Under these acts, although from want of system and of adequate means of enforcement they are often very imperfectly executed, a large amount of useful information is collected. It is scattered, however, through many disconnected reports, and consequently fails to yield the full advantage which might be derived from it. To combine this, and collect other similar information, and to present the whole, so arranged as to exhibit the mutual relations of facts and classes of facts, together with their general bearing upon the public welfare, is the proper function of a Bureau of Statistics. I can perceive no insurmountable obstacle to the collection of all, or nearly all, the information required through agencies already existing, without incurring much new expense. For the present, little more would be necessary than to provide for the appointment of a thoroughly qualified person to superintend the whole work, prepare and prescribe all necessary forms, and to receive,

classify, and report the returns. I cannot doubt that such a provision for the collection and publication of the statistics of the State, Agricultural, Industrial, Social and Educational, would repay ten fold its cost in benefits" [208, 1856, I, pp. 438–39].

6. "Among the ablest statisticians and practical economists in the country was Edward Deering Mansfield (1801–1880). Educated at West Point and Princeton, lawyer and teacher and editor by turns, he possessed an intellectual equipment and a practical training almost unequalled in the West. While his pen with equal facility wrote newspaper articles and books of a historical, biographical and educational character, he was mainly occupied with his duties as editor of the *Railroad Record* and as State Commissioner of Statistics, an office created in 1857. No one possessed a wider knowledge of Ohio's economic growth and prospects or recorded his facts with greater care. His reports as Commissioner of Statistics are invaluable to the historian and economist today" [225, p. 173].

7. He helped to take a census of Cincinnati in 1825 and participated in the preparation of a brochure and trade directory [181, p. 190 ff.]. While investigating marine statistics in New Orleans and in Portland, Maine, in 1852, he encountered local officials who had for convenience "regularly copied into the last report all that was in the former one; so that in his report of what should be the then steam marine of New Orleans, he had put fifty or a hundred steamboats destroyed or lost years before." Difficulties were traced to "want of a supervising officer" with interest and ability for the work [181, p. 227 ff.].

8. The Secretary of State assumed responsibility for the bureau by an act of the state legislature dated 17 April 1868 [208, I, 1868, p. 178]. For complaints about the burden of handling this part of the "rubbish of state government" see [208, I, 1870]. For an extended statement of the reasons why the functions of the bureau required expert administration and adequate funding, see [208, I, 1869, pp. 139 ff.]. The 1869 legislature failed to provide sufficient funds to permit printing of extra copies of the report to be sent to county officers whose cooperation was needed [208, 1870, p. 221].

9. A later report identifies the statistician of the department in 1888 as Davis Collings who collects "with as great care as is possible" and compiles "with accuracy" the statistics of Ohio. This statistician was paid the munificent salary of $1,500 yearly and shared the office of the Secretary of State with a chief clerk and three clerks for "stationery, recording, and corporation." There was a "book-room" superintendent at $800 yearly and $400 allowed for extra clerk hire. Later an "assistant statistician" was added. See [10, 1889, pp. 16, 19]. Later holders of the office were C. M. Smith (1900), J. I. Allread (1902), C. D. Cain (1908), and S. M. Johnson (1910). These officers were appointed for relatively short terms by the elected officeholder. See [10, 1900, p. 10; 1902, p. 15; 1908, pp. 12f.; 1910, p. 39; 1914, p. 613]. No archives or records of the statistical bureau are available in the present office of Secretary of State nor do archives of the state contain papers or records of the bureau.

10. This system of assessment was commenced in 1846 legislation and held in essentials through the property tax reform of 1910–14 [23, pp. 216–56]. See [290]; *Acts of a General Nature–53rd General Assembly, State of Ohio*, Vol. LVI (Columbus, Ohio), 1859, "An Act for the Assessment of all Property in

This State," pp. 175–218; [294]; *Report of the Honorary Commission Appointed by the Governor to Investigate the Tax System of Ohio* (Columbus, Ohio) 1908; *Report of the Tax Commission of Ohio—1893* (Columbus, Ohio), 1893.

11. Thus the number and dollar value of mortgages for 1871 and 1872 are as follows:

	Number of Mortgage Recordings	Value Secured (Thousands of dollars)
Railway 1871	50	316,739
Railway 1872	80	560,462
Other 1871	42,886	49,765
Other 1872	45,463	63,619

12. [134, p. 446]. Another noted real estate authority reports that "in the past when a freehold was transferred the deed customarily set forth the actual amount of the 'valuable' consideration" [91, p. 118].

13. See basic explanation in [41, pp. 116–28].

14. See the experiment practiced in the effort to establish 20 temporal relationships for monthly series between 1903 and 1914. Series were stripped of trend and standardized for amplitude by reduction to units of standard deviation. Cycle charts drawn on translucent materials were placed over a lighted box with a glazed top. Twenty cycle charts were compared in this way, making 190 comparisons by each of three independent observers. The variances were slight when the "correspondence between the curves was simple and regular" but wide in the more frequent cases of a variable lag. See [123, pp. 121 ff.].

15. The use of correlation coefficients to determine lead-lag was most thoroughly explained in the initial publication of the Harvard group [123, pp. 120–39]. In work carried out within the National Bureau of Economic Research the method was evaluated in Mitchell's 1927 work on business cycles and was intensively employed in the early NBER work of Harry Jerome [146]. See also the instructive use of correlogram analysis in Zarnowitz [295, pp. 8 f., 14 ff.]. Burns and Mitchell in their basic treatise noted that the method "is more objective and elegant" but was marred by "three grave shortcomings": (1) failure to distinguish between time-periods which are turn points, (2) variations in timing from cycle to cycle, and (3) presupposing trend-adjusted data. The first two shortcomings argue against *exclusive* reliance on correlation analysis, not against its use along with NBER measures. The third can be met in part by correlating without adjustment for trend and then making a separate adjustment of the correlation coefficients to allow for trend [41, p. 127].

16. This conversion formula was developed by Jacob Mincer, member of the Senior Research Staff of the National Bureau. The formula involved the following terms:

R = correlation coefficients including trends

r = correlation coefficients adjusted for linear trends

k_x = time slope of series X

k_y = time slope of series Y
n = number of observations
$\sigma(X)$ = standard deviation of X
$\sigma(x)$ = standard deviation of the residuals from linear time trend

$$c_x = \frac{\sigma(X)}{\sigma(x)}$$

$$c_y = \frac{\sigma(Y)}{\sigma(y)}$$

It turns out that:

$$(1)\; r = \frac{R \cdot \sigma(X)\, \sigma(Y) - 1/12\, k_x k_y\, (n^2 - 1)}{\sqrt{[\sigma^2(X) - 1/12\, k_x^2\, (n^2 - 1)]\, [\sigma^2(Y) - 1/12\, k_y^2\, (n^2 - 1)]}}$$

This is the best formula for calculation, given R, $\sigma(X)$, $\sigma(Y)$, k_x and k_y are easily estimated, freehand.
Formula (1) can be rewritten as:

$$(2)\; r = c_x c_y\, R \pm \sqrt{(c_x^2 - 1)(c_y^2 - 1)}$$

with + when both trends are in the same direction. Since c_x and $c_y > 1$, the *spread* of the *adjusted* correlogram will be less the spread of the unadjusted, by a multiplicative factor $c_x\, c_y$. The level, however, will depend on c_x, c_y, and R. Usually the larger c_x or c_y, the smaller will be r relative to R, given similar trends.

17. The inquiry whose results are presented in this appendix was carried out and written up, under my general direction, in 1962–63 by William M. Landes, then research assistant at the National Bureau of Economic Research, now member of the Department of Economics, University of Chicago, and member of the NBER Senior Research Staff.

18. [51, pp. 104, 95–96, 99–100]; emigration to these four countries accounts for over 90 per cent of English and Welsh total extra-European emigration.

Bibliography

1. Abramovitz, Moses. *Evidence of Long Swings in Aggregate Construction Since the Civil War.* New York, NBER OP 90, 1964.
2. ———. *Inventories and Business Cycles.* New York, NBER, 1930.
3. ———. "The Passing of the Kuznets Cycle," *Economica,* Nov. 1968.
4. Adams, T. S. *Prices Paid by Vermont Farmers for Goods and Services . . . 1790–1940. . . .* Vermont Agricultural Experiment Station, Bulletin 507. Vermont, 1944.
5. Adelman, Irma. "Long Cycles—Fact or Artifact," *American Economic Review,* June 1965.
6. Aftalion, A. *Les Crises Périodiques de Sur-production.* Vol. 2, 1913.
7. Altschul, Eugen. "Konjunkturtheorie und Konjunkturstatistik," *Archiv für Sozialwissenschaft,* 1926.
8. Anderson, Nels. *The Urban Community.* New York, 1959.
9. *Annuaire Statistique de la Ville de Paris.* Paris, 1952.
10. *Annual Report of the Secretary of State.* Columbus, Ohio.
11. Ashton, T. S. *Economic Fluctuations in England, 1700–1800.* Oxford, 1959.
12. Balboa, M., and Fracchia, A. "Fixed Reproducible Capital in Argentina, 1935–55." In *The Measurement of National Wealth.* London, 1959.
13. Bemis, A. F. *Economics of Shelter.* Vol. 2 of *The Evolving House,* 3 vols. Cambridge, Mass., 1933–36.
14. ———. *History of the Home.* Vol. 1 of *The Evolving House,* 3 vols. Cambridge, Mass., 1933–36.
15. Berlin Statistisches Amt. *Statistisches Jahrbuch 1908/11.* Berlin.
16. Berry, T. S. *Western Prices Before 1861.* Harvard Economic Studies, Vol. 74. Cambridge, Mass., 1945.
17. Beveridge, William. *The Trade Cycle in Britain before 1850.* Oxford Economic Papers, No. 3, March 1940.
18. Bezanson, A.; Denison, M. C.; Hussey, M.; and Klemp, E. *Wholesale Prices in Philadelphia 1852–1896.* Philadelphia, 1954.
19. *Biographical Cyclopedia and Portrait Gallery.* Cincinnati, 1883.
20. Bird, R. C. et al. "Kuznets Cycles in Growth Rates, the Meaning," *International Economic Review,* May 1965.
21. Blank, David M. "Relationship Between an Index of House Prices," *Journal of the American Statistical Association,* March, 1954.
22. Blank, D. M., and Winnick, H. "The Structure of the Housing Market," *Quarterly Journal of Economics,* Vol. 67, 1953.
23. Bogart, E. L. *Financial History of Ohio.* Urbana, Ill., 1912.
24. Bogue, Donald. *The Population of the United States.* Glencoe, Ill., 1959.
25. Bonbright, J. C. *The Valuation of Property,* Vol. 1. New York, 1937.
26. Borrie, W. D. "Trends and Patterns in International Migration." UN World Population Conference, Belgrade, 1965. Mimeographed, 1965.

27. Borts, G. *Regional Cycles of Manufacturing Employment in the United States, 1914–1953.* New York, NBER OP 73, 1960.
28. Bowley, Marion. *Housing and the State, 1919–1944.* London, 1945.
29. Bremischen Statistisches Landesamt. *Bremen 1900–1927.* Bremen.
30. ———. *Statistisches Jahrbuch.* Bremen.
31. ———. *Verwaltungs und Wirtshafts berichte.* Bremen.
32. ———. *Vierteljahrshefte Bremischen Statistik.* Bremen.
33. Bruck, W. F., and Vormbrock, H., eds. *Deutsche Siedlungsprobleme.* Berlin, 1929.
34. Bry, G. *Wages in Germany 1871–1945.* New York, NBER, 1960.
35. Buckley, K. *Capital Formation in Canada 1896–1930.* Toronto, 1955.
36. ———. "The Role of Staple Industries in Canada's Economic Development," *Journal of Economic History,* Vol. 18, 1958.
37. ———. "Urban Building and Real Estate Fluctuations in Canada," *Canadian Journal of Economics and Political Science,* Feb. 1952.
38. Bureau of Business Research. *Real Estate Transactions in Franklin County, Ohio, 1917–1937.* 1943.
39. Burns, Arthur F. "Long Cycles in Building Construction." Unpublished manuscript. New York, NBER files.
40. ———. "Long Cycles in Residential Construction." In *Economic Essays in Honor of Wesley Clair Mitchell.* New York, 1935.
41. Burns, Arthur F., and Mitchell, Wesley C. *Measuring Business Cycles.* New York, NBER, 1946.
42. ———. "Statistical Indicators of Cyclical Revivals." In Geoffrey H. Moore, ed., *Business Cycle Indicators.* New York, NBER, 1961.
43. Butlin, N. G. *Private Capital Formation in Australia.* Canberra, 1955.
44. ———. "Some Structural Features of Australian Capital Formation," *Economic Record,* Dec. 1959.
45. Cairncross, Alexander K. "Fluctuations in the Glasgow Building Industry," *Review of Economic Studies,* 1934.
46. ———. *Home and Foreign Investment in Great Britain, 1870–1913.* Cambridge, 1953.
47. Cairncross, Alexander K., and Weber, B. "Fluctuation in Building in Great Britain 1785–1849," *Economic History Review,* Dec. 1956.
48. Cameron, Rondo E. *France and the Economic Development of Europe.* Princeton, N.J., 1961.
49. ———. "Some French Contributions to the Industrial Development of Germany, 1840–1870," *Journal of Economic History,* Sept. 1956.
50. Campbell, Burnham O. *Population Change and Building Cycles.* Urbana, Ill., 1966.
51. Carrier, N. N., and Jeffry, J. R. *External Migration.* General Register Office, Studies, No. 6. London, 1953.
52. Chawner, L. J. *The Residential Building Process: An Analysis in Terms of Economic and Other Social Influences.* National Resources Board. Washington, 1939.
53. Chicago Local Improvement Board. *Report 1915–1918.* Chicago.
54. ———. "A 16 Year Record of Achievement 1915–1931." Chicago.
55. Chicago Public Works Department. *Annual Reports.* Chicago.

56. Ciriacy-Wantrup, Siegfried von. *Agrarkrisen und Stockungsspannen.* Berlin, 1938.
57. Clapham, J. S. *An Economic History of Modern Britain,* 3 vols. Cambridge, 1926–38.
58. Clawson, M.; Held, R. B.; and Stoddard, C. H. *Land for the Future.* Baltimore, 1960.
59. Coale, Ashley J. "Factors Associated with the Development of Fertility: An Historic Summary," *Proceedings of the World Population Conference.* Belgrade. Aug.–Sept. 1965. New York, 1967.
60. Cole, Arthur H. "Durable Consumer Goods and American Economic Growth," *Quarterly Journal of Economics,* August 1962.
61. ———. *Wholesale Commodity Prices in the United States 1700–1861.* Cambridge, Mass., 1938.
62. Colean, M. I., and Newcomb, R. *Stabilizing Construction: The Record and Potential.* New York, 1952.
63. Commons, John R., et al., eds. *Documentary History of American Industrial Society.* Vol. 6. New York, 1958.
64. Conklin, W. D. "Building Costs in the Business Cycle," *Journal of Political Economy,* Vol. 43, 1935.
65. Conrad, M. *Die Entwicklung der Häuserpreise in Freiburg I Br. Während der Letzten Hundert Jahre.* Jena, 1881.
66. Cooney, E. W. "Long Waves in Building in the British Economy of the Nineteenth Century," *Economic History Review,* Dec. 1960.
67. Cramer, D. *Personal Income During Business Cycles.* Princeton University Press for NBER, 1956.
68. Croxton, F. E., and Cowden, D. J. *Applied General Statistics.* New York, 1942.
69. Daly, D. J. *Long Cycles and Recent Canadian Experience.* Royal Commission.
70. De Bow, J. D. B. *Statistical View of the United States . . . Compendium of the Seventh Census.* Washington, D.C., 1854.
71. Deane, P., and Cole, W. A. *British Economic Growth 1688–1959.* Cambridge, 1962.
72. Derkson, J. B. D. "Long Cycles in Residential Building: An Explanation," *Econometrica,* Vol. 8, 1940.
73. Donner, Otto. *Die Kursbildung am Aktienmarkt,* Viertelsjahrsheft 2. Konjunkturforshung, No. 36, Berlin, 1934.
74. Dunham, A. L. *The Industrial Revolution in France, 1815–1848.* New York, 1955.
75. Duon, Gaston, "Évolution de la Valeur Vénale des Immeubles Parisiens," *Journal de la Société de Statistique de Paris,* Sept.–Oct. 1943.
76. Dupriez, Léon H. *Des Mouvements Économiques Généraux,* 2d ed., 2 vols. Louvain Institute de Recherches Economiques et Sociales. Louvain, 1951.
77. Easterlin, Richard. "The American Baby Boom in Historical Perspective," *American Economic Review.* Dec. 1961.
78. ———. *Population, Labor Force, and Long Swings in Economic Growth: The American Experience.* New York, NBER, 1968.

79. Eberstadt, Rudolf. *Handbuch des Wohnungswesen und der Wohnungfrage.* Jena, 1910.
80. ――――. *Die Spekulation in neuzeitlichen Städtebau.* Jena. 1907.
81. ――――. *Städtische Bodenfragen.* Berlin, 1894.
82. Eckstein, Otto, and Wilson, T. A. "The Determination of Money Wages in American Industry," *Quarterly Journal of Economics,* Aug. 1962.
83. Eversley, D. E. "Population in Worcestershire." In *Population in History,* edited by David Glass and D. E. Eversley. Chicago, 1965.
84. Ezekiel, M., and Fox, Karl A. *Methods of Correlation and Regression Analysis.* 3rd ed. New York, 1959.
85. Falkner, R. L. *Wholesale Prices, Wages and Transportation.* . . . March 3, 1893, 52 Cong., 2nd Sess., Pt. I.
86. Feig, J. *Die Verhältnisse des Grund und Bodens in Düsseldorf unter dem Einflusse der Wirtschaftskrise von 1900.* Schriften des Vereins f. Sozialpolitik, Bd. 111, 1903.
87. Feig, J., and Mewes, W. *Unsere Wohnungsproduktion und ihre Regelung.* Göttingen, 1911.
88. Ferenczi, I., and Willcox, W. F., eds. *International Migrations,* 2 vols. New York, NBER, 1929.
89. Firestone, O. J. *Canada's Economic Development 1867–1953.* London, 1958.
90. ――――. *Residential Real Estate in Canada.* Toronto, 1951.
91. Fisher, E. M. *Urban Real Estate Markets: Characteristics and Financing.* New York, NBER, 1951.
92. Fitzsimmons, P., and Simone, J. J. "Legal Aspects of Marriage." In *Marriage and the Family,* C. S. Milhanovich, ed., 1952.
93. Flaus, L. "Les Fluctuations de la Construction d'Habitations Urbaines," *Journal de la Société de Statistique de Paris,* May–June 1949.
94. Frickey, Edwin. *Economic Fluctuations in the United States.* Cambridge, Mass., 1942.
95. ――――. "The Pattern of Short Time Fluctuations in Economic Series, 1866–1914," *Review of Economic Statistics,* Dec. 1934.
96. Fuchs, K. J. *Der Wohnungsfrage.* Leipzig, 1910.
97. Gayer, A. D.; Rostow, W. W.; and Schwartz, A. J. *The Growth and Fluctuation of the British Economy 1790–1850,* 2 vols. Oxford, 1953.
98. Geddes, P. *Cities in Evolution.* London, 1915.
99. General Register Office, *Census of England and Wales 1911.*
100. George, Dorothy, M. D. *London Life in the XVIII Century.* London, 1925.
101. George, Henry. *Progress and Poverty.* New York, Modern Library Edition, Random House, 1938. Originally published 1879.
102. Giffen, Robert. *Stock Exchange Securities.* London, 1877.
103. Glick, P. C. "The Life Cycle of the Family"' *Marriage and Family Living,* Vol. 17, 1955.
104. Goldsmith, Raymond W. *The Flow of Capital Funds in the Postwar Economy.* New York, NBER, 1965.
105. ――――. *A Study of Savings in the United States,* 3 vols. Princeton, N.J., 1955.
106. Goldsmith, Raymond W., and Lipsey, R. E. *Studies in the National*

Balance Sheet of the United States. Princeton University Press for NBER, 1963.

107. Gottlieb, Manuel. "Building and Housing Cycles," *Proceedings of the Business and Economic Statistics Section, American Statistical Association,* 1959.

108. ———. "Building in Ohio between 1837 and 1914." In *Output, Employment, and Productivity in the United States After 1800.* Conference on Income and Wealth 30. New York, NBER, 1966.

109. ———. *Estimates of Residential Building, United States 1840–1939.* New York, NBER Technical Paper 17, 1964.

110. ———. "New Measures of Value of Nonfarm Building, U.S.A., Annually 1850–1939," *Review of Economics and Statistics,* Nov. 1965.

111. ———. "Price and Value in Industrial Markets," *Economic Journal,* March 1959.

112. ———. "Review of 'Evidences of Long Swings in Aggregate Construction Since the Civil War' by Moses Abramovitz," *Quarterly Review of Economics and Business,* 1963.

113. Graziani, A. "Il rapporto capitale e prodotto nell' economia italiana 1861–1957," *Rassegna Economica,* 1958.

114. Grebler, Leo; Blank, D. M.; and Winnick, Louis, *Capital Formation in Residential Real Estate: Trends and Prospects.* Princeton University Press for NBER, 1956.

115. Guttentag, J. "The Short Cycle in Residential Construction 1946–1959," *American Economic Review,* June 1961.

116. Habbakuk, H. J. "English Population in the Eighteenth Century," *Economic History Review,* Vol. 6 (2d ser.), 1953.

117. ———. "Fluctuations in Housebuilding in Britain and the United States in the Nineteenth Century," *Journal of Economic History,* June 1962.

118. Haber, William. *Industrial Relations in the Building Industry.* New York, 1930.

119. Hajnal, John. "The Marriage Boom." In *Demographic Analysis,* edited by J. J. Spengler and O. D. Duncan. Glencoe, Ill., 1956.

120. Hall, A. R. *Building Cycles in Australia and Great Britain.* Mimeographed. 1952.

121. Hamburg Statistisches Landesamt. *Statistisches Jahrbuch.* Hamburg.

122. Hart, Albert. *Anticipations, Uncertainty and Dynamic Planning.* Chicago, 1940.

123. Harvard University Committee on Economic Research. "Index of General Business Conditions," *Review of Economic Statistics,* April 1919.

124. Henderson, J. M. *A Report on Stabilization of Rents in the United States.* Washington, D.C., 1953.

125. Hexter, M. B. *Social Consequences of Business Cycles.* Boston, 1925.

126. Hickman, Bert; Campbell, Burnham O.; and Williamson, J. G. "Postwar Growth in the United States in the Light of the Long-Swing Hypothesis," *American Economic Review, Papers and Proceedings,* May 1963.

127. Hicks, U. K. *Public Finance.* Cambridge Handbook Series. London, 1947.

128. Hoagland, H. E. *Real Estate Principles*, 3d ed. New York, 1955.
129. Hoffman, W. G. *British Industry*. Originally published in German in 1939. In English translation, Oxford, 1955.
130. ———. *Das Wachstum der Deutschen Wirtschaft Seit der Mitte des 19. Jahrhunderts*. 1965.
131. Hoover, E. D. "Prices in the 19th Century." NBER. Mimeographed, 1957.
132. Hoover, Edgar M., and Vernon, Raymond. *Anatomy of a Metropolis*. Cambridge, Mass., 1959.
133. House Report, 83rd Congress. *HR275*. Washington, D.C., 1953.
134. Hoyt, Homer. *One Hundred Years of Land Values in Chicago*. Chicago, 1933.
135. ———. *The Urban Real Estate Cycle—Performance and Prospects*. Urban Land Institute, Technical Bulletin No. 38, June 1960.
136. Hunscha, K. *Die Dynamik des Baumarkts*. Institut für Konjunkturforschung, Sonderheft 17. Berlin, 1930.
137. Husband, W. H., and Anderson, F. R. *Real Estate*, rev. ed. Homewood, Ill., 1954.
138. Illsley, R., et al. "The Motivation and Characteristics of International Migrants," *Milbank Memorial Fund Quarterly*, April 1963.
139. Institute for Social Sciences, University of Stockholm. *National Income in Sweden 1860–1930*.
140. International Labor Organization. *European Housing Problems since the War, 1914–1923*. Geneva, 1924.
141. ———. *Housing Policy in Europe, Cheap Home Building*. Geneva, 1930.
142. International Statistical Institute. *Statistique International des Grandes Villes*. The Hague, 1960.
143. Istituto Centrale di Statistica, *Annali di Statistica*, Series VIII, Vol. 9, Rome, 1957.
144. Jacobs, A., and Richter, H. *Die Grosshandelspreise in Deutschland von 1792 bis 1934*. Institut für Konjunkturforschung, Sonderheft No. 37. Berlin, 1935.
145. Jacobson, Paul. *American Marriage and Divorce*. New York, 1959.
146. Jerome, Harry. *Migration and Business Cycles*. New York, NBER, 1926.
147. Joint Economic Committee, U.S. Congress. *Employment, Growth and Price Levels*. Washington, D.C., 1957. [See statement by Moses Abramovitz.]
148. Jones, G. T. *Increasing Returns: A Study . . . with Special Reference to the History of British and American Industries, 1850–1910*. Cambridge, 1933.
149. Keiseritzky, Ernest. *Das Gelände der Ehemaligen Festung Breslau 1813–1870*. Breslau, 1903.
150. Kelly, Allen C. "International Migration and Economic Growth: Australia, 1865–1935," *Journal of Economic History*, Sept. 1965.
151. Kendall, Maurice G., and Stuart, A. *Advanced Theory of Statistics*. New York, 1968.
152. Keyes, S. "Fluctuations in Land Development in Allegheny County," *Pittsburgh Business Review*, March 1935.
153. Keynes, J. M. *General Theory of Interest, Employment and Money*. New York, 1936.

154. ———. *Treatise on Money,* 2 vols. London, 1930.
155. Kindleberger, C. F. *Economic Growth in France and Britain 1851–1950.* Cambridge, Mass., 1964.
156. Klaman, Saul B. *The Postwar Residential Mortgage Market.* Princeton University Press for NBER, 1961.
157. Klein, L. R. *Economic Fluctuations in the United States, 1921–1941.* Cowles Commission Monograph. New York, 1950.
158. Knowles, L. C. Z., and Knowles, C. M. *The Economic Development of the British Overseas Empire.* London, 1930.
159. Kollman, P. *Die Kaufpreise des Grundeigentums in Grossherzogtum Oldenberg von 1866–1893.* Tübingen, 1895.
160. Krause, J. T. "The Changing Adequacy of English Registration, 1690–1837." In *Population in History,* David Glass and D. E. Eversley, eds. Chicago, 1965.
161. Kuznets, Simon. *Capital in the American Economy.* Princeton University Press for NBER, 1961.
162. Kuznets, Simon, and Rubin, E. *Immigration and the Foreign Born.* New York, NBER OP 46, 1954.
163. Labrousse, E., ed. *Aspects de la Crise et de la Dépression de l'Économie Française au Milieu du XIX Siècle, 1846–1851.* La Roche-sur-Yon, 1956.
164. Lange, Oscar. *Introduction to Econometrics.* Elmsford, N.Y., 1959.
165. Lavington, F. A. *The English Capital Market.* London, 1921.
166. League of Nations, *Urban and Rural Housing.* Geneva, 1939.
167. Lewis, J. Parry. *Building Cycles and Britain's Growth.* London and New York, 1965.
168. ———. "Growth and Inverse Cycles: A Two Country Model," *Economic Journal,* March 1964.
169. ———. "Indices of House-building in . . . Great Britain 1851–1913." Mimeographed. January 1961.
170. Liesse, Andre. "Evaluation of Credit and Banks in France." *Publications of the National Monetary Commission,* 15. Washington, D.C., 1911.
171. Lindahl, E.; Dahlgren, E.; and Kock, K. *National Income in Sweden, 1860–1930,* Part 1. London, 1937.
172. ———. *National Income in Sweden, 1860–1930,* Part 2. London, 1937.
173. Long, Clarence D., Jr. *Building Cycles and the Theory of Investment.* Princeton, 1940.
174. ———. "Seventy Years of Building in Manhattan," *Review of Economic Statistics,* Vol. 18, 1936.
175. ———. *Wages and Earnings in the United States, 1860–1890.* New York, NBER, 1960.
176. Lorenz, Paul. *Der Trend.* Institut für Konjunkturforschung, Sonderheft 21, 2d ed. Berlin, 1931.
177. Macaulay, F. R. *Some Theoretical Problems Suggested by the Movements of Interest Rates, Bond Yields and Stock Prices in the United States Since 1856.* New York, NBER, 1938.
178. Maisel, S. "An Approach to the Problems of Analyzing Housing Demand," Ph.D. dissertation. Harvard University, 1948.

179. Mangoldt, R. V. *Die Städtische Bodenfrage Eine Untersuchung über die Tatsachen, Ursachen, und Abhilfe.* Göttingen, 1907.
180. ———. *Aus Zwei Deutschen Kleinstädten.* Jena, 1894.
181. Mansfield, Edwin D. *Personal Memoirs 1803–1843.* Cincinnati, 1879.
182. Marget, A. W. *Theory of Prices.* Vol. 2. New York, 1942.
183. Marjolin, Robert. *Prix, Monnaie et Production, Essai Sur les Mouvements Économiques de Long Durée.* Paris, 1941.
184. Marshall, Alfred. *Principles of Economics,* 8th ed. London, 1938.
185. Mattila, J. M., and Thompson, W. R. "Residential Service Construction: A Study of Induced Investment," *Review of Economics and Statistics,* Nov. 1956.
186. Maverick, L. A. "Cycles in Real Estate Activity," *Journal of Land and Public Utility Economics,* May 1932.
187. Melnyk, M. "The Problems of Long Cycles and Residential Construction," *Land Economics,* Nov. 1968.
188. Mewes, Wilhelm, *Bodenwerte, Bau- und Bodenpolitik in Freiberg I. Br.* Karlsruhe, 1905.
189. Meyer, J. A. *Die Wirtschaftlichen Verhältnisse des Grund und Bodens in der Stadt Giessen in den Letzten Fünfundzwanzig Jahren.* Giessen, 1903.
190. *Michigan Business Studies.* July 1928.
191. Mildschuh, W. *Mietzinse und Bodenwerte in Prag, 1869 bis 1902.* Vienna and Leipzig, 1909.
192. Mitchell, Wesley C. *Business Cycles, The Problem and Its Setting.* New York, NBER, 1927.
193. ———. *What Happens During Business Cycles, A Progress Report.* New York, NBER, 1951.
194. Morgenstern, Oscar. *International Financial Transactions and Business Cycles.* New York, NBER, 1959.
195. Morton, Walter A. *Housing Taxation.* Madison, Wis., 1955.
196. Muth, R. F. "Economic Change and Rural-Urban Land Conversions," *Econometrica,* Jan. 1961.
197. Myrdal, Alva. *Nation and Family.* New York and London, 1941.
198. NBER, *Investing in Economic Knowledge.* 38th Annual Report. New York, 1958.
199. ———. *Problems of Capital Formation: Concepts, Measurement, and Controlling Factors.* New York, 1957.
200. ———. *The Study of Economic Growth.* 39th Annual Report. New York, 1959.
201. ———. *The Task of Economics.* 43rd Annual Report. New York, 1963.
202. ———. *Tested Knowledge of Business Cycles.* 42nd Annual Report. New York, 1962.
203. ———. *The Uses of Economic Research.* 43rd Annual Report. New York, 1963.
204. New York City Real Estate Board. *History of Building, Real Estate, and Architecture* . . . . New York, 1898.
205. New York State, Temporary State Housing Rent Commission. *High Rent Housing and Rent Control in New York City.* Albany, 1958.
206. Newman, W. H. *The Building Industry and Business Cycles.* Chicago, 1935.

207. North, Douglass C. *The Economic Growth of the United States 1790–1860.* Englewood Cliffs, N.J., 1961.
208. *Ohio Executive Documents.*
209. Paasche, E. *Über die Entwicklung der Preise und der Rente des Immobiliarbesitzes zu Halle a.g.* Halle, 1877.
210. Phillips, A. W. "The Relation Between Unemployment and the Rate of Change of Money Wage Rates in the United Kingdom, 1862–1957," *Econometrica,* Nov. 1958.
211. Pinkney, D. H. "Money and Politics in the Rebuilding of Paris, 1860–1870," *Journal of Economic History,* March 1957.
212. Predetti, A. "Sul comportamento ciclo ed il valore congiunturale degli investimenti lordi per impianti ed attrezzature," *La Industria,* 1959.
213. Pribam, K. "Housing." In *Encyclopedia of the Social Sciences,* Vol. 7. New York, 1932.
214. Quinn, J. A.; Eubank, E.; Elliott, L. E. *Cincinnati Building Permits—Trends and Distribution, 1908–1938.* 1941.
215. Quittner-Bertolasi, Ellen. *Das Verhältnis von Trend und Konjunkturzyklen.* Leipzig, 1933.
216. Rapkin, C.; Winnick, L.; and Blank, D. *Housing Market Analysis.* Washington, D.C. 1953.
217. Ratcliff, R. *Urban Land Economics.* New York, 1949.
218. Rees, Albert. *Real Wages in Manufacturing, 1890–1914.* Princeton University Press for NBER, 1961.
219. Reich, Emmy. *Der Wohnungsmarkt in Berlin von 1840–1910.* Munich and Leipzig, 1912.
220. Renauld, J. R. V. *Beitrage zur Entwicklung der Grundrente und Wohnungsfrage in München.* Leipzig, 1904.
221. Renne, R. R. *Land Economics.* 1958.
222. Riggleman, John R. "Variation in Building Activity in the United States Cities," Ph.D. dissertation. Johns Hopkins University, 1934.
223. Robinson, Herbert W. *The Economics of Building.* London, 1939.
224. Roos, C. F. *Dynamic Economics.* Monograph of the Cowles Commission, No. 1. Bloomington, Ind., 1934.
225. Rosenbloom, E. H. *The Civil War Era 1850–1873.* Vol. IV of *The History of the State of Ohio,* C. Wittke, ed. 1944.
226. Rossi, Peter H. *Why Families Move.* Glencoe, Ill., 1955.
227. Rousseaux, Paul. *Les Movements de Fond de L'Économie Anglaise, 1800–1913.* Brussels, 1938.
228. Schmoller, Gustav G. *Grundriss der Allgemeine Volkswirtschaftslehre II.* Leipzig, 1904.
229. Schumpeter, Joseph. *Business Cycles,* 2 vols. New York, 1939.
230. Senate Committee on Banking, 81st Congress, 2d session. *Senate Report 1780.* Washington, D.C., 1950.
231. Shannon, H. A. "Bricks: A Trade Index, 1785–1849," *Economica,* August 1934.
232. Sombart, Werner. *Die Deutsche Volkswirtschaft im 19 Jahrhundert.* Kohlhamer, 1954.
233. ———. *Der Moderne Kapitalismus. Das Wirtschaftsleben im Zeitalter des Hoch-Kapitalismus,* Vol. 3. Munich, 1927.

234. Sorokin, Pitirim. *Society, Culture and Personality.* New York, 1947.
235. Sorokin, Pitirim, and Zimmerman, C. C. *Principles of Rural-Urban Sociology.* New York, 1929.
236. Soule, George H. *Men, Wages, and Employment.* New York, 1954.
237. Spengler, J. J. "Effects Produced by Pre-1939 Immigration." In *Economics of International Migration,* edited by B. Thomas. London, 1958.
238. Spensley, J. C. "Urban Housing Problems," *Journal of the Royal Statistical Society,* March 1918.
239. Spiethoff, Arthur. *Boden und Wohnung.* Heft 20, Bonner Staatswissenschaftliche Untersuchungen. Jena, 1934.
240. ———. "Business Cycles," *International Economic Papers,* No. 3, 1953. Originally published 1925.
241. Statistika Kontoret. *Stockholms Stad Statistik.* Stockholm, 1949.
242. Steinbruck, R. *Die Entwicklung der Preise des Städtischen und Ländlichen Immobiliarbesitzes zu Halle (Saale) und im Saalkreise.* Jena, 1900.
243. Summerson, John. *Georgian London.* Rev. Pelican edn., 1962.
244. Talmona, Mario. *Fluttuazioni Edilizie E Cicli Economici.* Rome, 1958.
245. Thomas, Brinley. *Migration and Economic Growth, A Study of Great Britain and the Atlantic Economy.* Cambridge, 1954.
246. ———. *Migration and Urban Development.* London, 1972.
247. Thomas, Dorothy S. *Research Memorandum on Migration Differentials.* SSRC. New York, 1938.
248. ———. *Social Aspects of the Business Cycle.* London and New York, 1925.
249. Thomas, D. S. *Social and Economic Aspects of Swedish Population Movements, 1750–1933.* New York, 1941.
250. Thompson, W. S., and Whelpton, P. K. *Population Trends in the United States,* New York, 1933.
251. Thorp, Willard. *Business Annals.* New York, 1926.
252. Tinbergen, Jan. *Statistical Testing of Business Cycle Theories,* 2 vols. League of Nations. Geneva, 1939.
253. Tinbergen, Jan, and Polak, J. *Dynamics of Business Cycles.* Chicago, 1950.
254. Tooke, Thomas, and Newmarch, William. *A History of Prices.* London, 1857. Cited from the 1928 reprint.
255. Tostlebe, Alvin S. *Capital in Agriculture: Its Formation and Financing Since 1870.* Princeton University Press for NBER, 1957.
256. Turvey, R. *The Economics of Real Property.* London, 1957.
257. Unger, M. A. *Real Estate.* Cincinnati, 1954.
258. Ungern-Sternberg, R. V., and Schubrell, U. H. *Grundriss der Bevölkerungs Wissenschaft.* Stuttgart, 1950.
259. United Nations. *The Determinants and Consequences of Population Trends.* New York, 1953.
260. ———. *United Nations World Population Conference, 1965.* Vol. 4. New York, 1967.
261. U.S., Bureau of the Census. *Census of Governments, Taxable Property Values in the United States.* For the 1956 Census, Vol. 5, published in 1959; for the 1961 Census, Vol. 2, published in 1963.

262. ——— . *Historical Statistics of the U. S., 1789–1945.* Washington, D.C., 1949.
263. ——— . *Historical Statistics of the United States: Colonial Times to 1957.* Washington, D.C., 1960.
264. ——— . *Marriage and Divorce 1867–1906.* Washington, D.C., 1909.
265. ——— . *Real Estate Mortgages in the United States.* 11th Census. Washington, D.C., 1895.
266. U. S., Bureau of Labor Statistics. "History of the Wages in the United States from Colonial Times to 1928," *Bulletin* 499.
267. U. S., Department of Agriculture. *Report on Senate Resolution 311* (by the Forest Service, 1920).
268. ——— . *Year Book,* 1922.
269. U. S., Department of Housing and Urban Development. *Statistical Yearbook, 1966.* Washington, D.C., 1968.
270. U. S., Department of the Interior, Census Office. *Compendium of the Eleventh Census: 1890,* Part III. Washington, D.C., 1897.
271. U. S., Department of Labor. *Cost of Living and Retail Prices of Food.* 18th Annual Report of the Dept. of Labor. Washington, D.C., 1904.
272. U. S., Immigration Commission. *Abstract of Reports,* Vol. 1. Washington, D.C., 1911.
273. Voigt, A., and Geldner, P. *Kleinhaus und Mietkaserne.* Berlin, 1905.
274. Voigt, Paul. *Grundrente und Wohnungsfrage in Berlin und seinen Vororten.* Jena, 1901.
275. Wagemann, Ernst. *Struktur und Rhythmus der Weltwirtschaft.* Berlin, 1931.
276. Walras, Leon. *Elements of Pure Economics.* American Economic Association Publication, 1954.
277. ——— . "Theorie Mathematique de Prix des Terres et de leur Rachat par L'État," *Études D'Economie Sociale.* Paris, definitive edition, 1936.
278. Wander, H. "Migration and the German Economy." In *Economics of International Migration,* edited by B. Thomas. London. 1958.
279. Warren, George F., and Pearson, Frank A. *Prices.* New York, 1933.
280. ——— . *World Prices and the Building Industry.* New York, 1937.
281. Weber, Adolf. *Boden und Wohnung.* Leipzig, 1908.
282. ——— . *Über Bodenrente und Bodenspekulation in der Modernen Stadt.* Leipzig, 1904.
283. ——— . "Die Wohnungsproduktion," In *Grundriss der Sozialökonomik,* pp. 351–68 Abt. VI, Ch. XI. Tübingen, 1914.
284. Weber, B. "A New Index of Residential Construction and Long Cycles in Great Britain, 1838–1950," *Scottish Journal of Political Economy,* II, 1955.
285. Wendt, Paul F. *Housing Policy—The Search for Solutions, A Comparison of the United Kingdom, Sweden, West Germany, and the United States Since World War II.* Berkeley, Calif., 1962.
286. White, W. H. *Wholesale Prices at Cincinnati and New York.* Cornell University Agricultural Experiment Station, Memoir 182. Ithaca, N.Y. 1935.

287. Wilkinson, Maurice. "Long Swings in Swedish Population," *Journal of Economic History*, March 1967.
288. Willcox, Walter. *Introduction to the Vital Statistics of the United States, 1900 to 1930*. U.S. Bureau of the Census. Washington, D.C., 1930.
289. Williamson, John. *American Growth and the Balance of Payments*. Chapel Hill, N.C., 1964.
290. Woods, John. *Tax Laws Relating to Assessment of Personal Property and the Duties of Township Assessors with Instructions*. Columbus, Ohio.
291. Woytinsky, W. C. *Die Welt in Zahlen, I*. Berlin, 1925.
292. Wright, A. J. *Economic Geography of Ohio*. Bulletin 50, 2d ed. Ohio Geological Survey, 1956.
293. Wright, Carroll D. *A Report on Marriage and Divorce in the United States*, rev. ed. Washington, D.C., 1891.
294. Wright, F. M. *The Tax Laws of Ohio—Assessment of Personal History—Revised Instructions to Township Assessors*. Columbus, Ohio, 1858.
295. Zarnowitz, Victor. *Unfilled Orders, Price Changes, and Business Fluctuations*. New York, NBER, 1962.

Index

Abramovitz, Moses, 3, 12, 35f., 46, 49, 212, 237
Alameda County, 85, 94
Amplitude. *See* Cycles
Amsterdam, 4, 10, 12, 37, 116
Ann Arbor, 85
Argentina, 192, 194–197, 204
Ashton, T. S. 5, 215f.
Australia, 5, 45, 217, 219; conformity, regional to national, 208, 211; cycle patterns, long, inversion of, 15; marriage, 2, 224, 226, 236; migration to, 238; surveyed series, 37f.
Austria, 226

Babson-Bradstreet, 160
Berlin: building cycles, 10, 12, 37; foreclosure, 107ff., marriage, 116; mortgage credit, 96–100, 110; real estate, 145, 178; rental market, 146, 172f.; study of, 1; vacancy, 23f., 125ff., 182
Belgium, 226
Birmingham, England, 37
Blank, David, 179
Borts, G., 64
Bradford, England, 37
Brick production: England, 193f., 196, 204; Australia, 208
Brooklyn, 52
Building materials: cycle patterns of, 215; price of, United States and Germany, 155–161; series surveyed, 145f.; summary of, 28f., 185
Burns, Arthur F., 2f., 5, 41, 43f., 49ff., 161, 209
Business Cycle (or short cycle): building in Germany in regard to, 144f.; demographic fluctuations in regard to, 114ff., 224ff., 229ff., 238ff.; duration of contraction, 62f.; England 18th century, 215f.; rates of change of, 203ff. *See also* Local long building cycle; National long building cycle

Cairncross, Alexander, 4, 130, 181f., 184, 237, 239
Campbell, Burnham, 212

Canada, 45, 192f., 195ff., 203, 216f.; indexes of building activity, 327ff.; migration to, 238; study of, 5
Chicago: building cycles, 12, 37; building cycles duration and amplitude, 52, 62; industrial influence on building, 71f.; land development, 85; marriage and migration, 116; realty sales, 94ff.; rental market, 146, 172–176; site value, 147, 153ff., 185; street paving, 78f.; vacancy, 182
Chronology, 41ff., 46f.; reference, list of, 12f.; reference, theory of, 44f.; reference, via residential building, 44f., 54f.; short cycles, use of, 40f.; summary, 10f.
Cincinnati, 12, 37. *See also* Ohio
Cleveland, 85. *See also* Ohio
Conrad, M., 1
Correlation analysis, 55f.; correlograms, 56, 119, 173f., 232; Jerome study, 238f.; marriage data, 229; methods, 301–314; Paris data, 119ff.; used in vacancy data, 182f. *See also* Trend adjustment
Cost of new construction: behavior compared, 161–164; labor cost component, 28f., 161ff., 185; rentals related to, 169; series surveyed, 38f., 147f.; site values related to, 179f; summary, 28f., 186f.; supply function related to, 142ff.
Correlogram. *See* Correlation analysis
Credit Foncier, 149
Cycle. *See* Business cycle; Local long building cycle; National long building cycle; Reference cycle; Specific cycle

Denmark, 191f.
Detroit, 12, 37, 52, 85
Duration, 11–15. *See also* Business cycle; Local long building cycle; National long building cycle

Emigration, 238f., 241ff. *See also* Migration
Easterlin, Richard, 9, 35, 49, 212, 229
England: brick production, 193f., 196, 204; building cycles, 3, 12, 14, 62, 201, 203f., 207f.; building cycles, inversion of, 10f.,